Voices from the
HOME FRONT

Voices from the
HOME FRONT

Felicity Goodall

David & Charles

A DAVID & CHARLES BOOK

David & Charles is a subsidiary of F+W (UK) Ltd.,
an F+W Publications Inc. company

First published in the UK in 2004

Distributed in North America
by F+W Publications, Inc.
4700 East Galbraith Road
Cincinnati, OH 45236
1-800-289-0963

A catalogue record for this book is available from the British Library.

ISBN 0 7153 1708 3 hardback

Printed in Great Britain by Antony Rowe Ltd
for David & Charles
Brunel House   Newton Abbot   Devon

Commissioning Editor   Jane Trollope
Head of Design   Ali Myer
Desk Editor   Lewis Birchon
Production Controller   Jennifer Campbell

Visit our website at www.davidandcharles.co.uk

David & Charles books are available from all good bookshops;
alternatively you can contact our Orderline on (0)1626 334555
or write to us at FREEPOST EX2 110, David & Charles Direct,
Newton Abbot, TQ12 4ZZ (no stamp required UK mainland).

CONTENTS

September 3rd 1939 – I am writing this while listening to
Chamberlain at 11am. To have grown up for this!
(Mary Ross, 1939)

When Mary Ross wrote those words to her fiancé, little did she
think that World War II would last for almost six years. She and
the rest of her generation would have their lives overtaken by the
machine of war. This book is an album of 'oral snapshots' from
the lives of some of those who lived through the years 1939–45.

This book is dedicated to my mother, who lost her youth to World War II.

Author's Note: Because most of these personal experiences were recorded
either in letters or diaries, where words tumble on to the page in a rush
to capture the thoughts and feelings of a moment, spelling mistakes have
been left unaltered. Such documents are often typified by long sentences,
so punctuation has been added where necessary to ensure clarity.

INTRODUCTION

Take yourself back to the summer of 1939. A teenager picks flowers in a country garden, little dreaming that she will lose a cherished brother, or that she will nurse burnt airmen. A young woman works in a music shop, unaware that the handsome lifeguard she is walking out with will be shot down. A mother of four, who lost a fiancé in the Great War, will leave her comfortable home to run a canteen for troops resisting invasion. There are few cars; homes are left unlocked in the countryside; and it is a matter of pride to men that their wives do not need to go out to work. Washing machines and refrigerators are for the wealthy only; children can leave school at 14; and there is as yet no vaccination against childhood diseases like polio and meningitis. There are few homeowners; the rent man, the bailiffs and the Means Test are the scourge of the majority; and the previous two decades have been dominated by recession. Gracie Fields, Deanna Durbin, Cary Grant and Errol Flynn are among the stars who entertain cinema audiences. Witty plays by Noel Coward entertain London theatregoers. Britain has an empire, and India is the gem in its crown, but the movement for independence is gaining momentum. King George VI has been on the throne for three years, Neville Chamberlain is Prime Minister, and Winston Churchill is waiting in the wings. Across the English Channel, ugly events have been brewing since Hitler rose to power in 1933. Germany has been re-arming. Britain has not. A war is about to erupt, though nobody wants to believe that it can, or will, happen.

Mrs Walters (left) and Mrs James make camouflage nets, one of many tasks taken on by the WVS, which also included teaching soldiers how to darn socks, skiing to remote anti-aircraft batteries with hot meals, and fishing for tyres in village ponds when rubber became scarce.

1
THIS NATION IS AT WAR

I stood on the footway of Hungerford Bridge across the Thames, watching the lights of London go out. The whole great town was lit up like a fairyland, in a dazzle that reached into the sky, and then one by one, as a switch was pulled, each area went dark, the dazzle becoming a patchwork of lights being snuffed here and there until a last one remained, and it too went out. What was left us was more than just wartime blackout, it was a fearful portent of what war was to be. We had not thought we would have to fight it in darkness, or that light would be our enemy.
(Mea Allan, September 1939)

The world had watched and waited throughout the summer of 1939, as events unfolded on the continent of Europe. Some British families had gone away as usual, snatching what was going to be the last seaside holiday for many years. But bags were soon packed, tent pegs pulled up, as families returned home to prepare for the civilian war. There was none of the flag-waving enthusiasm witnessed when World War I was declared. Twenty-five years later, a new generation had grown up with the knowledge of the casualties and death toll of that Great War. As they listened to Chamberlain's announcement on the wireless, declaring that 'this country is at war', they knew what it would cost. They did not know that within a year Britain would stand as the last bastion of Western freedom, an isolated island on the fringes of Nazi-occupied Europe. They did not know that in this war thousands of civilians would be killed, as Hitler tried to batter the British into submission. They did not know that the demands of the Home Front would leave the British population exhausted, dressed in threadbare clothes and ill-fitting shoes. They did not know of the inner resources that would keep them soldiering on, giving rise to the wartime spirit that has since become legendary.

Making and hanging blackout curtains was the first massive war effort by women all over Britain. Even before war was declared, yards and yards of dark blue, black and dark green material were being stitched by hand and machine to hang at every window from which light might spill at night. On 31 August 1939 Miss Andrews, who was living quietly in Tonbridge, Kent, recorded in her diary:

> **We make curtains busily and finish ten minutes before the wireless order for universal blackout as from tonight. Everyone rushing for curtain material, torches etc.**

Those unable to buy cloth could use black card and secure it round the window frame with battens, sealing in the light and sealing out the fresh air. Blackout curtains could not be washed, as this was apt to make them let the light shine through. The Government issued instructions in a leaflet telling people to 'hoover, shake, brush then iron' – the latter to make them more light-proof. Nowadays light streams out into the streets and skies from shop windows, empty office buildings and traffic on the streets. Wartime buses and cars had their headlights covered to show only a crack of light, and they passed through empty streets like ghost vehicles. Phyllis Warner kept her diary as a basis for the articles she sent to American newspapers.

> **The density of the blackout these cloudy moonless nights is beyond belief. No one in New York or Los Angeles can successfully imagine what it's like. For the first minute after going out of doors one is completely bewildered, then it is a matter of groping forward with nerves as well as hands outstretched.**

Teacher Grace Dennithorne knew the feeling well. She was just one of those who had an accident in the blackout.

> **I have had the unusual and unwelcome experience of having a 'rest' in Moorfield Eye Hospital – blindfolded for 2½ weeks. I walked into a door in the blackout and when I recovered from the stun I found that one eye could not see – at first I thought it must be due to the shock.**

Forces switchboard operator Mollie Wilson described finding her way out to the YMCA in the unfamiliar surroundings of Corsham, a military town in Wiltshire.

> It was pitch dark at about 8.40 when we set out, and it was pretty difficult to find the gate so Louie and I sort of crept along. We bumped into bushes and plenty of walls before we reached the road. Then we said, 'Oh, I'm beginning to see properly,' and walked bang into another wall. After that we weren't too bad 'cause we got on to the main street. We were walking gaily along the pavement, when suddenly bang!! – The two of us fell over a sandbag barricade. I nearly split my sides with laughter.

Broad white stripes were painted round doors of underground trains as they were practically invisible in the dark, and railway carriages were blacked out. One Essex farmer even painted white stripes on his cattle so that they might be more visible in muted car headlights. Those walking in the streets took an essential item: a torch. Mrs Peg Cotton, a wealthy American living in London and Devon, kept a vivid diary of daily life, including such an everyday experience as walking down a country road in the blackout.

> The tissue came off my torch and since the light is prohibited thus, I hid it under my coat. The light shining out from below my skirts thus made me look like a crawling lightening-bug.

An added complication later in the war was the scarcity of torch batteries. Even after four years of blackout, fitter's mate Frank Forster found that it was still easy to become disorientated walking round Chester in 1943.

> Every journey one makes across the city during blackout, especially on a very dark night is a great adventure – although one is aware of certain landmarks, many of them are of no use whatever, unless one is possessed of a good torch – without a good light every step must be taken carefully – one never knows what is in front of one beyond a distance of about 3 feet – and when there is need for hurry then the adventure is increased

Massive hydrogen-filled barrage balloons dwarf the recruits being trained to control them. The operators were taught how to splice ropes and wires, and mend tears in the fabric. These unwieldy balloons lived up to their soubriquet, 'pigs', particularly in bad weather.

for visibility is so poor that street corners, kerbs of pavements and other matters for consideration present themselves slap bang in front of one's face and a great deal of adaptability manoeuvrability and cleverness is needed to avert them.

In the few days before the declaration of war on 3 September 1939, Frank Forster was employed building huts for troops, and making camouflage nets for the nearby RAF (Royal Air Force) station – a job that was also done by the WVS (Women's Voluntary Service). Thousands of soldiers were pouring into Chester and he was concerned for the safety of his fiancée, Lyn.

Drunkenness is on the increase. I must confess that I feel rather uneasy when Lyn has to move about the town and so many troops are about. One cannot help feeling that they have very little sense of responsibility.

Church bells were silenced; they would be rung only in the event of invasion. As the nation geared up for that anticipated event, milestones were boxed in, aeroplane-trapping poles were built alongside roads and in flat fields, and enormous barrage balloons appeared in the sky – gigantic fabric balloons filled with hydrogen and designed as visual and physical barriers to enemy bombers. In Glasgow, Dr JP McHutchison waxed lyrical about these strange objects.

I should record my impression of the strange beauty of the balloons over Glasgow – silver stars in the morning sunlight. Seen against a glowing sky as dark shapes in a welter of colour, they make a picture to my mind somewhat more typical of our war landscape than even the long fingers of searchlights at night.

The barrage balloons, which became such a familiar and arresting sight, were cumbersome beasts. Their enormous bulk was harnessed by teams of men and women in parks and fields near potential enemy targets. Rosalind Desch helped to run a YMCA mobile canteen, which took welcome refreshments to these teams in Surrey. She kept a scrapbook of the activities of the canteen, including this brush with a barrage balloon in 1940, just as she was serving tea.

An alert was sounded – they immediately left us and went about the jobs and we started to pack up to leave for the next place. We heard guns firing in the distance and saw the crews getting the balloon higher – no easy task in the gale that was then blowing. I had turned my back and was engaged in buttering the buns when the van received a terrific crump – it shook and shuddered all over, seemed to right itself and then finally slowly tottered over on to its nearside, incidentally smashing the serving hatch, which we had not yet shut. Mrs Clouston and myself, almost too surprised for speech, found ourselves lying at very queer angles in the van covered with stock which had fallen in all directions, and tea, milk and sugar which was everywhere but in the cups. We found the door of the van had jammed, but willing helpers soon released us and we crawled out to learn the balloon, momentarily out of control, had hit the top of the van, and that for an instant the wheels had been entangled in the guy ropes.

Urban streets became cluttered with green canvas sandbags piled round lampposts as a precaution against firebombs. Because of the perils of these sandbags, Londoner Lylie Eldergill accompanied her blind husband to work and back every day. Lylie had lived through World War I and was depressed at having to go through domestic preparations for a second war. She busied herself preserving her most precious possessions.

I have packed my glass and china away – so really it looks like Christmas Day in the Workhouse. I am glad we had our holiday, I don't know when we shall have another. Eddie [her younger brother] is twenty two years old today. I think that it will just about break my mother up when he goes to war.

But go to war he did, joining the RAF as a pilot. The dreadful screech of air-raid sirens sounded across the country as their machinery was tested; searchlights probed the skies for enemy planes; and anti-aircraft batteries were installed in such incongruous places as London's Hyde Park.

Aware of the momentous times they were living through, many people began diaries to record the daily minutiae of wartime life. The population stepped into their new wartime roles. Will Dineen became the chief ARP

(Air Raid Precautions) warden in Streatham in London, but his wife's role was as chaperone to hundreds of evacuated schoolchildren. The couple were to be separated, so Mollie Dineen sadly packed up her London home.

> My home looked very dejected and untidy, I was feeling very tearful and unhappy about this, but I soon began to clean up. One sad moment was when he [Will] told us he had had to have our dog Pat put to sleep, as there was no one to look after her, she was a good dog and we loved her, and I'm sure she loved us, but we have to be cruel to be kind in these sad times. As I write I try to remember what the last war was for. I was only eight years of age, and now my son is eight, will he think us right to go to war to stamp out Nazism, and will there be someone else rising up to give trouble to the world after all this is finished? I pray to God that after this Peace may come to us and stay for all time.

The Home Front went to war, donning the uniforms, helmets and armbands of their new roles in Civil Defence, carrying identity cards, and one vital piece of equipment – a gas mask. Carrying gas masks would become routine, but first they had to fit properly. Peg Cotton, living in London with her two daughters and her granddaughter Penny, described the routine in her diary.

> A few days ago a young Air Raid Precautions officer came in to test our gas masks. Those of us who were here, had to try them on and breathe in and out, etc. Then the young woman took the average number of people here during the day and at night – as memoranda for 'trapped casualties' – that is, the ARP unit assigned to our particular area would look in the 'ruins' for 4 or 5 after a day raid, and 5 or 6 at night. Elegant and comforting thought! And today an 'Animal Guard' appeared. We have now a 7 weeks kitten that Alix [her daughter] rescued from a watery grave in Regents Park a few days ago.

Babies were catered for with special care.

> Penny has a huge 'protective helmet' – a contrivance that covers her completely – then we pump oxygen into it.

Gas was one enemy weapon anticipated by the authorities, after its use with such brutal effect in the trenches during the Great War, and as a precaution, Royal Mail pillar boxes were painted with pale green gas-detector paint that would turn red on contact with drops of mustard gas. According to a London County Council leaflet, *Anti-Gas Precautions for Civil Defence*, mustard gas was the most difficult to detect but it smelt faintly of horseradish, onions or garlic.

Local authorities secretly stockpiled cardboard coffins; and the population responded to a huge campaign to donate blood in preparation for inevitable casualties. The Local Defence Volunteers (LDV) were formed in preparation for possible invasion and speedily acquired the soubriquet, the Home Guard. Initially these volunteers were poorly equipped, and in June 1940 a wireless appeal was made for the loan of shotguns to the Home Guard. But as the demand for regular troops increased many would find themselves taking the place of Army regulars, serving in anti-aircraft batteries in British cities. At the outbreak of war, journalist Leonard Marsland Gander had moved his family out of London to Angmering-on-Sea, in Sussex, where he applied to join the volunteers.

I was asked if I would like to join the foot patrols but in view of the fact that the family are coming back to town I see no chance of getting down for duties. So I contented myself with typing out a list of phrases in German which I thought might be useful to the Home Guard, as Churchill calls them. Such as 'Hands up.' 'You are my prisoner.' 'You are surrounded by superior forces.' ' Surrender or you will be wiped out.' 'Surrender your arms.' Could not make out whether the locals thought this really useful or whether they thought I was mad. Of course there is the question of pronunciation, but after all this is what the Germans are doing with their English booklets.

The Home Guard was celebrated throughout the war with Home Guard Sundays, where the ranks of World War I veterans, now middle-aged, marched shoulder to shoulder with teenagers too young to enlist. Brian Poole was a teenaged member of the Home Guard in Cheshire and wrote to his American penfriend, Trude, in August 1940:

The best news yet, I am in the Home Guard (ex Local Defence Volunteers). I've had three rifle drills up to now and I do my first duty from 9pm to 6am on Wednesday, three hours duty, the rest a sleep on the floor ready for action. We are hoping to be in the fight night fronts!!! What we want is not to shoot the Bosche but to bayonet him. That which the Germans don't like, cold steel. The General in Command said our motto should be 'Kill the Bosche' and shoot to kill. Done a fine bit of work today, cleaned 20 rifles with Dad. Not so bad eh? Our house is simply littered with field dressings, supplies of uniforms, steel helmets, ammunition and I don't know what.

The Home Guard harnessed such enthusiasm on manoeuvres. They were taught to charge with bayonets, and took part in exercises with the regular army. Switchboard operator Mollie Wilson in Corsham found herself a bystander at a Home Guard Practice.

It was most exciting. There was a dive-bombing attack on the village. Mrs Taylor ducked every time the planes came low, and bombs kept going off. Every time they burst, ambulance men rushed out with stretchers and bandages. Several children were hurt. Others had to be sent to rest centres. Then the parachutists (regulars from the regiment here who crept in from the outskirts) tried to capture the place.

The Home Guard and the 'Germans' kept taking pot shots at each other round the war memorial. Some of the 'Germans' climbed into Lady Methuen's garden and came down that way. I saw one shadowy figure creeping through the shrubbery and nearly had a fit, as there was a member of the Home Guard standing with his back to the railings. Then a rifle butt crept round the wheel of a van and someone was killed. I couldn't see who. Then some 'Germans', two all splattered with blood and bandaged up, came creeping down from the Priory, and were making fine progress, towards the capture of the Town Hall, but they became too sure of themselves. One of them, a corporal, had the bright idea to throw a bomb. While he was lighting it and the others were reloading, a lance corporal of the Home Guard made a sudden dash and machine-gunned them all. He even held up and shot a Colonel who came up behind unintentionally.

So the day was won, and the Ambulance people carried out their task of collecting up the wounded and dead to be bandaged by the Red Cross nurses. One soldier I noticed was lying on the ground for about half an hour. Other soldiers kept coming up to look at his label (broken thigh or something) and going away again. It was so funny for us, but so sad for him.

One of the men said that a large scale practice like this one is the best thing that could happen, for they find lots of remedies from every time. It won't be so funny when it really happens and there won't be so many spectators to get in the way.

With a defiant stare, two German airmen are marched through a London railway station. Many German prisoners were not repatriated until 1947, and returned to a shattered nation that would spend the next fifty years trying to expunge the guilt of the Nazi regime.

This was 1940: Hitler's army was aggressively making for the English Channel, and Mollie Wilson (like most people) used the preposition 'when' rather than 'if', when talking of invasion. It was a very real threat. Brian Poole was trained to tackle incendiary bombs.

> I had to go inside a building and put out a bomb. Two men pump outside and you concentrate a spray of water on the bomb. You don't put a direct stream on it or else it flies about in red hot pieces. You crawl about on the floor so as to get fresh air.

It was not long before Brian and the rest of his Home Guard platoon were putting their training into practice. In the middle of the Liverpool blitz they were called out to search for German airmen, who had baled out of a Junkers 88 after it was shot down by a British fighter plane.

> We jumped into a cart and followed it until it crashed and burst into flames. We were amongst the first to arrive there and we helped put the flames out. What a Godsend it had crashed in a field of oats.
> We found no bodies in the machine. So we began to search, then news came through that two had escaped by parachute, one had been captured by soldiers and the other by members of our Home Guard Platoon. That left two to find as the captured airmen said there was four in the machine.
> We spread out and Dad found another parachute, open, and the harness undone. So he called me and three others to search, we were going to turn past a stream when someone shined his torch in the water, and there was a body lying face upward in the water. He was dead. I've never felt like being sick in all my days as at that moment. I turned away and someone said to me, 'I shouldn't be sorry for him if I were you, he's killed lots of women and children tonight.' And my heart hardened and I turned towards him. He had been badly shot, and how he found the effort to crawl from the parachute to the water nobody knows. He was an NCO [non-commissioned officer] about 23 years of age and very broad and well built. The other man, the pilot, was found by a dog, his parachute had failed to open.
> These two are to be buried with full military honours

tomorrow, by the men of the squadron that shot him down.

Millions of young lives were overtaken by the war machine. When Brian Poole left school he enlisted with the RAF. Kenneth Walsh joined the navy and had celebrated his engagement two months before war was declared. His fiancée, Miss E Williams, worked as a private secretary for the LMS (London Midland Scottish) railway. She wrote to her brother Ellis in British Somaliland:

20 Feb 1940 – The number of marriages on the LMS are going up by leaps and bounds now girls are being retained. One supervisor who has been courting a man through thick and thin for 17 years and is now 42, got married yesterday. He has joined up and is a lieutenant, having been a captain in the last war.

This was an era when women did not stay on at work after marriage, a convention that soon disappeared, however as the nation's demand for manpower increased.

People are getting married by the dozen now the single girls only decree has been rescinded. Daddy has been giving long talks on the stupidity of war widowhood. Apparently war widows get very bad reputations.

The bluntness of Miss Williams's father seems extraordinary, but widowhood was a practicality also discussed by teacher Mary Ross and her fiancé, Ben Hooper, during the early months of war. She wrote to him with the memory of the Spanish Civil War fresh in her mind:

There are still people alive loving and laughing in Spain and how long did they fight? Wars often help individuals darling. And just think dearest how you'll enjoy telling your family about what you did when you were a soldier. Darling, I know it's beastly and miserable but it can't be always wartime and the very worst that can happen is death, which is probably better than life.

Mary was consolingly philosophical. But she was also aware that fiancées and girlfriends were not automatically notified if men were missing in action or killed.

> I wish we had married in September at the beginning of the war now, but it doesn't really matter does it dear. Things might not be as bad as they seem and they might be worse but it doesn't really matter to us. Oh one horrid awful thought – (I know you'll want to hit me) but if anything did happen to you – do you think you could make some arrangements (beforehand) to have me notified fairly quickly.

Mary was evacuated with her pupils, far from her beloved Ben. Although she had little time to brood, she nevertheless found herself dwelling on this subject, and was brutally honest in her letters.

> I must marry you quickly, cos oh darling just think if you were killed and I hadn't. That's pure selfishness – I mean it's not a case of trying to make you happy before you possibly die – that sounds noble but it was me I was thinking of, cos darling, I don't think it'll help you in any way being married will it? But I don't really think it will harm you either. And then darling if you were badly hurt I know they wouldn't let me marry you but if we were already, they couldn't do much could they? All very morbid darling but always there in the back of my mind – everyone else's too I believe.

Ben and Mary were married in 1941. The Germans looked unstoppable in the spring of 1940 and, with a similar sense of fatalism, the thoughts of Miss E Williams also turned to her marriage.

> Kenneth has his commission after all, and we are to be married as soon as he can get leave, which he hopes will be the last week in June. This is very indefinite as he may be sent abroad before then, but on the other hand he may not, so I am preparing for marriage. Daddy and Mother want me to be married in white, although it isn't quite the right thing in wartime. Our sudden decision to marry was due to the fact that we shall probably have no money or job after the war,

and may not live till then in any case, so there seems nothing
to wait for.

Her cheerful optimism of April turned to pragmatism at the end of
May, as the British Expeditionary Force was trapped on the beaches of
Dunkirk, between the English Channel on one side and the German Army
on the other.

> As things are getting blacker and Harold Nicholson MP tells us
> to expect thousands of German troops here; I had better write
> and tell you how cheerful everyone is. The Belgian refugees have
> come here but where do we go – just stick I suppose.
>   The Office have given me a beautiful Queen Anne silver
> teapot, sugar basin and milk jug. If the German's come I
> must bury it at the bottom of the garden with my trousseau
> nighties, my watch and engagement ring. Not that we shall
> be beaten but we might get a bit pushed about before we
> win. Don't think by all this tomfoolery that I am not terribly
> miserable about the men left in the lurch in Belgium, but we
> can't help our country by being depressed.

All ages were drawn into the preparations against invasion. Joan Strange, a
middle-aged physiotherapist in Worthing, Sussex, recorded in June:

> Boys at Windlesham School have cut their hay and stacked
> it in the middle of their cricket field as is being requested by
> the Government as obstructions to enemy aircraft.

Journalist Leonard Marsland Gander was scornful of what he regarded
as rather futile measures against invasion, spotted on the outskirts of
London.

> Near Chessington they seem to be building concrete tank
> obstacles of the superior sort right across country and across
> the road. Are they making a sort of Siegfried Line as London's
> last defences? On the Kingston by-pass, added to the muck,
> are a large number of strange objects like galvanised iron
> chimney pots. Cannot imagine what they are for. But I am

again dismayed by the sight of the derelict motor cars with baulks of timber thrust through the windows and the old carts standing by the road ready to be used for barricades. An ancient Morris car filled with earth seems a feeble, inefficient means of defence incredibly crude and messy by comparison with a battleship or a Spitfire.

On the way to his office at the London headquarters of *The Daily Telegraph,* there was evidence of preparations for the desperate defence of the city centre.

Pillboxes of various types have been constructed on the Embankment. One at the end of New Bridge Street is particularly ingenious as it is partly disguised to look like the entrance to a Tube subway and even has newspaper placards painted on one side. Numerous brick air raid shelters have been built on the pavements. The work on Waterloo Bridge goes on but there are also the beginnings of emergency pontoon bridges at several points.

The Government had exhorted people to buy shelters in the summer of 1939. Some were given away to those on low incomes; many families pooled their resources. Dolly Howard in Liverpool described her family shelter: their reinforced garage.

We filled hundreds of sandbags – I had blisters on my hands and Lillian's shoulders ached so much that she could not stand up straight for a week. Well now it is like a little refuge room, walls papered with waterproof paper, electric light dim and bright, and beds. James has a camp bed at one side and there is a big double bed for Lillian and me. So after the nightly alerts, we just go to bed. Puss comes as well. We take supper and we knit if we do not want to go to sleep. Lillian and James just put their heads down and sleep through everything, but the guns keep me awake a bit. Jim goes on ARP duty, so I have put him a bed in the sitting room, and he pops in when there is a lull. If we feel cold in the winter we shall put a little radiator in the shelter, but so far we have been too warm.

We started with a lot of bedclothes but have been peeling [them] off ever since.

In London, May Britton and her husband Ernie had to content themselves with a refuge room, inside the house.

We can't get a shelter built because of a shortage of cement, so Ernie has done his best to strengthen our dining room with heavy timber supports and the window is barricaded with about three tons of cement blocks. How I hated having to shut the sunshine out of this room – it's the best in the house and now it never gets daylight – let alone sun.

As well as reinforcing their homes and building shelters in the garden, people covered their windows with netting, strips of gummed paper or celluloid solution, to reduce the danger of flying glass.

As they prepared for siege, inevitably people's thoughts turned to food. Rationing had been introduced during World War I, as Britain struggled to feed its population. Those in the know began to stockpile. As an American, Peg Cotton had not experienced those shortages during 1914–18.

Within a few months of the declaration of War people began to think of laying in a few stores of those commodities which, in time, were likely to become scarce. My grocer in London recommended tinned goods, sugar, candles, soap and toilet paper. The latter article made me smile. 'I remember the last War very well, Madam,' he admonished me. 'And there wasn't even a telephone directory to be had!'

2

IN THE FRONT LINE

Once we thought of a front-line village as a heap of shattered ruins in a pockmarked earth bordering the tumbled wilderness of No Man's Land. Now there are hundreds of British front-line towns and villages along our coasts, in the shadow of a menace, but as yet preserved from the worst of war's ravages. No Man's Land is our own protecting element, the sea, where the Royal Navy rides and rules.
(Leonard Marsland Gander, **Daily Telegraph**, May 1940)

Britain's coastline stretches for 11,232 miles. While the sea may act as a No Man's Land, this enormous coast with thousands of tiny bays and inlets required constant vigilance to counteract invasion attempts. The watchers have gone, but the crumbling shells of the pillboxes remain, scattered along the coast. While the population on land experienced the phoney war – all preparation and no action – Britain's first months of war against Germany took place at sea. The first enemy aggression was the sinking of the SS *Athenia* by a German U-boat four hours after war was declared. Five days later Bessie Skea, a 15-year-old schoolgirl in the Orkney Islands, recorded in her diary some of the action in her small corner of the British Isles.

Britain has caught two German ships and taken them into Kirkwall. They put both crews on one ship and sank the other one. Three Germans somehow got away in a motor boat, and they spent the night in the Bay of Sandsgarth. Tommy Nicholson saw them and reported it. Tom Sinclair and Bill Nicholson (both first-war veterans) gave chase in Bill Nicholson's boat. A tug came from Kirkwall with armed men on it, touched here and set off too. The village people went into a 'steer' because the Germans were said to be armed and Bill and Tom weren't! They caught them near Stronsay.

When the Shapinsay men came up to the Germans, they found
them unresisting and friendly. They gave them cigarettes,
and were about to make them a pot of tea when the tug-boat
appeared, and unceremoniously ordered the Germans aboard
at gun-point.

Bessie Skea's home was on the island of Shapinsay, a short ferry ride from
the Orkney capital, Kirkwall.

There are eleven ships lying in Kirkwall Bay, quite a few of whom
have been captured round Orkney. One big tanker was said to
have been lying off Westray supplying German U-boats. She was
caught and a submarine thereabout as well.

The Orkney Islands were in a vital strategic position, and the influx of
service men and women boosted the islands' population to 60,000 – three
times the peacetime population. Some of these troops were billeted on the
local population.

We hear that Miss Balfour is making the private soldiers who
are billeted with her eat their food outside in the cold. She
even refused to let them put their stoves in the courts outside
the kitchen door – the stoves are in the tennis court and the
men must eat there in the rain! And the Lieutenant is treated
like a gentleman, while he would prefer to be out with his
men. They must take their boots off before coming indoors!

Bessie Skea often saw troops on their way to the anti-aircraft battery not
far from her home.

The lorry went past here a little while ago with men and a
big trailer behind. The men were singing, and they all waved.
Mother lectured me for waving back, and when they returned she
wouldn't let me go out in case I waved to them again! The men
have been planning to hold a dance on Wed night, but I won't be
allowed to go.

From her coastal vantage point, Bessie watched with excitement as planes buzzed overhead, and great convoys of ships steamed past en route to Kirkwall.

> Hitler is sure to bomb Kirkwall; Orkney is a dangerous place to live in. The King was in Scapa Flow and Kirkwall last week; Churchill was here the week before. There are rumours that Churchill said Orkney was half-fortified – with the result that we are to have more coastal guns – one in Shapinsay too.

Her prediction was correct. Ten miles from Shapinsay is Scapa Flow, a natural harbour deep enough for larger ships and encircled by islands. The German Navy had scuttled their own fleet there during World War I. It was the British Navy that suffered on 14 October 1939.

> There were two air raids over Kirkwall while I was in town. The Royal Oak was blown up in Scapa and about 800 lives lost – many young boys in training. The war is only beginning now.

When ships were sunk and planes shot down, the crews (British or German) were unlikely to survive in freezing waters. Their unidentified decomposing bodies came to rest on the shoreline.

> Three bodies have come ashore on Shapinsay, two in Sands and one near Hillside. Finding the bodies has rather scared the Sands' people. Bill Nicholson (coastguard), going past the place where the bodies lay one dark night, nearly jumped sky high when something gripped his trouser leg! It was only a wee white dog – but it frightened Bill!

Thousands of troops were billeted along Britain's south and east coast, as defences were strengthened in the summer of 1939. A string of circular Martello towers, grim remnants of the last threat of invasion during the Napoleonic Wars, found a new role as positions for anti-aircraft batteries. In 1940, as German troops roared victorious across Europe, frontline towns became restricted areas, barbed wire appeared on sea fronts and beaches were mined. The genteel seaside resort of Worthing, in Sussex, had been considered a safe destination for evacuees in 1939, but on 27 May 1940, physiotherapist Joan Strange began to record the changes in her diary.

Worthing is being prepared! All the bathing huts have been trundled off the beach, filled with stones and put to block roads leading up from the sea! All boats have been removed from the beach and no bathing is allowed.

May 28th – Our pier has been closed by the military authorities and mined. No one is allowed to sit on the seats on the front in a given area round the shore end of pier.

May 30th – Worthing looks different! The front is being cut up for 'pill-boxes', there's a lookout on top of county café, soldiers and sailors abound. People are leaving the coast hotels very rapidly and some residents with small children are going too.

The police logbook in Felixstowe records how ditches were dug on the town golf course as tank traps, and elsewhere on the Suffolk coast huge cubes of concrete were constructed on beaches to trap invading military hardware. The German Army had reached the coast of France. Trapped on the beaches round Dunkirk were members of the British Expeditionary Force. At 11am on 30 May the crew of the Margate lifeboat were called out to help with the evacuation of troops. Equipped with steel helmets, cigarettes and rations, the crew launched the boat and set off. Ted Jordan had been on the crew for 18 years.

The boat was launched at 5.20pm and put off into Margate Roads where we made fast to a naval craft, we proceeded in tow to Dunkirk, arriving there just before midnight. As we approached, we could smell the fires which were raging in the town and about the docks, and the whole sea front was one mass of dense smoke and flame. We got in as close as possible, and saw masses of troops assembled at the water's edge, and we got about 80 aboard at first, and then got them aboard a nearby craft. A British officer swam to us, and came aboard, telling the coxswain that he had a large number of men further along the shore and guided us to the spot. He instructed his men how to make their way to us, telling them it was their last chance. Among them were several badly injured, and their mates were holding them shoulder high, on improvised litters.

They ferried the wounded to a hospital ship with German planes buzzing overhead, then set off to look for survivors clinging to rafts and bits of wreckage closer to the shore.

> Everywhere around one could see sunken craft, and could hear the bursting of shells from German guns. Troops on the beach were frantically trying to dig out all sorts of small boats which had been left high and dry, cattle were wandering along the water edge bewildered and quite near to us were the charred remains of one of the popular pleasure steamers, *Crested Eagle*. The whole job was at times awe-inspiring.

The Margate lifeboat brought off 600 survivors. It was just one of an estimated 100 civilian boats that crossed to Dunkirk. Sub Lieutenant A Carew Hunt, RN, was one of many in the forces who dashed to help. After several trips he volunteered as Lewis gunner in the War Department speed boat *Marlborough*.

> The *Marlborough* had a crew of four subs, two solicitors from the treasury, four leading stokers and two sergeants of the RAF. We went alongside a jetty and took about 40 poilus [French soldiers]. One of the solicitors spoke French which assisted the operation considerably. The next day our solicitors had to return to the treasury so we signed on an army officer and a retired colonel who had the reputation for being a crack shot with a Lewis.

In his official report to the Admiralty, Carew Hunt described the actions of one man who was typical of the civilians who helped to make Dunkirk such a very British 'victory'.

> I'd like to recommend highly the civilian cox of the *Thark* a man by the name of Ambler. This man who had only river experience succeeded in taking the boat to Dunkirk and back with no officer on the boat. He took the boat over again on Monday night and it was sunk, but I believe the crew was saved.

According to writer Noel Streatfeild, there would have been even more boats in the flotilla. On 13 June 1940 she wrote to her brother and sister-in-law in Bangkok:

The disgruntled who didn't go have appeared on the scenes. It seems to those hundred odd little ships that made up our Armada, there were countless hundreds more, that were screaming to be allowed to go, and whose owners, presumably because they were already in useful jobs were not allowed to take them. Whatever may happen to the owners of those boats for the rest of their lives, I don't think anything will ever compensate for them missing Dunkirk. They seem to feel like racehorses who should have run in the Grand National, and were not given the chance.

As Dunkirk survivors arrived ashore, civilian workers of all sorts rose to the occasion. Arthur Mowbray, head postmaster at Dover, recorded how postal, telephone and telegram services coped.

Foreign mails, labelled and unlabelled, outward and inward, sealed and unsealed were dumped in the Sorting Office as they were brought from France in anything that could float. Many bags were riddled and torn by bomb splinters, others salved from the sea were in a saturated condition, the contents like paper pulp, but with careful drying and a little imagination in deciphering addresses, the majority of items were sent off on a second journey. Special arrangements had to be made on the spot; as boats of every size imaginable were emptied of their human cargoes, hundreds of telegrams were handed in; 1,500 such messages were handed over in one day at a quayside office. The average daily traffic of 850 telegrams dealt with at the Head Office jumped to over 4,000. No appreciable delay occurred in disposing of the traffic, due to the wholehearted co-operation of the staff, who worked long hours at high pressure. Teleprinter speeds of 109 and 110 messages per hour were obtained: meal reliefs went by unheeded, for who could handle such messages and remain unmoved by the urgency of their appeal; the senders, somebody's fathers, somebody's sons, were indeed straight from the jaws of Hell, back from the gates of Death, and the little we could do to assist them to relieve the anxiety at home was gladly undertaken.

The nation had lived through the retreat from Dunkirk with the stranded army. Once on land, survivors were desperate to speak to their families on the telephone.

> The increase in telephone traffic was phenomenal. Lengthy queues
> of troops stood at the six telephone kiosks at the Marine Station,
> and at other kiosks in the vicinity of the Harbour. Much difficulty
> was experienced in dealing with this traffic, as owing to delays
> through congestion, callers frequently had to leave by train before
> their calls matured and generally did so without notifying the
> Exchange that the call would have to be cancelled. I let one young
> fellow use my 'phone to advise his fiancée of his safe arrival. The
> Counter was thronged from morning till night and the hours
> of business were extended to cope with the situation. Most of
> the pressure was due to evacuated troops, and refugees in their
> hundreds who accompanied the troops. People of British, French,
> Belgian, Dutch, Polish and unidentifiable nationalities turned
> the Public Office into a Tower of Babel. Queerly clad, many wet
> through, tired to the point of exhaustion, dirty and wounded,
> many were so excited at their miraculous escape, they found our
> currency and language a bit of a difficulty.

Arthur Mowbray was particularly impressed by worker in particular: a 16-year-old Girl Guide, who volunteered to tend some of the rescued men in one of the town's pubs.

> The Inn was swamped with troops, wet, wounded and exhausted;
> every chair, form, table, and available floor space was occupied;
> any place to rest was heaven. This child stayed several nights,
> after her working hours, taking off men's boots and wet clothes
> and drying them. She did what she could. To some it may have
> been their last taste of human kindness.

Mrs Iris Phillips, from the WVS, was one of many who helped the wounded on to hospital trains, serving refreshments donated by shops and local inhabitants.

> As soon as the patients were put down on the platform they
> began to look anxiously round, first for a cigarette, which we

instantly provided, and secondly for their particular pal. It made all the difference to those pitifully wounded men to know that however painful and miserable the journey might be their friends would be beside them to share it. Many of the patients were unable to sit up, and the nurses were all busy, so we knelt down where we were, and supported the men with one arm, and fed them with drinks with the other.

Kathleen Crawley had been on holiday when war broke out, and was evacuated from her home in London to Ashford in Kent.

All the soldiers coming home from Dunkirk came through Ashford station. Crowds of people wait along the line for them to give them refreshments and to collect souvenirs. They throw lots of things out of the trains. When Doris was there one threw an old German Army boot and Doris claimed a buckle and a piece of leather off the sole.

This was evidence of the thrifty nature of wartime living even in June 1940.

Further along the railway line, Ann Reeves was nursing at a military hospital, when the wards were suddenly emptied of patients. The hospital staff didn't have to wait for long.

One lovely May Day they came – filthy, unshaven, tattered and verminous. Most slept as they walked, unless they groaned in agony on stretchers. They collapsed on the beds, some lying for 48 hours before waking. Time ceased to exist. The only means of sterilisation – the primus – must be lit and kept going and the blood-soaked, fly-ridden dressings removed.

Dunkirk was a military defeat, but to the nation became a cause célèbre, as men returned to their families and home towns. On 1 June 1940, Joan Strange joyfully recorded in her diary the safe return of 'a number of Worthing men'. Captain Tommie Kerr described his welcome at a London railway station in a letter home.

Somewhere about 8 o'clock we arrived at Victoria. There were crowds and crowds with policemen keeping open a lane. I toddled down in my tin hat and bedroom slippers, haversack and revolver still strapped round me. Someone shouted 'The Good old Naivy' and some woman kissed me and they cheered and I wanted to cry. Then a man got hold of me and said 'Where do you want to go, I will look after you'. He led me to a taxi and brought me to the Admiralty and paid the taxi off. I went up to see Claud and he led me off to his flat and gave me dinner, and I told him all about it and thanked him for the honour he had done me in sending me over, and so back here to get some clothes and bath. My stomach hasn't been too good, some filth I have eaten, and I have been sick a number of times. This morning I had a couple of boiled eggs and I won't eat any lunch but will now lie down and sleep again. My only clean linen is in that suitcase I took to Dover and I don't know when I will get that. I have sent a pile of washing and will get it on Tuesday. I don't think I can write any more.

What remained of the British Expeditionary Force was safely back from France, but the invader was still poised on the French coast. The Government issued orders to all those in coastal areas to immobilize parked cars, in case they unwittingly offered transport to enemy parachutists. Removing the rotor arm from the engine of her car became routine for Joan Strange as she went on her physiotherapy rounds in the Worthing area. These coastal towns were packed with troops to defend British shores. Energetic Joan Strange was one of the many civilian volunteers who leapt into another wartime role.

I drove the YMCA mobile canteen to Shoreham beach this evening. I felt a bit scared as it is all heavily land mined there and there have been a few fatal accidents. However all went well and we did brisk trade for about an hour. Bungalow Town is no more – the bungalows and houses proved troublesome to the gunners who fire into the sea from the Downs so they have all had to be demolished.

During the summer of 1940, people on the south coast watched dogfights in the skies above their homes as the 'ragged RAF' fought the Battle of Britain. In August, journalist Leonard Marsland Gander was astonished at the contrast between London and his Sussex home at Angmering-on-Sea.

> The atmosphere in London is unbelievable. The enemy is making
> mass raids on our coasts and here it is quiet. I heard yesterday
> that a German airman had baled out at Angmering and landed
> somewhere on the Willowhayne Estate. I made numerous inquiries
> by telephone and discovered that there had been a terrific fight
> over the village at about 6.30 in the morning, lasting roughly
> half an hour. About twenty Jerries came in at an immense height
> invisible most of the time from the ground. Apparently they were
> intercepted right over the coast and below the locals could hear
> the continuous rattle of machine guns but see little except an
> occasional arching speck. Mrs Wells, the air raid warden, said that
> a German badly wounded in the hip landed in a cornfield. Air raid
> warden and the military captured him and Dr Ashby attended to
> his wound on the spot. He is said, apocryphally, to have given a
> weak Nazi salute. Mrs Wells said that he and another German pilot
> were taken to the institution for treatment. The second chap was
> truculent and threw off the British khaki greatcoat offered to him.
> Official reports showed that 78 German machines were brought
> down yesterday – a record.

Contemporary diaries and letters often include this day-by-day tally of the
'score' of the RAF versus the Luftwaffe, as the nation held its collective
breath. The place in the vanguard of these frontline towns was Dover, only
26 miles from the French coast. Enormous German guns were positioned
across the Straits of Dover at Cap Gris Nez, jutting out into the English
Channel, with their sights set on Dover. It was a matter of great pride
to head postmaster Arthur Mowbray (later awarded the MBE) that even
under this barrage his staff carried on working.

> Following a severe bombing attack on the harbour, barrage
> balloons were provided and these proved a comforting deterrent
> to the Luftwaffe tactics until the 31st of August, when a
> determined attack was made by enemy aircraft on the balloons
> over the town and port. Twenty three balloons were shot down
> between 8.30am and 9.00am, one of which fell in flames on the
> office roof and parapet near to the Telephone Exchange. It was

somewhat alarming to the operators, to see the blazing balloon hanging over their window, and as the machine gunning and anti-aircraft barrage were very intense, the Switchroom was evacuated and work continued for 23 minutes on the Emergency Board. This was the first time the Dover Exchange had been abandoned since the outbreak of war. Prompt action by members of the male staff, who pushed the remaining portion of the burning balloon off the parapet into the street below, prevented further damage. In the evening a further attack was made and nine more balloons were shot down, one starting a fire at a house near to the office. In this attack one plane dived and machine-gunned the Post Office Garage and Mail Entrance. The masonry over the lintel was hit by a small shell, and one door jamb bears the marks of twenty three machine gun bullets. The plane continued firing down the street and the Post Office Home Guard used their rifles with great relish. This day's five raid warnings lasted over nine hours, with hardly a dull moment.

Dover was bombarded with over 1,700 shells from the Cap Gris Nez guns in the second half of 1940. Lookout posts on the cliff tops were manned night and day by wardens who watched the flash of guns on the French Coast. The coastline was marked out in sections on a map, and when a flash was spotted in that section, the control centre in Dover itself could alert ambulances and rescue workers to the section of town where the shells from that particular gun site would fall. Despite the intensity of the bombing, the post never failed to be delivered, though on one occasion it was 50 minutes late! Even when the railway line was bombed, lorries were on standby to replace the mail trains. Writing daily, Arthur Mowbray catalogued the added disruptions faced by post office staff.

Add to this 552 air raid warnings, plus many of the homes of members of the Staff have been badly damaged, necessitating living in semi-darkness or in patched rooms. Many of the men have evacuated their wives and families, yet in no case has Hitler been cited as an excuse for failure to report for duty. One girl who was off at 8.00pm, reported back at 9.00pm with a request for permission to sleep at the office as her home had been demolished by a shell that evening – that was all – back on duty the next morning as usual, the only unusual feature being that she had to wear the same jumper and skirt as on the previous evening; but this girl's attitude is typical of them all. One postman had his home destroyed by a bomb; then the gas main in the street caught fire, adding to the destruction. His misfortune was only one of many.

The Nazi flag and sword of the German naval commander of Cap Gris Nez were presented to the town after the Allied invasion of Normandy, in commemoration of the courage and endurance of the inhabitants. Constance Logan Wright visited Dover in November 1944.

> During the five years of war the population had gradually dropped from 42,000 to 14,500. Many people left after the outbreak of war, but very many others did not leave till their homes were destroyed or made uninhabitable by the shelling.

She was particularly impressed by the tunnels in the famous and symbolic White Cliffs, which had originally been quarried to provide ballast for ships, then used as an arsenal during the Napoleonic Wars, and in this war used as air-raid shelters by the people of Dover.

> On the outbreak of the present war, the tunnelled cliff-face was hurriedly extended into great long galleries radiating from a kind of central hall, and into these galleries were put three-tier sleeping bunks. The shelter we saw could accommodate 2,300 men, women and children and was wired with electricity throughout. It had a complete operating theatre and first aid post, independent water supply from deep springs within the cliff, kitchen, clothes and bedding space. With 100 feet of cliff towering above it, it gave its shelterers a wonderful sense of security, and these caves have literally saved many hundreds of lives.

A mass of tunnels was cut into the hill below the 19th-century Fort Southwick at Portsmouth, as an underground communications centre for the navy. t qualified as a coder in the WRNS (Women's Royal Navy Service – the women were known as Wrens) in December 1942 and was based there for the rest of the war.

We only work 12 out of every 48 hours. We work in underground tunnels which have daylight lights and are air conditioned but it makes you feel rather sleepy until you get used to it. When you're on the long night watch, you sleep on double deckers near to the office, but tonight we shall be sleeping in this Recreation hut which is outside and we'll get plenty of air.

Veronica, daughter of a Commander in the Royal Navy, described the work as 'dull and steady', coding and decoding signals that came in from all over the world. When there was an incident in the English Channel, Veronica and her fellow coders could be called into the plotting room - a scene familiar from wartime films, with gigantic maps where ships were pushed into position with a croupier's stick. Re-reading her wartime diaries later, she wrote:

My memory is of the excitement and interest, and I was surprised on reading the letters and diary of the tedium which I apparently felt at the time.

Most of those working in these tunnels - plotters, wireless telegraphists, messengers and cypher officers - were Wrens. Every watch meant a journey down 166 concrete steps into the ground to offices that looked like underground Nissen huts. To compensate for the conditions, the underground Wrens had three days of 'stand-off' a month, and compulsory sunray treatment! When George VI visited in November 1944, Veronica recorded that the place was spruced up.

He walked through the coding office looking in a glaze of exhaustion but spoke to 2 or 3 people. There were double the number of people below ground than normal, and the whole tunnel had been painted in glossy off-white paint a few days before. It was extremely hot, small and stuffy. The tunnel rumour was that the King had declared the place 'not fit for human habitation'. Whatever he had said, the number of air ventilators, certainly in the Coding Office and probably throughout, was doubled within 2 to 3 days - the improvement was noticeable.

Although Veronica did not complain in her letters home, these conditions

Wren Veronica Owen (third from right) with fellow members of A Watch in the Coding Room at Port Southwick, Portsmouth. The naval base made the city a target for the Luftwaffe. On 10 January 1941, 450 bombs were dropped in a single raid.

must have been hard, particularly as she revelled in the fresh air, taking long bike rides on her days off.

Maureen Bolster, another naval daughter and fellow Wren, was thrilled to be selected as a naval despatch rider, as she wrote to her fiancé Eric Wells in July 1942.

> There are very few despatch riders indeed, and we are a complete speciality – 'the darlings of the Navy'! You are attached with a couple of others to a Port, and you run about all over the place. All traffic gives way to you. You don't have to work very long hours – 9–5 as a rule. The equipment provided is superb – breeches and shiny leather leggings and a tailored jacket, nipped in at the waist. Unfortunately, a crash helmet as well (Cor!) then for cold weather, a great big lined mackintosh, windproofed etc. One gets two ordinary Wren outfits, with special markings, to show your superiority over the rank and file. When you've been

qualified three months you get wings. One can be reasonably assured of a good time socially. It all sounds so wonderful, I can't wait to go . . . I pray nothing will happen to stop me!

When she wrote that, Maureen had been eager to leave her current job as a billeting officer for a factory – a job to which she brought a natural determination and sense of humour. In October 1942 she became a woman in uniform, and began her probationary period with the WRNS. The glamour wore off pretty quickly, as she wrote to her fiancé in November.

Am in a cabin with 14 others – all couriers. Except for this other girl who's 25 none are under 30!!! Six are over 40! They're tough, strong and ugly. Some of them are ladies, but queer, their conversation is dreadful – lots of them, apparently use their job as a means to another end – if you get me! They're all as dull as dishwater and so ugly. I'm as lonely as hell.

It wasn't only her living conditions that Maureen found a strain. As a secret courier she had to travel all over the country, not only by motorcycle but also by plane, train and ship.

You don't know what it was like that particular kind of mental strain – taking things that cost vast sums of money – taking things that you were told a ship were waiting for, before they could sail – new inventions – highly secret dispatches, having to have things in a certain place by a certain hour. Taking enormous quantities of gear, coping with porters, working parties, transport.

Rail travellers were plagued by delays: trains travelled at speeds of 15mph over parts of the line in case of bomb craters; carriages and corridors were crammed with people; and there was always the possibility of air raids. Maureen's fiancé was a squadron leader in the Middle East, and her own experiences as a courier during those ten months were a close parallel to those of men fighting abroad in at least one respect.

The lack of sleep. Have you known what it's like to keep on going without it and never making it up? Sitting up through the

night, maybe several nights running – having travelled all day
your eyelids red and sore, the muscles of your face all strained
– probably hungry because you hadn't the money to get yourself a
decent meal. And then – when back in quarters, unable to get rest,
being in a noisy dormitory – not companionship, as the others
were so old and ugly, and forever quarrelling and fighting.

In October 1943, after she had been transferred from the courier service,
she expressed her relief to Eric and revealed that she had been suffering
from . . .

> . . . a shocking nervous exhaustion, the like of which I hardly
> knew existed. I can't imagine what my letters were like. Eric I
> can assure you this – if I'd gone on there any longer, I'd've had
> a breakdown. I can't tell you what the strain was like. Quite
> honestly, I don't know how I carried on for 10 months. I can
> see now that I was left in a state of extreme exhaustion, mental
> and physical.

Maureen Bolster became a stoker. In the dust and heat of RAF Headquarters
in the Middle East, her squadron leader husband must have felt refreshed
reading these exuberant words:

> I've had a wonderful day. I've spent it driving round
> Portsmouth Harbour in a speed boat! Whizzing along the
> water and a long wash of foam behind. There's nothing to it
> – clutch rudder wheel and throttle. Easy! Crew of 3 sailors –
> Coxswain (instructor), stoker and deckhand. I took them to
> Gosport and nearly to Spithead. The exhilaration was terrific.
> This morning we went over the water to get the rum ration for
> our establishment, but I wasn't allowed even a smell! I adore
> this life. I love the water – the sea – the boats, the dockyard,
> the old salts and the yarns they spin – the movement and
> colour. I like sitting on the gunwale, swinging my legs and
> talking to the tough seamen in the little boats.

Finally Maureen had found her niche.
  As homes to ships of the merchant and Royal navies, ports were constant

targets for Luftwaffe pilots. Dolly Howard lived in West Derby, a suburb of Liverpool – the destination for many convoys.

> Liverpool seems to be well-defended, glory be; and when Jerry comes we bump him about a bit. The sound of the guns is sweet music to our ears. We seem to get several visits when the convoys come in.

After one raid she wrote to a friend:

> Most people's water systems 'went west' here. In fact we have been waiting for a plumber for four weeks. I heard of one plumber with 500 names on his list, and he was taking them in strict rotation. We were so tired of waiting that yesterday Jim borrowed a blow lamp and solder, begged petrol (as we have no coupons) and set to work himself. He finished a short while ago after repairing three broken pipes, and looks gorgeous – as black as a sweep. So now we can have a fire downstairs again, and can pull the lavatory chain. It has been a procession of buckets.

Low water pressure was a recurring problem for the fire service in many towns and cities. In Liverpool, the council laid pipes in the main streets, so that a continuous supply of water could be taken from the River Mersey. It posed a particular problem during a massive raid on the east coast in 1943. In the early hours of 14 June, 101 people were killed and 300 seriously injured in Grimsby and Cleethorpes, in Lincolnshire. An anonymous diarist in Grimsby recorded the damage, as high explosives, incendiary bombs and anti-personnel bombs fell for an hour.

> Most damage in the docks by fire, portion of two pontoons burned out. Hospital gutted. In town anti personnel bombs caused deaths through people kicking or moving them. For several days afterwards anti-bomb squads were exploding bombs found in offices and private houses. The NFS [National Fire Service] and Civil Defence people were overmatched and much of the theoretical organisation went 'phut'. Fire brigades came from Mansfield, Lincoln and Leicester. There was much criticism of

the NFS, but low water pressure contributed to the comparative failure in some cases. After the raid notices were posted about touching strange objects. If they had been posted *before*, many lives would have been saved. The Chief Constable had received notice about them but instead of giving the matter publicity treated it as all very hush hush and secret – the fool.

A few days after the raid this anonymous observer discovered an unexpected hero among the Cleethorpes citizenry.

> Mr AA Beardsall, well known chartered accountant and a leading man in Cleethorpes Civil Defence, was one of a party of ARP men, soldiers, police, who swept fields at Stallingborough for anti-personnel bombs, and also sands at Cleethorpes. Through growing corn they searched for bombs with sticks and found about 100 in two fields. Bomb squad exploded them by fastening long lengths of string to each. Beardsall made light of it, although he admitted he got the wind up. While on the sands he found his foot on something hard which had sunk in soft sand. It turned out to be a bomb, but luckily it didn't go off.

A month later Grimsby and Cleethorpes were hit again, making 3,000 people homeless, killing 65 and leaving 173 injured. Schools, churches, the fish docks and numerous residential streets were hit, as the area was dive-bombed. British bombers limping back from raids on Germany were also a danger as they crash landed in the surrounding countryside.

The port's fishing fleet also ran the gauntlet of German bombers. Among them was the *Volesus*, which had landed a record catch in April 1941.

> Skipper J Walters died in Grimsby Hospital following wounds inflicted by Nazi airman when he machine-gunned the trawler *Volesus*.

The following day:

> Minesweeper *Corfield* sunk, destroyer cut in half by bombs towed into Immingham.

On Christmas Day 1941 the same observer noted that 80 men were rescued from three ships sunk off Humber, but most seamen did not survive in the North Sea for long. His brief notes catalogue a trail of casualties at sea, which brought the dreaded telegram – 'The Admiralty regrets . . .' – to so many wives and families.

> Trawler *Lord Shrewsbury* given up with crew of ten hands. Skipper IH Noble and son IJ Noble lost; Charles Perritt (mate) married; John C Elliott (third hand) married, two children; Leonard Sparkes (trimmer); Sidney Allan Rodgers (trimmer); William Judge (deckie); Henry V Gerwaney (cook), wife two children; George Robertson (chief engineer); Thomas Jobson (second engineer).

Many fishermen joined the merchant navy, their trawlers converted into minesweepers and coastal patrol boats. The years 1939–45 brought some of the coldest weather on record and led to teams of women knitting for victory. Mollie Baker was one of the many women who formed knitting groups for 'adopted' ships of the merchant navy. Seamen were delighted with the supplies of sweaters, balaclavas, gloves and socks that were sent to them. Sam Gibbs, gunner on HMT *John Stephen,* was a former deep-water fisherman used to the icy waters round Bear Island, Greenland and Iceland. He was 'adopted' by Mollie Baker in September 1940.

> I want to thank you for the woolens you sent for the boys. I hope this finds you and your two children in the best of health also your lady friends, if any of them care to write I will always be pleased to answer these letters. I'm married with five children, three have been evacuated to Gainsborough, my home is in Grimsby, I was a fisherman before this bit of bother started. You asked if we would like to be adopted, I'll say we would, then we could say that *John Stephen* has a few sweethearts. The lads and myself will always be thankfull for a few woolens and books. I had to smile when I saw the stocking without heels, but one cannot look a gift horse in the mouth. I hope I'm the lucky one to get that sweater you wrote about. I know what the winter is like at sea after spending the last 20 Christmases in the North regions.

Merchant seaman Sam Gibbs, with the gun he proudly called 'my baby': a 12-pounder that was the crew's only defence as they patrolled the waters round Britain. He served on the HMT John Stephen, *a converted trawler pressed into service in 1939 as a minesweeper.*

In his jokey letters, Sam introduced her to the intricacies of deep-water trawling and sent photos of his wife and children. His pride and joy was the 12-pound gun, which was the former trawler's only defence against enemy aircraft and U-boats.

> I been real busy catching my work up, what with cleaning my
> baby, that's my 12 pounder, then the small gun and stowing
> ammunition I'v been kept at it. I dare say you would like my
> baby, she a beauty, the commander complimented me on it
> last trip, since when I painted it blue grey the colour of your
> eyes I hope. We are presently at sea, and being night-time we're

patrolling, we pulled in our sweeps about two hours ago. Up to now we've had a quite time but I don't know how long it will last, the weather is beginning to get his winter grip now so we get a few more brezzes, and don't this old tub roll she makes you think your in a rocking chair, but not so comfortable.

In November Mollie and her knitting group knitted woolly hats for the crew of the *John Stephen*.

Thank you for the caps ect they were just what we needed, I shared them out to the lads and told them you sent them, they said thank you. I dare say it comes hard on you people knitting things your not accustomed to but your doing well keep it up but don't tire yourselves you kneed your rest the same as other people.

We have been working a different sweeping system this last day or two, the lads called it the sewiside squad, how would you fancy cooking dinner with a life belt round you but I was taking no risks. I didn't want to have to walk back to shields [North Shields]. I can swim but there are times when one may be hurt and not able to, so safety first.

In December Sam wished Mollie 'a Jolly Time' at Christmas, and told her things were getting 'a bit warmer' out in the North Sea.

We left harbour this morning and about 5 minutes after we left there was a nasty crack just behind us, towards where we had left but we didn't see anything and when we got back this afternoon we found two big ships had struck a mine each, but luckily only 1 killed and 4 injured on one ship which was a large 2 funnelled Passenger carrying a lot of passengers, and on the other 4 were killed, 6 injured, but both vessels have been brought to land. We have to go to ships that are in trouble through enemy action the last one we went to had lost 65 men, previous to that we went to one that had been bombed, we had to blow them up and it wasent very nice seeing the bodies after the explosions, but I suppose its all in a days work.

The dirt and danger of his job played only a small part in these letters. Instead Sam told anecdotes of drunken shipmates, wrote poetry and showed concern for the welfare of Mollie and her family, all tinged with the humour and affectionate intimacy of an old friend.

> Well Dear, regards the stocking, I should say the men would prefer them with heels and if you make the foot, say to fit a man taking 9 in shoes I don't think you'll be far wrong. I'v worn them all my life being a fisherman in peace time so I hope you don't get offinded at me telling you how to knit them. I thank you for promising me the sweater, I want to tell you I'm not very fat. I stand 5ft 8, and weigh 10 stone, so I'll leave you to guess the size but whatever size it is I shall be proud to wear it because you made it for me. I'm very proud to have someone like you to write to. I hope you feel that way about mine. A letter allways cheers one up and if you have someone you can rely on to write to you well youv something to look forward to.

William Lind was the chief engineer on the MV *Angularity*. On her way to Newcastle with a cargo of phosphate, the ship was torpedoed between Harwich and Lowestoft, on a freezing cold evening in February 1941.

> It was a bitterly cold night and a snowstorm was raging with a heavy sea on. At 20:30 hours GMT there was a muffled explosion. I opened my cabin door to see what had happened, but no sooner I did this a solid wall of water drove me back into the cabin. The next thing I knew was I was trapped in my cabin under water. Fortunately, my cabin got air locked through the vessel going down bow first. I reckoned the whole thing happened within ten seconds. Strange enough I did not panic. I was swimming in circles in my waterlogged cabin with just enough air space to keep the water below my nose. My head was bumping the bulkhead. I took one deep breath and dived through the open doorway. It seemed ages before I broke surface. The seas were high and the water was bitterly cold. When I came to the surface I could see the stern of the doomed ship sticking out above water, the strong tide was carrying me away from her and suddenly she disappeared. There was nothing in sight except the dim outline

of the Suffolk coast. I kept swimming without a life belt. Sooner or later I too would come to an end, nothing but a miracle could save me. Just when things began to look black for me a hatch from the doomed ship came floating towards me. I grabbed at it and hung on for dear life . . . I thought of my wife and children, very soon I would be leaving them for ever.

As he recited stanzas from *The Rubaiyat of Omar Khayyam*, he saw two shapes 50 yards away in the gloom.

I shouted, they heard me, and one of the dark forms came in my direction. With some difficulty they hauled me on board, I could not help myself owing to my numbed legs. They bundled me in blankets when they got me below. I was laid in one of the crews bunks. Then three sailors sat on top of me to impart the warmth of their bodies. They offered me a bowl of hot soup, and a glass of schnapps.

After his rescue by the German E-boat (a torpedo boat), William discovered that he and the second engineer were the only survivors. He spent 4½ years as a German prisoner of war.

The years 1940 and 1941 saw a horrifying loss of life and ships, as convoys bridged the gulf between Britain and her transatlantic cousins, Canada and the USA. Ships carrying munitions, oil and food travelled in convoy at the speed of the slowest vessel. Out in the vast Atlantic wilderness they were hunted by U-boats (submarines). Rough seas were another danger, but mountainous waves also brought a degree of camouflage. One eyewitness described a direct hit on a ship carrying aviation spirit.

A sheet of flame, a roar as the blaze spreads across the water and no chance of saving either life or the ship.

Convoys were ordered not to stop or make detours to pick up survivors. Merchant ships and escorts were supplied with snowflake rockets, which illuminated the sea in a burst of white light in a bid to hunt the hunters, but with the risk that the rest of the convoy became more visible and more vulnerable. Warwick Brookes was a trimmer on the SS *Beaverford* on the transatlantic run to Canada. A month after war broke out he married his 21-year-old fiancée, Mary, and for a year the couple shared the brief shore leaves and frequent partings common to maritime marriages. On 18 November 1940, Mary Brookes received the dreaded telegram saying that the *Beaverford* had been sunk, and her husband was reported 'missing believed killed'. In March 1941 the General Register and Record Office of Shipping and Seamen sent her notification that 'Warwick T Brookes is supposed to have died on November 5th 1940'.

> That word *supposed* sustained my hopes, for never at any time had I been informed that, quite categorically, all the crew had perished.

She was unable to come to terms with her husband's death until in 1944 a friend sent her an eyewitness account of the sinking published in the *Evening Standard*. The captain of the last ship in the convoy had watched from his bridge as he steamed away.

> At 5pm on November 5th 1940, in the North Atlantic, the enemy raider encountered the British convoy. Instantly the *Jervis Bay* (the escort ship from the Royal Navy) headed for the foe, her guns blazing. The whole weight of the raider's guns were concentrated upon her, but the desperate twenty minutes of her noble effort to draw the raider's fire gave the convoy time to disperse.

Within 20 minutes the *Jervis Bay* went down.

> Vengefully, the foe singled out the *Beaverford* for concentrated attack. So it fell to her to take the place of the *Jervis Bay* and to carry on the delaying action against the enemy by which so many of the convoy were saved.

The *Beaverford* and a neighbouring ship put out a smokescreen to give the rest of the convoy a chance to run for safety.

> For more than five hours the *Beaverford* stayed afloat firing and fighting to the last, pursued by the raider. Using the big reserve of engine power for speed, and steering and manoeuvring to baffle and evade the enemy's aim, she held her own, hit by shells

but hitting back, delaying the raider while the rest of the convoy made their escape into the rapidly gathering gloom. The unequal engagement lasted until 10.45pm when there was a burst of flame from the *Beaverford*.

On Christmas Eve 1940, Mary Brookes received a parcel: a bundle of her letters, returned by the shipping company. They had never reached her husband.

The letters that Bill Crowther sent to his wife Bette at their home at 31 Tyne Street, Hull, reveal the homesickness men could suffer at sea, even when the ship was in sight of English shores.

> There was a doleful figure of a man on the poop as we slipped
> through the locks and headed out to sea. His head was bent
> and the look on the poor man's face would have put Dismal
> Desmond [a cartoon Dalmatian dog] to shame. His heart was left
> in 31 Tyne Street and his actions in giving orders were those of a
> robot. Well such is life in the Merchant Navy.

Bill had married his sweetheart Bette only two months earlier, in September 1941. Throughout the next 15 months he travelled back and forth across the Atlantic.

Easter Sunday, Somewhere at sea [1942]
Time marches on and here we are rolling along like an ocean
greyhound, homeward bound and feeling quite pleased about it.
The sun is shining and if it wasn't for our escort nosing around
the convoy, one would hardly believe there was a war on. I didn't
send any letters to you over on yon side [the USA], as we weren't
in port very long, and we would have arrived home before them,
but I hope you received my cable OK. I received some letters
from you over on the other side, they were old ones posted last
December, but I enjoyed them just the same. I often get them out
and read them over again, they are as good as a tonic to me and
my hair sort of takes on another curl. It is hard being married to
a sailor Bette, long months of parting from each other but I pray
to God that I can make up for it when we are together for the few
days leave I get, and so long as you are happy with me that is all

that matters. I bought a few things for you. I didn't have time to look round but I hope you will be pleased with them. I didn't buy much in the way of food, only a couple of tins of orange juice and two tins of biscuits and four packets of tea. I forgot all about sugar, butter and such like so I hope you will not be disappointed, my dollars didn't go very far.

Bill was at sea when his wife gave birth to their first child.

I only wish I could have stayed at home for our happy event, to comfort you and welcome the new arrival to the home, but such is life. No one knows the heartache which a sailor has to silently bear in missing such times which are normal in the ordinary man's life.

In September that year his ship was torpedoed and sunk by a German U-boat on its way back from America. He and the rest of the crew were rescued and he returned home on 'survivor's leave' to meet his baby daughter Carol for the first time. They celebrated the Christmas of 1942 together. Bette joined him aboard ship while it was in dock at Birkenhead. It sailed on 11 January 1943 and spent the next 14 months in the waters off South Africa, India, Egypt and Australia. In September 1943 Bette gave birth to their second daughter. At noon on 29 February 1944 Bill Crowther's ship, the SS *Ascot*, was torpedoed by a Japanese submarine in the middle of the Indian Ocean. Four of the crew were killed instantly, 52 boarded the ship's life rafts. The submarine's captain ordered the survivors be machine-gunned. Eight survived, but Bill Crowther was not among them.

3
OCCUPATION

Someone in Jersey has been imprisoned for keeping a diary!
(Douglas Ord, 1943)

A shocking photograph appeared in the *Daily Express* on 28 April 1942. It depicted the familiar British bobby standing next to a jackbooted officer of the German army in a British street. This was not propaganda designed to make British hearts skip a beat. The picture had been smuggled out of Jersey and it recorded a sight familiar to Channel Islanders - loyal to the Crown since the 13th century. The Channel Islands were occupied in a fashion that can only be called ignominious. The British Government decided that the islands would be too costly to defend, lying only 15 miles from the French coast, and declared them a demilitarized zone.

Iris Bullen was 25 years old, and a mother of two young children, when she heard the British Government's statement at five o'clock on 19 June 1940. She wrote in her diary, as boats were being readied for evacuation:

> It was a very unsettled evening for everyone, we couldn't make up our minds, and also the difficulty was that in some families all did not wish to leave, therefore many had the chance to go, and yet felt they could not leave some of those dear to them behind, which also meant leaving homes and animals etc behind.

Like many Channel Islanders, her husband John was serving in the British Forces. On 25 June he returned to Jersey on special leave to see his family.

> We were still undecided as to whether we should go back with

him to England. John had a strong view that the Germans were coming to pay us a visit soon, which meant that if they occupied the island I should be cut off from the mainland. After much thought over it, we both decided it would yet be safer for the children and myself to remain behind.

When the boat left at 9.30 the following morning, John Bullen was on board.

> I felt the parting very much. I said goodbye to John at the gate, as I did not want to upset him by going to the boat – his family was there to see him off.

On the island of Guernsey, a few miles closer to the advancing Germans, Methodist Minister Douglas Ord recorded the arrival of French evacuees, followed by people from the tiny island of Alderney. But, simultaneously,

> . . . in the opposite direction an unceasing stream of women and children went down to the harbour to embark. Beasts have been left in some fields tethered in Guernsey fashion, but without arrangements for milking. The vets have put so many pets to sleep that they have run out of the wherewithal to continue this unhappy task. Many took swift decisions. Leaving beds unmade and tables uncleared they made a dash for the boats. Among these were some who will one day have regrets.

His standing in the community made him an obvious source of wisdom and advice for parishioners. On 22 June he wrote in his diary:

> An unforgettable day. From early morning to midnight and after, our house was besieged by people of all classes seeking advice. Tearful mothers brought grave-faced children. Parents came to ask if it might be risky for daughters to remain. Some merely called to say goodbye.

Posters circulated imploring people to remain in the islands: 'Don't be yellow!'. That Sunday the Methodist church was full.

In the afternoon, in concession to the circumstances, I married two of my young people from the church. They wished to face the future together. As might have been expected there has been a rush of weddings this week.

About half the population left Guernsey in that exodus. Among them was Mr E Hamel, a telephone engineer from the island's capital, St Peter Port.

I needed no telling that to abandon everything we possessed was almost too terrible to contemplate, but what was the alternative.

Hundreds of Channel Islanders were evacuated to Bradford. Once Mr Hamel and his family reached the relative safety of Yorkshire, they listened avidly to the wireless for news.

The first news of enemy action was unexpected and horrifying – St Peter Port had been bombed. Reports said that many had been killed and injured. The quayside was littered with a mass of blazing tomato-laden lorries.

The island's famed tomato crop was at its peak and just before the invasion 1,800 tons had left the island bound for England. Islanders watched and waited. German troops landed first on Alderney, then Guernsey, where Douglas Ord saw them arrive on 1 July 1940.

All day long planes and troop carriers have been coming over from France, flying very low with deafening din to impress us. As we went to town car after car went by, packed with officers and NCOs. The men were fetched in local buses as they arrived and stared open-mouthed at the well-dressed civilians, the clean, freshly-painted houses and at the shops with their windows invitingly full of good things.

Germans are everywhere – eating, eating, eating. They prove their prowess as trenchermen, ordering omelettes made with eight eggs. From time to time they go out into the street to be sick and then valiantly resume their place at the festive board unless ousted by others. It was instructive to see Germans eating butter in half-pound packets without bread as they went about the streets.

On 1 July, when news of Guernsey's occupation reached her, Iris Bullen managed to send a final telegram from the post office to her husband in England. Moments later, communications with the mainland were severed.

> The most tragic time of the day, was when we were all informed that we had to have a white flag of surrender flying from every house in the island, by 7am on Tuesday morning [2 July] the time when the Germans were to occupy the island, so we were all busy making and erecting this unhappy flag. We also thought it best to take away any pictures of Royalty or Military origin as we did not know what our invaders were going to do, many papers etc we burnt.

Channel Islanders were quickly subjected to curfew; their clocks had to be moved an hour forward to German time, and their wireless sets tuned to German stations. Iris Bullen thought these restrictions 'very lenient'. But as the occupation progressed the Germans forbade tuning in to the BBC; they announced that anyone caught in possession of British propaganda pamphlets would be imprisoned for 15 years; and they confiscated cars and lorries. Iris wrote in September 1940:

> What absurd robbery. We are all very upset, especially those concerned, some have worked very hard to have a car, though a written receipt is given for each one, we know it is a dud bargain.

A month later, there was an apparent concession from the occupying power. Iris was in a quandary.

> We are now able to send a letter of a few words to our relations in England to tell them we are well, but so far I have declined from writing as it seems to me it would be wrong to disclose John's military address.

Such patriotic restraint was very much in character, and she recorded with elation that her mother had picked up one of the forbidden pamphlets dropped by the British. But her immediate concern was feeding and clothing her two children, Roy and Monica.

> Everyone has started to raid the shops of all sorts in the clothing and grocery line. Some shops had people queued up for hours outside and many were buying much more than their immediate requirements as they were afraid of not being able to get such articles later on. Elastic, darning wool, cotton and salt were soon stripped from the shops.

Flyers from the German Luftwaffe bragged in streets and shops of the imminent invasion of the mainland. Douglas Ord was woken by the roar of enemy planes flying north towards England on 9 July.

> Could this really be confirmation of the boast of those Luftwaffe fellows? I lay balancing arguments for and against in my mind. With some anxiety I awaited the early news on the wireless. Nothing to report!

On 14 August he wrote:

> Our confidence in the futility of invasion grows. Several damaged planes have gone down round our shores while occasionally, as yesterday, a plane limps back to the airport. Many Germans, like the cranks who foretell the world's end from Daniel and Revelation, are now betting on August 15th when London will be entered. Hotels here have been booked for dinners and dances to celebrate.

But they had underrated the RAF as opponents. As the Battle of Britain continued over the Home Counties, Channel Islanders had pressing domestic concerns: food was becoming increasingly scarce. In September Douglas Ord was warned that:

> . . . Germans were likely to make domiciliary visits to check

on private food stores. We therefore hid some of our precious tinned stuffs, bought before the Occupation, as people were advised to do, in the lower part of the piano!! In the garden I also constructed a rockery with such plants as summer snow, arabis, etc trailing attractively over. But inside was a fairly strong metal deed box, quite three feet in length. It was a useful cache.

German rules and regulations were tightened, and there were fears of further requisitions. Many island houses stood empty and Germans were reportedly helping themselves.

> Many quite sound and indeed brave people are beginning to
> be jumpy. Even G [his wife] hates to have to be left alone, as
> do so many. It becomes second nature to lock all doors even
> in daytime.

Morale was boosted as a boatload of people escaped from Guernsey to the mainland, landing at Start Point in South Devon. The news was brought to the islanders by one of the forbidden pamphlets, dropped by the RAF. Morale dipped when wireless sets were confiscated in November. Iris Bullen bravely hung on to her set.

> Today we have the dreadful news that all wireless sets have
> to be given up. It has shocked us all, as it was the greatest
> comfort we possess, to be able to link ourselves with England.
> How eagerly we listen to the familiar announcer's voices, and
> the good news they have at times is like a tonic to the dreary
> and hard times which we are going through now. We love to
> hear of the assurances given to the occupied, that we shall be
> delivered from this awful tyranny, but, alas, our lives are to be
> gambled again by the power of these tyrants, who love to make
> strife among men, but we are still British, and it will take more
> than taking our property to break our spirits and our belief in
> the outcome of this struggle.

In May 1945, as the Channel Islands waited to be liberated, she was able to confess to her diary:

During the evening we dug up all John's wireless, which has
been in the ground for two years! I had kept it in the house
for one year, after the orders to send them in, but as I heard of
suspicions that some neighbours (friendly with the Germans)
had, that I had some wireless, I thought it was time to do
something about it, so dismantled quite a few sets and buried
the parts in a tin trunk etc.

Douglas Ord had found friendship with a German officer through their
shared love of music and books. The officer was a frequent visitor to the
minister's home.

Again he warned me against hearing or retailing the BBC
news. 'There are many civilian spies around who would betray
you for a penny. Our police give rewards and sometimes
other "persuasions" to informers.' In his billet they have a
new corporal – a pukka Nazi. He issued an ultimatum 'The
moment anyone turns on London I go for the police!'

Ordinary islanders braved informers and German reprisals to hang on to
their sets, and listen secretly to the BBC. This is what Douglas Ord heard as
he tuned in on New Year's Day 1942:

At the end of the news last night the Secretary of State for
Scotland referred to us in passing. It is puzzling that so little
mention is made of the Channel Islands and that we never get
any more leaflets via the RAF. We try to imagine this is owing
to policy and that we are an infinitesimal pin-point in the map
of world affairs. Still we are a loyal folk and would welcome
a chance of defying orders in picking up anything the RAF
might drop, from daily newspapers to a side of bacon, though,
greedily, we would expect them to drop the latter in the bounds
of our garden.

An evacuated islander kept a scrapbook of articles that did appear
in English newspapers. Most appeared in the Methodist Church press,
and naturally the most column inches were devoted to dramatic escapes

from the islands in tiny boats. But as one correspondent wrote to the *Daily Express* in 1941:

> I'm still waiting for some of our leaders to remember the Channel Islands when they speak of the various oppressed peoples. Even the Archbishop of Canterbury, on the Day of National Prayer, when he expressed sympathy with the invaded countries and mentioned several by name, omitted them. So did the Prime Minister in his last broadcast. The Channel Islanders have given their men to the forces, and have always been loyal to the British Empire. Now they are under the Nazi heel, yet we never hear of anything being done for them.

An octogenarian Guernsey peer, Lord Portsea, managed to get limited publicity by offering to parachute into the Islands. But diarists and letter writers on the mainland rarely even mentioned the occupation. In fact, publication of newsworthy stories of escapees was likely to bring reprisals on those left on the Islands. On 16 September 1941, two Guernsey men and two French girls had escaped. Douglas Ord heard them on his wireless.

> A wretched blunder on the part of the BBC will assuredly have its effect on us. Two men and two French girls were allowed to tell the story of their experiences of their escaping by boat to England a fortnight ago. One of the girls said the Germans were permitting civilians in billets to listen to London. Muller will know just what to do to stop that leak. But why mention the escape at all? Surely London will know this may bring reprisals on us all, while any information that party took would probably not add greatly to the stock of knowledge in the Intelligence. It is not very long since they issued menaces against escapers, and the probability of their being put into operation against innocent folk is enough to deter all but the utterly selfish.

The Germans subsequently demanded a deposit on all boats from fishermen in the islands. Iris Bullen recorded her reaction to this.

> It seems obvious that they are still afraid that some boats might
> escape, and so they use these cunning tactics, which makes us like
> children under their commands.

The terror, daily uncertainty and anxiety of occupation was increased as lists of deportations were announced through the *Evening Post,* which had been taken over as the main arm of German propaganda. People deported as 'undesirables' included Jews and ex-officers, but those who contravened German regulations were also sent to the camps. Iris Bullen was great friends with Eddie and Olive Muels. At the end of the war she felt able to record what had happened to Eddie.

> Tried and accused of giving civilian clothing to a German
> soldier, December 43/January 44. In prison in Jersey, taken to
> concentration camp just prior to D-Day. As I was so friendly
> with Olive his wife, I became mixed up as a suspect of hiding
> the soldier, and had visits by the Germans and cross-questioned
> by the Gestapo, even though I could swear that I had never had
> anything to do with the soldier whatsoever.

Eddie Muels died in a concentration camp. A total of nearly 570 Channel Islanders were deported to camps such as Auschwitz and Ravensbruck and 31 were murdered or died as a result of the ill treatment they suffered.

Despite her own hardships, Iris managed to be sympathetic towards the occupying soldiers.

> It is a frequent site to see batches of worn out soldiers marching
> past. Some are simply staggering along with sweat pouring down
> their faces. Some seem to drop out, and have to pull themselves
> up in a state of dilemna. Though they are the enemy they have my
> pity when I see them treated in this way. Whilst the officers are
> alongside on bycicles.

Some German conscripts committed suicide, particularly when news reached them of the deaths of loved ones as German towns and cities were flattened by Allied bombing.

There were many deaths among Channel Islanders under the occupation. Douglas Ord regularly officiated at funerals in Guernsey.

> Dr Revell, Medical Officer of Health, has sent me a copy of his printed Report for 1940. Although the population fell from 43,000 to 24,000, deaths in the second six months were more than double the number recorded in the first six. Deaths among the elderly were naturally more numerous.

Food shortages were part of the problem. German troops had the lion's share of supplies shipped from the French mainland. By May 1941, when the islands had been under occupation for less than a year, Ord noted that rations were already inadequate.

> A doctor has put up a notice in his surgery advising women not to engage in Spring cleaning in view of the urgent needs for conserving energy against next winter when we shall probably be on much shorter rations and may have to do without lighting.

People's need for food was so desperate that, in that same month, Ord heard of a breeding rabbit being sold for £16.

> A man, barefoot, clad only in pyjamas, was found wandering about at two in the morning in St Peter Port, utterly exhausted, he told the policeman, one of ours – that he was cold and his feet ached. He was taken to the hospital and a brief examination shewed that he was an extreme case of undernourishment. Many others who are in a like condition do not appear before the public. Many say they feel as if they had been beaten with truncheons all over them. I find it extremely difficult to lift my head from the pillow in the mornings. Falla the florist confessed to having lost four stones and to being racked with pain. Some have shrunk so much that their clothes hang loose about them.

Iris Bullen's diary is a snapshot of her own struggle for survival. She queued for a day to buy shoes for her growing children, but emerged with a pair of slippers two sizes too big for Monica and nothing for her son Ray. The family made butter with the cream of the milk, scraped breadcrumbs from the table to make a pudding, and made flour from potato peelings. Basic foodstuffs available to the civilian population would have been deemed inedible under any other circumstances.

> The potatoes that we are eating are only fit for pigs. We are still on the old [Jersey] Royals of last year, which normally are finished well before Christmas. They are watery, and transparent when cooked. After eating a plateful, we are still hungry half an hour later.

Even after a trip to the Island's communal kitchen, where she had a meatless meal for ninepence (less than 4p), Iris was still hungry.

> I could have managed another 9d worth as the plates were not very full. We had tomato soup and potatoes, cabbage with a little herb cake comprising mostly potato, and after we had a little tapioca pudding, which just covered the bottom of my fruit dish – though this was a luxury for me as we have not been able to buy anything to make puddings with for months. Times are so hard that we have to even make our own salt as it is unobtainable except at few intervals when we get 2oz per person. So we have to put sea water in a saucepan and let it evaporate. In the end we have about 2 tablespoons of salt.

The sea provided some treats for the table: occasional shellfish, shrimps and the abalone or ormer (a mollusc that was a Channel Island delicacy). It was a way to make a little money too.

> Had a picnic at Samares. Ivy and I spent the afternoon looking for a special kind of seaweed, which, when bleached, is good for making milk jellies. There is a great demand for it. The hospital needs it. I understand that they are drawing some oil from it for medicines. When it's quite ready, after the process of bleaching, it

fetches 10/- a pound, so if I can get sufficient, I am going to try to sell some.

Like all those on the Home Front, islanders grew what food they could. But digging, harvesting, and foraging in hedgerows required energy. Starving, exhausted islanders were forced to walk to the shops when the bus service was cut to a minimum to save petrol (some buses were modified to run on charcoal). So the trusty bicycle was in great demand, but people had to resort to using rope and pieces of hose to replace worn-out tyres.

All bycicles are being bought at extraordinary high prices. I thought it was a chance to sell John's and keep the money for him to buy a new one after the war. Tyres too are very scarce, so I thought I had better sell it whilst it was yet complete, so I polished it up a bit, and also an old relic of a ladies bike that we have had for a long time in the shed, with a hope of selling it also. However when we arrived at the dealers, he gave me 15/- for the old crock which he said was 40 years old, and could only make use of the parts. For John's he gave me £5 so I thought it was worth the trouble.

Iris heard nothing from her husband John for a year. Then on 20 June 1941 there was a summons.

This morning I had a shock when the postman brought me a red cross envelope with an enclosed slip of paper asking me to go to the Bureau, as there was a request for information there. As I had not heard of anyone previously having such a request, I became alarmed, as I thought that if it were a message to me from John I should have had it handed to me at home, and so I imagined that all was not right with John, and was rather upset.

I went to town on the 2pm bus. I had to go to an office over Burton's. My legs were shaking when I went up the stairs, but was soon releaved when told that it was an enquiry from John concerning his family.

Iris composed a suitable reply to be sent via the Red Cross in Geneva, but sometimes these messages could take two years to reach the recipient. In July 1942 Douglas Ord sent a Red Cross message, ingeniously using biblical verses as a sort of code.

> Last two verses Acts, Moffatt's version. 'Now this reads:
> for two full years he remained in his private lodging
> welcoming any who came to visit him. He preached the
> reign of God and taught about the Lord Jesus Christ, quite
> openly and unmolested.' Some of these passages seem
> designed for the conveyance of messages, if only they are
> not censored!

Two months later his 'unmolested' status was threatened.

> An evil day for Guernsey. I was doing my best to prune the
> fruit bushes in the garden, feeling very tired and unlike effort,
> when I became aware of a German coming down the path with
> a grave face.
>   Someone had just rung up to ask if I knew anything about the
> Order for the Deportation of the English-born people. We had
> heard nothing.

English-born Douglas Ord had been a German prisoner of war in the closing stages of World War I in 1918.

> I confess I did not sleep all night. Memories of the
> imprisonment in 1918 and of the dreadful train journey to
> Germany haunted me, tired out though I was, and feeling far
> from well. The shock together with the thought of all G would
> now face, what I had once been through, weighed me down.
> And now this morning the rain is coming down in sheets and
> all seemed black.

Thanks to the duties of his ministry, Douglas Ord won a last-minute reprieve. Iris Bullen, 26-year-old mother of two small children, was also English-born. There is no clue in her diary as to how she escaped the

Iris Bullen was only 26 when this photograph was taken for her German identity card. After a year of occupation she looks considerably older. It is a mystery why she was not deported to a German internment camp along with the 2,000 other British-born Channel Islanders.

attentions of the authorities, but she was aware she was in danger, as illustrated by this diary entry.

> Sewing very hard making clothes for the children, as I fear that perhaps my turn will come to be sent to Germany as I am British-born.

The deportation included some of her friends and neighbours.

> They have lost no time in mustering the people they want. They sent constables, along with a soldier late last night, waking up people to be ready to go this afternoon. We are very distressed at these inhuman actions. Vera Whiting, her husband and little girl have gone today. In town there were people in groups looking very sad, some crying, and nearly crazy with anxiety. All families of English men have to go.

Iris was one of those who went to St Helier, the Jersey capital, to watch the exodus.

> Observed a very distressing sight of people making their way down to the pier with their little luggage, including a blanket. We gave them some hearty cheers as a send off from Library Place as we couldn't get any nearer to the pier, the Germans had barred us off. However the Germans must have observed our unbroken spirit in that pilgrimage to the boats. I heard that on last Wednesday's boat, as it left the pier heads, they struck up as loud as they could the song 'There will always be an England' and 'God save the King'.

Over 2,000 British-born Channel Islanders were deported to internment camps, and more than 40 died.

For those left behind, conditions grew worse. The Germans requisitioned homes at a few hours' notice to accommodate troops; gas and electricity supplies became increasingly intermittent; and firewood was in short supply. It was sometimes a choice of getting warm or having a hot meal.

One anonymous 70-year-old woman left a diary for the year 1944. It is a pathetic record of her loneliness (she received few visitors, thanks to the lack of petrol and lack of transport), misery (as her family was in England) and cold and hunger (she went to bed in the late afternoons and remained there till the next morning in order to keep warm).

> I generally feel starved about 3:30pm and have some thick gruel (flour milk and water) how I long for a good rump steak.

The Germans employed men to harvest what little wood there was on Jersey, and this was rationed. Iris and her neighbour, Olive Muels, set out to a wooded valley with a handcart to supplement the ration.

> A lot of chippings are left about, so we piled our carts up, branches and some pieces being quite thick. We got a lot of fun out of it, and even more going home especially the hills we had a job to get up and the lanes were so muddy!

Iris managed to sound upbeat in her diary on these odd occasions, but as the war wore on her diary entries became shorter and less frequent. She explained at the end of the war that she could have been arrested for writing 'certain things', and indeed for keeping a diary at all.

Guernsey and Jersey have highly fertile agricultural land, but the occupying forces were busy fortifying the islands at the expense of agriculture. Douglas Ord watched in horror.

> Tractors are busy hauling long-range artillery to points of vantage all over the island, without regard to crops. In one place they cut across a field of standing corn and in another right through a whole field of cauliflower. Anxious however, for the production of food, the German authorities issue an order most obligingly permitting the cultivation of gardens by their dispossessed owners, though the troops are occupying the dwellings. Who will reap the harvest? Already thieving is taking place on a wide scale and civilians cannot keep watch after curfew.

Slave labourers of many nationalities were brought in by the Germans for these building works and thousands died. Iris Bullen and others treated the forgeigners with astonishing compassion, especially as the islanders were hungry themselves.

> We have lots of Spanish and French men which have been brought here by the Germans for what reason, is not quite clear. When I went to the shop today to get my bare weekly rations there was a negro and another man also going into the shop. They looked pitiful, Miss Vanberg had previously met them, and taken them to her home and given each a slice of bread, They had not had anything to eat since 6pm the day before and have only soup and ¼ loaf a day. They are half starved, and in camps guarded by soldiers. They could not get anything from the shop as everything is rationed on coupons.

By the end of 1942, Iris Bullen was only able to buy swedes during her trips to the market. These were desperate times.

There are a lot of robberies going on in the island. In the west of the island last week, a man was killed and his sister injured, when they attacked two men (believed to be Russians, as they have brought a lot here to work). They were after the fowls.
It is not money they are after, but food as some of them are starving. It is not always the foreigners that rob, the German soldiers often do themselves as they are on small rations, and after curfew are at liberty to scour the fields and farms. Shops and stores also have robberies.

Iris's children both suffered from frequent bouts of diarrhoea. On Guernsey, Douglas Ord recorded frequent gastritis. He also witnessed a harrowing sight.

How serious the food shortage has become, was rudely illustrated this morning when I saw two bricklayers trying to haul a handcart with some bricks and cement. The men were just skin and bone, their facial bones protruded and their legs wobbled with sheer weakness. As they struggled uphill cars filled with officers and NCOs flashed past – men in prime condition, fed on the best that can be plundered in fair France before they come here to do the like. It isn't good for one to feel the intense resentment within at such contrasts. The wet season is producing potato disease and the outlook for winter is none too good.

Limited passive resistance was recorded in these diaries. A neighbour buried his supply of tyres under a concrete floor rather than let the Germans requisition them. Telephone wires were cut, and downed Allied airmen were given food and sometimes shelter. News of D-Day brought muted feelings of excitement. This was a double-edged sword: liberation could be at hand, but German supply ships from France were cut off. Rations were cut – morale was high but Iris had to go gleaning to put food on the table. On 1 September 1944, she wrote:

The gas supply of the Island failed at 7:30am on Aug 4th. This means a great hardship on the population with practically no fuel available. We are registered to have one meal a day cooked at the bakehouse in a container without handles for 3d. We have only an open grate, and what we can get hold of for fuel, such as sticks and peelings, we use to warm up some porrage for breakfast, boil milk etc.

Could things possibly get worse? Six weeks later:

Everything is in a critical state, no leather for shoe repairs and no boots or shoes available. Clothing very scarce. People get what they can from second hand shops. Also a lot of bartering is going on including black market. Some unpatriotic people have been watched during the occupation years, and had their houses daubed with tar and swastika's just to remind them their day of payment is coming for their black marketing and co-operation with the Germans.

Reprisals would soon be taken on the girls known as 'gerrybags' who fraternized with the Germans. In January 1945 Iris Bullen did not know that World War II would soon be over, and she could only think of keeping warm.

On January 25th the electric came to an end, though we have only had it in the evenings, with half hour cut off, for some time, so now we have to go to bed with the dark, about 7pm and remain there till 8am when there is light enough to get the breakfast. The [*Evening Post*] has also had to cease publication. Really the island is now in a critical condition, almost everything is at a standstill, and with the end of Electric current, has put hundreds out of work. We have had a very cold month and no fuel ration, still waiting for December ration!

Transport is a great problem. The buses ran one trip on Saturday Morning and evening. Mother and I have to gather twigs along the hedges in order to make a little fire to cook a hot meal. We spend most of our days in coats, and are shrivelled up with the cold. The children are still on holiday, as they are unable to heat the schools.

Relief ships carrying food, tea and other basics signalled that liberation was at hand. On 8 May, Iris was able to write:

> Truly this is the greatest day of our lives, for most of us in these islands. Wireless sets opening up from everywhere. And we heard Mr Churchill's speech. Our emotion was overwhelmed when he mentioned the dear Channel Islands would be freed today. After the speech which was just after 3pm, we all put up our Union Jacks, and flags of the Allies.
>
> Any one that has not had the experience of occupation such as we have had, do not realise what it meant to us, to hoist our flags once again. For five years we had our patriotism suppressed, we could only show our faith in the future by our acts and forbearance. In the evening I walked into town and back with some friends. We expected the fleet to arrive today, but were disappointed though we enjoyed ourselves immensely, and thought it was wonderful to be free and without 10 o'clock curfew. We arrived home about 11:30pm. It was wonderful to see the electric on once again and no blackouts!

The following day the Channel Islands of Jersey, Guernsey, Alderney and Sark were liberated.

> As the soldiers landed they were simply mobbed, and could hardly move, and I was jammed in the crush complete with cart, children, and a dog – which I had difficulty to control. We heard that there were six Jersey men on board, so all who had loved ones in the Forces were eagerly looking if they could spot one. I saw a touching seen of a mother who found her son. We all cried, it was a touching episode. We had a good time shaking hands with the Tommies and cheering! We could barely move in the crowd. Eventually we arrived back home past 11pm very tired.

As excited islanders returned from exile on the British mainland, they found that many of their homes had been looted and wrecked by the occupation forces. Post Office engineer E Hamel had been warned when he landed on

Guernsey soil that his house had been requisitioned by the Germans, but he was eager to see it nonetheless. His first visit was in darkness when he could see little but empty rooms.

> Daylight served only to add to the problem. The eye more than confirmed what the nose had suggested on the previous evening. Dirt was laid on thick on all sides. Scorched floors marked the position where the German stove had stood; a rough hole in the chimney breast showed where the stove pipe had entered the main flue. The Germans had 'wired' the house for electricity the easy way by bashing a hole through the ceiling and floor to reach the next level. Nails abounded, driven at random in mantle shelves, windowsills and doorframes – chiefly the latter. There were twenty-two nails of various sizes in one doorframe! I wondered if the German Command used our house as a training centre, and detailed several men to hammer in nails simultaneously to simulate gunfire. How these troops moved around the place without tearing their uniforms to shreds is a problem I have never been able to solve. There was no gas meter. Lead gaspipes had been ripped away from the walls; fittings had, no doubt, long been melted down to provide shell cases. A house completely furnished from top to bottom had been reduced to two items – a cane bedside table and the kitchen linoleum. I actually HOED the muck off the kitchen floor – it was quicker that way.

It was a poor homecoming, but there were others who fared worse, returning to find that their homes had been demolished because they impeded the sight of German guns.

4
A PLACE OF SAFETY

We were slowly let down into the stormy Atlantic alongside of the now
rapidly sinking City of Benares *and then the sailors tried to row away,*
but the boat was sadly overloaded with the children and passengers from
the smashed lifeboats, the boat soon became waterlogged and we were
sitting in water up to our chests. The poor little children hadn't a dog's
chance. It was awful.
(Bess Walder, September 1940)

Suitcase and teddy bear in hand, wearing labels with their name and age, scores of British children were taken from their homes and evacuated to the homes of strangers. The plan was well intentioned: to safeguard the rising generation from the worst of war. During World War I, 1,400 people had been killed in air raids, and 18 children were killed when Upper North Street School in the East End of London was demolished by a bomb in 1917. So at the start of World War II, entire schools were evacuated from the cities to places like Cornwall and Wales. Most children were sent to rural areas, but others took long risky sea voyages to America, Australia, South Africa and Canada.

Twelve-year-old Bess Walder and her little brother were among the passengers on the *City of Benares* steaming for safety in Canada. The ship sailed in convoy from the River Mersey on Friday 13 September 1940. It was torpedoed four days later, 500 miles from land. Safely back on British soil she wrote a letter to her teacher and school friends, describing 'how I managed to escape what so many of my fellow seavacs had to go through'.

About 11.30 (at night) we were literally shaken out of our beds
by the explosion in the engine room where the U-boat torpedo
had cleaved the power engine in two. This was followed by louder
and terrifying detonations. I jumped up and put on my dressing

gown, and fumbled for my life jacket (as we were completely in
the dark as the lights were out) and grabbed hold of my mac.
Then I fished the other two that were in my cabin, got their
lifebelts and got one little girl onto the boat deck. Then I went
back for the other little girl Ailsa. I found that our wardrobe had
blocked the cabin door, I grabbed hold of something, (to this day
I don't know what it was) and hacked at the wardrobe. I managed
to squeeze through a hole, into our cabin, I found that Ailsa had
fallen over something and was bleeding to death. I wrapped her
in my coat that I wasn't wearing and tried to get her out. The
cabin was fast filling up with water and I found to my horror that
I couldn't get past the wardrobe.

One of the adults escorting the evacuees heard her frantic cries, and helped
Bess and Ailsa towards the stairs leading to the boat deck.

As we rushed along the passage the stairs that led to our boat
deck collapsed and so we had to rush back again and use the
other stairs to the lifeboat we were allotted and found that it had
been smashed to smithereens. By this time Ailsa had fainted and
was nearly ded. But she was such a brave little kid and game to
the end, which mercifully came while she was unconscious. The
escort lowered her into the sea and said a prayer for her, and then
hustled me into another lifeboat that was being lowered.

The overloaded lifeboat descended into the freezing Atlantic waters, but it
soon became waterlogged.

The poor little children didn't have a dog's chance. It was awful.
We had to put them out of the boat as we were loaded. So the
sailors could have a try at righting the boat and baling. But it
was of no use, for as fast as they baled out, the waves came
dashing up about as high as the average sized house and filled
her up again.

Those with nothing to hang on to were washed out of the boat. Finally the
boat capsized, throwing the remaining 20 passengers into the sea.

I decided to swim for it. It was really surprising how strong
I felt when I swam against the waves, I suppose I knew it
depended on me to keep myself alive. I swam until I reached
the upturned lifeboat, when I tried to scramble on to it I found
I had sprained my ankle, so I had to use my arms and only
one leg. When I had regained my breath I saw my pal Beth
Cummins trying to get on. I held out one hand and by hanging
on with the other I fished her up on top of the boat, where we
both hung onto the keel with all our might. At last the waves
calmed a bit and we were able to see by moonlight the other
people on the boat. Two Indian seamen, one was dead and the
other was half-alive.

The two girls clung on all night in increasingly rough seas.

When dawn broke, there was just us and the Atlantic. Perhaps
you know that creepy feeling that comes over you when you are in
a lonely field at night with nothing but fields in sight.

Four hours later the two girls were picked up by a British destroyer.

I saw my brother on the destroyer. He had been picked up later. I
was so relieved, as I was wondering what I should tell mother if he
was lost. I came out of hospital yesterday and am staying with my
brother and mother at this very beautiful mansion house. I think
we are staying for some time, as my nerves have gone to pot but it
won't take me long to pull myself together again. If the occasion
arises that I feel I should like to go to Canada, mother will let me
go by plane if I still want to go.

The sinking of the *City of Benares* on 17 September 1940 stunned the
nation. Of the 90 children on board only 13 survived. The reaction of
Phyllis Warner was typical of many at the time. She wrote on Friday 27
September 1940:

We are all thrilled to hear that there are 46 more survivors of the
City of Benares. I don't know why the torpedoing of 77 children at

sea should fill us with even more horror than the thousands of children killed in air raids, but it does, perhaps because the point of safety had been so very nearly reached.

The *City of Benares* was one of several ships taking 'seavacs' to Canada and America as war in Europe began to hot up. Veronica Owen was 15 and reluctant to leave Britain. Her father, a Commander in the Royal Navy, wrote to her explaining the logic behind the evacuation abroad.

> If you were four or five years older, I should like to think of you nursing the wounded in some hospital or hospital ship – as it is, I think it's very much better that people of your age should be out of England – to ease the work of ships bringing food and so on, and to make more room for the soldiers to fight and for the workmen who have to be here. It means that we shan't see one another for some time – that can't be helped, and let's hope it won't be for really so very long. After all, lots of people don't see their children for two or three years at a time in the Navy.

In her letter, Veronica's mother stressed that the younger generation needed to be saved for postwar roles.

> Your object in life must be to fit yourself for the future – you may feel you can do all sorts of things here which are of direct help – like you are doing now in weeding, washing up etc – but you will be able to do that just as much in Canada, as Canada will put, in fact is doing so already, every ounce she has into helping the mother country – You will be spared the immediate horrors of war, such as air raids etc. I know you will say 'I don't want to run away', but you are not – the world of the future is going to depend on your generation, therefore we want you to have every advantage. Purely from the practical reason of defending this country it is better that there should be as few people as possible who cannot by reason of their age be directly helpful – your duty, darling, lies in the future, ours is in the present.

Julie Kemp was 5¼ years old when she was evacuated from her Cheshire home to Vancouver in July 1940. In a stream of transatlantic correspondence, her mother, Lucy Kemp, tried to keep in touch with the tiny but important details of her daughter's life as she grew up thousands of miles away. It had been a difficult decision to send her little daughter so far away, as she admitted in 1941.

> We knew that she would be as safe there as anywhere, we knew that she would be well-looked after and well fed, and we knew she was a serene little person, likely to settle down without undue homesickness, but I certainly have been worried the last few months – hence my letters have, I know, degenerated into sheer questionnaires. I will try to be more patient – it is impossible not to be 'down' at times about a child who is so far away. I think of her continually, longing for news and living for the day she will return.

Julie was to spend five years in Canada, and eventually returned to her mother in England with a Canadian accent. During the war years Lucy Kemp devoured every crumb of news that came from the Canadians who were caring for Julie, as her daughter grew up so far away.

> Thank you so much for your letter of December 21st, which arrived yesterday. This is a grand letter though and well worth waiting for – I am so delighted to hear of your Christmas preparations, and lovely party Julie enjoyed so much. So Julie has the *House at Pooh Corner*, my hand has hovered over it many times in bookshops, to send to her. Does she remember about Piglet, we had a lot of his adventures in Children's Hour on the radio. About babies – please tell Julie whatever is necessary to keep her abreast of her own development, my views are yours to steer a middle course between ignorance and precocity. I was one of the 'shocked' at 11–12 years old, and resolved never to let that happen to my children. I am deeply interested in Julie making her First Communion – her father and I have expected to hear something about it now she is nearly seven. I would not hurry her for the world, but if Sister thinks she is ready, she is the best

On a sunny July day in 1940, five-year-old Julie Kemp poses for her father on the ship that will take her to spend the war in America. Julie returned five years later with an American accent, but to her mother's joy still remembered her favourite soft toys, waiting on her bed.

person to know. We really only expect little children to grasp in their own way what is to happen and whom they are receiving – the doctrine etc can come later, as long as they are reverent, and understand, as children so beautifully and innocently do. I would give anything to be there.

Although Julie's father, Teddie, was in the merchant navy on the transatlantic convoys, he rarely went to Vancouver. He did manage to buy gifts for his daughter, such as a pair of slippers, but when Julie tried them on they were the wrong size. Her parents were missing out on the formative events of their daughter's life.

He saw many children making their First Communion at a Philadelphia Church not so long ago, and told me he felt so wretched about missing Julie's, he nearly had to come out.

Teacher Grace Dennithorne was in Ireland when war clouds started to gather. She realized that she must return to help to organize her school's evacuation.

We hurried home from Donegal when the news began to look ominous. For a week we assembled at school wondering what every minute would bring and rehearsing the carrying of luggage etc to the station (we walked round and round the school garden for 20 minutes with luggage) to see whether the children could carry their loads. When the day for evacuation came we had to meet at 8am at school – waited until 1pm not knowing where, or exactly when, we should be told to go and finally when we departed we were not certain of the place although we thought it was to be Bedford. In the end it was a mystery drive and we finally alighted at Kettering at about 5 or 6pm. The first load of us was taken to the wrong school and so we were billeted in the wrong part of the town – quite away from the rest of the school. After a hectic week of readjustments and re-billeting we were told that the whole school must move to Wellingborough since Kettering was overcrowded with secondary schools (6 evacuated schools and only one girls' high school in the town!). For the last month we've been trying to readjust here in Wellingborough and it hasn't been easy.

Mollie Dineen accompanied her son Bryan and the rest of his Streatham primary school to Eastbourne, in Sussex. She wrote a vivid account of her experiences in her diary.

The great evacuation of schoolchildren from London began for us at 7.30am on September 1st 1939. We all arrived at school fully equipped with clothing, gas masks and food for the great unknown journey. Children were very excited, the older ones perhaps a little scared, helpers and teachers worried and mothers

> with sad eyes but brave smiles. Everyone was most anxious to be
> on our way and we really did start away from school at 9.5am all
> marching in fives and a helper in charge of two lines and arrived
> at the station in a very short time. All was very quiet here, no
> people on the platform, only lines of children all looking forward
> to a journey in a train.

As a journalist on the *Daily Herald*, Mea Allan covered the evacuation for
her newspaper and wrote about it in the notes she was assembling for her
unpublished autobiography.

> Trains ran all day from the main stations. I covered this
> wonderful exodus, rising early in the morning in the grey
> summer haze to see the first train out, and returning to the
> office in the stifling heat of evening, hoarse with cheering the
> last train off on its journey. Parents were not allowed on the
> platforms. 'No fuss, no tears,' was the motto of the London
> County Council. And it certainly worked for the children went
> away singing. It was all rather like a glorified school treat.
> Some of those mothers who had made the brave sacrifice of
> unloosening loving Cockney apron strings, came for a last
> peep at their departing Tommy or Violet or Billy. Pressed
> behind the barriers they saw little more than the rear-lamp
> of the guard's van.

Mollie Dineen and her charges had no idea of their destination as the train
pulled out of the station.

> From the window we watched London fade away and the green
> fields of Surrey and later on the hills of Sussex came into view.
> We realised we must be going to the sea as the stations flashed
> by, and presently we heard the cry, 'All change Eastbourne'. We
> marched from the station in our lines of five again, with crowds
> looking on, we might have been film stars arriving, the attention
> we received.

Volunteers provided a welcome cup of tea, and settled the children for a

Tearful mothers press against the gates at Waterloo station, trying to catch a last glimpse of their children boarding trains for the relative safety of the countryside. The authorities banned parents from the platforms, to ensure that there was 'No fuss, no tears'.

rest, before putting them through a medical examination – checking for head lice. First aider Miss Andrews was a volunteer who met two trains of evacuees at the station in sleepy Tonbridge in Kent at 5.30 on the morning of 1 September. Among them were expectant mothers, and mothers with babies.

> **The mothers are naturally far more bewildered and 'difficult' than the children – homesick as they felt the country was 'more unsafe' than London, being so empty.**

Billeting officers attempted to find homes for the evacuees. George Whiteman was a billeting officer in Saffron Walden, Essex. Writing in 1942, he admitted that billeting was something of a dirty word because in the past it had meant the 'demand for board and lodging for troops'. He summed up the difficulties of his job.

Our task is to make a better job of fitting the right sizes and styles and shoes on the customer's feet, and we shall find that we have requests for a second fitting instead of the usual tale of pinched and sore understandings. I cannot bear to think how much goodwill towards evacuees has been thrown away by 'dumpings' of evacuees in unsuitable areas and ill-chosen billets. The much publicised failure of evacuation should not blind us to its astonishing success. Although there were outcries and shocked letters to MPs, it [country hospitality] even rose above the invasion of clean homes by children with dirty habits. Billeting for long periods has been as genuinely altruistic a piece of service as any in wartime.

The government paid a billeting allowance to those who opened their homes to evacuees, but it barely covered a child's keep. In the village of Tonbridge, Miss Andrews recorded in her diary how billeting brought out the worst in some people.

A rich woman first refused to have anyone billeted in her mansion; then when billeting powers were used (in the form of the village constable) grudgingly agreed to four staff (eight were sent) but decreed that 'those women' should be quartered with the servants, provided no beds and threatened to turn them out if she was made aware of their existence.

The behaviour of some of the evacuees brought a smile to her face.

The family quartered on Mrs Leonard preferred to sleep on the floor, and the child won't eat at table because she had always taken her meals sitting on the doorstep.

After returning from Ireland, teacher Grace Dennithorne was billeted in a house in Wellingborough, Northamptonshire.

For the last month I have been anything but comfortable – the one virtue (an important one I grant) was that the house was clean. How I put up with it for so long I can't think now – except perhaps that I was so stunned by much bigger things, that mere home comforts and privacy mattered less for the time being – but it must have added to one's depression.

In 1939, before German troops had overrun Belgium and France and posed the threat of invasion by sea, children were still being sent to towns on the south coast. Doreen and Sheila Manwaring were sent to Deal in Kent. Doreen was a feisty young Communist sympathizer.

> I was billeted in the Rectory. The house and food was all right but the people were snobbish blue-blooded Tories. The Rectory is the biggest house in Deal, yet they only took in four children. There were seven large rooms in the house which were not used. Yet the lady of the house complained that 4 children were too much for her to manage (her maid did all the work) and said that Sheila and I would have to move to another billet.

There was no school for the girls in Deal, so they were shunted off to Folkestone.

> The billeting authorities moved us into a large hotel. Directly we were in, they started moving us out into private billets. I was in a lovely hotel, Barrelle House. We were treated exactly as guests; we had the same meals as the hotel visitors. Mrs Godefroy, the proprietress, treated us so well that she went bankrupt and had to close the hotel.

Constant changes of billet were one of the themes of the Home Front, as officials tried to match billet and billetees. Doreen's next billet was the Victoria Hotel on Marine Crescent in Folkestone, but she complained in a letter to her mother (whose name was also Doreen):

> The first few days at the Victoria were the worst I have ever experienced. I never knew what it was to feel hungry before. We had so little to eat we were reduced to eating anything, we were so hungry, lumps of dried bread, cake crumbs etc. Mrs Godefroy used to let us come back to the other hotel for food; she used to

give us cups of tea, bread and butter, plates of chips, apples and all manner of good things.

The sisters had been evacuated with Eltham High School and its staff.

> The evacuation scheme in Folkestone is rotten. Over 1,000 children have gone home. We told our mistresses that we had not enough to eat. As a result the hotel people called us liars and other things not fit to write. We protested so strongly that now our food is quite good. I feel certain that the hotel people must make a profit out of us though. We have no milk except in powdered form, then it is very little in our tea. We have no eggs or fresh food; it is all tinned food. One day we did have eggs but they were pickled ones and nearly all rotten. They are gradually moving us out. I am thoroughly sick of so much uncertainty; we will not be really settled down till Christmas. I have got past the stage of caring what food we have etc, now though. I console myself with talking Communism, reading Communism and thinking Communism all the time.

With hindsight, billeting officer George Whiteman felt that the authorities had failed in many ways when the great exodus was planned.

> They made little allowance for the essential difference between billeting schoolchildren and billeting mothers and children together. There was apparently no allowance for the different character of different reception areas, so that people from the dirtiest evacuation areas were quite possibly directed into the cleanest reception areas; or cities with a known preponderance of, say, Irish Catholics in their danger areas, allocated to country areas of rigid protestantism. I even suspect that Whitehall, in planning the reception of evacuees, never contemplated that they would need to be transferred from one billet to another. Transfers are of course inevitable. The record in my district was held by one boy whom we tried out in eleven different billets. In fairness to him, it should be said the parents were chief cause of his billets being upset. Four or five

changes of billet before the right one has been found have not
been uncommon.

Parents visited, despite the difficulties of wartime travel on overcrowded
trains and buses. One London parent wrote to thank George Whiteman for
their son's home from home.

> I came away on Sunday afternoon with the grandest feeling of
> content and I feel like a feather this week. The people the boy
> is with, made us most welcome and are extremely kind to him.
> I only hope he will appreciate it all his life. I sincerely believe
> he does because he asked if we would mind him coming back
> to Mum and Dad for weekends when the time comes for him
> to come home altogether. To me it is the most wonderful thing
> in the world to hear him call the people he is living with Mum
> and Dad. People here say I wouldn't care for my child to call a
> stranger Mum and Dad but I tell them Saffron Walden people are
> not strangers (somehow they make one feel that way) and it just
> proves that they really are Mums and Dads.

There were many others who were not so happy. This mother had been
billeted 'on the southern side of London'.

> We have been billeted the last place on God's earth that working
> class mothers and children should have been. Ninety five per cent of
> the mothers and children have returned home. The residents here
> are snobs who never wanted us here in the first place but thought
> it was their duty, the few modern shops are beyond our purse, and
> while the weather was fine we were able to walk about, but now it's
> damp and cold the householder dosnt even like the idea of us sitting
> in the cold kitchen. We are in the way, so it's better to go home to
> danger, but have our nice fires and comfort. They have tired of us
> and our children already. One cant blame any mother or child for
> returning home to a home and welcome, where our children arnt
> looked down on and untrue nasty stories arnt told.

Some children started to trickle back to their homes and parents, particularly as the phoney war dragged into 1940. Mrs Doreen Manwaring expressed the heartache of all wartime mothers.

It has been such a wrench for us to part with our children, but the press and wireless are forever begging us not to bring them home, so we do what we hope is for the best, and let them stay. We can only keep hoping that it won't be for long.

Her daughters Doreen and Sheila were still in Folkestone.

They have been away now for 15 months, and have now reached the stage when they never ask to come home. They are quite weaned from their mother now and I must say that I cease to be hurt any more by the long partings we have. It all seems so hopeless, and I can't see any hopes of them being home again for a long time yet.

By the summer of 1940 the south coast was deemed unsafe and children were re-evacuated. Doreen and Sheila were sent to Abertillery in Wales.

It is a mining town in Monmouthshire, lying in a valley between very high mountains. It is one of the distressed areas and has a high death rate from TB. But apart from these failings it is reckoned to be a safety area. The girls are living in a miner's home and are being very kindly treated. These people have had very hard times, and know what trouble is.

Despite the disruption of two evacuations, young Doreen passed her exams and left Abertillery to go to university. Her younger sister Sheila remained, safe but homesick.

She wants to come home, as indeed they all do. Most of the girls in her school are heartily sick of evacuation. I feel rather sorry for poor old Sheila. She wanted to be a ballet dancer, and as she said, she ought to be having the training now, but that's out of the question. She has her toe shoes with her, and she and two other girls practise each Saturday, but it's not enough of course.

She seems to have given up the idea now of ballet as a career, and wants me to let her come home and take a commercial course and then get a clerical job.

Bryan Dineen and his mother Mollie were also re-evacuated to Wales. The children had their school friends to socialize with, but Mollie was lonely, as she expressed in the diary she kept for the five years she was there.

> At home my friends are many and almost every evening someone would drop in for a cup of tea and a chat, now my time in the evenings is spent alone mending or reading in bed, but it's my job to be here.

Mollie was in for a culture shock. The Welsh village of Llandovery was so small that there was no radio, no newspaper, no cinema or theatre. She threw herself into the job, offering a prize for the tidiest child, becoming cub leader, and enjoying the simple pleasures of country life, like blackberry picking and the May Queen celebrations. She settled into village life so well that her return to London in 1945 was as much of a wrench as it had been to leave – she was homesick for Wales!

A year after the major evacuation of schoolchildren, a new evacuation was called for. Thousands were made homeless by the Blitz in 1940, and entire families arrived in Saffron Walden to be billeted by George Whiteman and his colleagues.

> The refugees had been travelling for four or five days, and many had slept on the ground in Epping Forest. Ours were the first Rest Centres, they said, where they were able to sleep on camp beds and not on the floor. Now in the midst of this problem of trying to billet families, nearly all large, averaging about 7 or 8, another problem was forced on us. We found men appearing who were chasing their families trying to get re-united. In the last three days we have had literally dozens of men and some women, who have been trailing from village to village, sleeping under hedgerows, determined to find their families at all costs. They're absolutely worn out, and when we've been able to put them on to where their families are their faces light up. The real difficulty

has been that Canning Town and Silvertown seem to have been completely evacuated during the day while the men were at work, or looking for work. One man with his wife and six children, including one baby of four weeks, has just got what he and his family stand up in. Their home is a heap of rubble – but he's got no sense of bitterness.

Two years later George recorded that a third to a half of those homeless evacuees were still in villages round Saffron Walden.

Those who found their way into billets stayed but a short time of course. It was the expedient of putting them in quarters on their own, which enabled them to 'settle in'. Condemned cottages were used in a good many areas.

Kathleen Crawley had been evacuated to Ashford in Kent at the beginning of the war, but as Kent came under fire she was sent to Llanelly in Wales.

It really is ridiculous sending us to Llanelly. We are surrounded by factories etc (careless talk may give away vital secrets) which the Germans are having a go at. They've stopped sounding the air raid sirens too and we never know whether the planes are British or not. We keep hearing thuds, which are mostly caused by some queer process in the steel works. Don't get alarmed will you, but some bombs were dropped round the docks etc. Thank goodness we are the other side of town. The people here are very jittery and the children won't go to bed at nights. Have you had any air raid warnings lately? They've had lots at Ashford I hear. I don't think there is a safe place anywhere in England now.

Phyllis Higgins, writing to her son Stephen in the Forces, described the evacuees she took into her large house in Hale, Cheshire, in August 1944, as the pilotless planes (V-1 rockets) were dropping on south-east England.

I have five evacuees, a mother and her three children and the grannie who is only 54 but oh terribly bomb-shocked. She is shaking all the time. They are an exceedingly respectable nice family so I have sent for another daughter and her 14-month-old son. They are having a ghastly time down in Kent where they come from. They love being here and the children are wonderfully good. The grandpa came last Sunday and returns tomorrow. The husband of their youngest daughter is here for his 48 hours. He is stationed at Chester so comes over every Saturday and Sunday. The flying bombs are coming over pretty frequently so it would be stupid for them to return home. The people round here think it marvellous of me to have so many, but I would rather have them, than two small children on their own to look after.

It was not just children who were evacuated. Whole villages gave up their homes in 1943 as plans for the Second Front became concrete. People living in farms, hamlets and villages round Slapton Sands, on the South Devon coast, were given six weeks' notice of evacuation. On 20 December 1943 the area was 'occupied' by American troops, who used the beach, countryside and buildings as a training ground for D-Day. Some farmers who returned to their land the following year found it impossible to restore their fields to their previous productivity. Further eastwards along the south coast, villagers at Tyneham in Dorset had to leave their homes as the British Army moved in to practise manoeuvres. Miss Lillian Taylor was the village Sunday school teacher.

Mr Churchill came round in his car on the hilltop, they wanted a training ground for the army. And he just said move all those people out and that was that. We had to be out by December 19th, just a few days before Christmas. We had a job to find a place for our family because my father had arthritis and had sticks, so we had to be careful. The thing was that anywhere with stairs and he would be housebound. It was depressing leaving home and coming to live among strangers, but we lost three brothers in the First World War. They hadn't had adequate training in England before they were sent abroad, better for men to be trained on their own ground than to go abroad to be trained.

Villagers evacuated from Tyneham were given compensation. Most did not own their cottages, which belonged to the big estate.

We got about £12 compensation for the garden, things we had left in the vegetable garden. Twelve pounds was quite a bit. We left several things behind, but we could go back and get anything we wanted the following week. So we went back to get a few cabbage plants and things that we had coming on. Somebody'd been there before us! Even the doors in our bedrooms were gone, we'd only been gone a week, and the copper – for doing the washing. Local builders went in. The soldiers told us, 'People came with horses and carts and took things.'

The evacuated Tyneham villagers never returned to their homes, and this quintessential English village is still used as a training ground for the British Army.

5
BLITZKRIEG

The planes are very determined. *One comes along and slows up,*
gyrating down and down, lower and lower, and slower and slower,
the engine gets louder and nearer and nearer. You are just expecting
a bomb when suddenly the guns let fly with a resounding crack like
the world blowing up. And all of us in the shelter – stiffening suddenly
in fright and then relaxing as suddenly, till the next volley. Of course
one can do interesting things – one can time the shells, from the moment
of firing until they burst into the sky. Meanwhile one would like to be
doing anything else – making a cup of tea, going to the lavatory.
(Mea Allan, September 1940)

Sporadic air raids were launched on Britain in June, July and August 1940, but Hitler's *Blitzkrieg* (literally, 'lightning war') began in earnest with a massive raid on London on 7 September 1940. What had been called the phoney war was over. Throughout the next five years there would be eerie lulls in the bombing, sometimes more difficult to cope with than the terror of the Blitz itself. It begged the question: when would it start again? It was far easier to go through the nightly routine of sleeping in an air-raid shelter. Some city dwellers succumbed to depression and nervous breakdowns, brought on by the relentless battering of eardrums. Others found comfort in the drone of bombers swiftly followed by the 'ack ack' of the anti-aircraft batteries. Civilians soon learnt to distinguish between the 'alert' and the 'all clear' as the sirens shrieked their chilling tunes. Pupils at the Kneller Senior Boys School in Twickenham had something new to write about in the autumn term of 1940, and R Turner entitled his essay 'Not Wanted Visitors'.

When an air raid siren goes off Mr Ellis beats a drum. We put

down our work, pick up our gas masks and run to the air raid shelters. When we get there we sit down and read comics or else we sing. If the air raid goes near the time when we go home, and we are down there quite a long time, the teachers come round with water and something to eat. But nearly all of us put some chewing gum in our gas masks to eat.

From their essays, it is clear that these 11-year-olds relished the adventure of war, but it did disrupt their education.

Since 'Goering's Blitzkrieg in the air' began we have found school life rather messed up. For one thing if there is an air raid between 12pm and 6am we do not come to school until 10.30am. We hardly have a whole lesson without it being interrupted, but we will have to put up with it for the 'duration'.

Sadly their essays also record the death toll in the streets around their homes, particularly that of a schoolfriend, Gordon Morgan, who died in the raid of 29 November 1940.

His mother died on the same night. He is the first boy of Kneller school to be killed in this war because of enemy action. His father died in the last war. Kneller boys subscribed over £2 and bought him a wreath. Each day before he went into school he would play on the swings in the Recreation Park in Kneller Gardens.

Older pupils were drafted in to help to dig their school air-raid shelters. Margaret Butler taught in a North London school where open trench shelters had been dug. These were considered by many to be safer than underground shelters, because there was no superstructure to collapse on top of shelterers in a raid. But neither teaching nor learning was easy under these conditions.

Each trench held 80 children facing each other. A teacher sat at each end of the trench, where sanitary accommodation was provided in the form of a bucket curtained off for privacy. The trenches were barely wide enough for a girl to walk from her seat to the nearest toilet corner. At intervals we let them stand and stretch as much as possible, for the slatted seats were very uncomfortable and we all felt very sore in the rear. After a patch of bad weather the trench began to hold water. Pumps were fixed up and the other teacher and I had to spend 15 minutes alternately outside the trench, at the mercy of Hitler, and pump vigorously.

Shelters were constructed at factories and offices, and many streets had their own shelter. Mr Piper was one of those running a church shelter in Hamilton Road, Everton, a poor area where few shelters had been erected and most of these 'had been captured by groups of people determined to keep them to themselves'.

This selfish monopolising of shelters was, partly at least, broken up by a group of young men, composed of Catholics and Unitarians; armed with short staves not unlike policemen's batons. They visited shelters which had the reputation of refusing admission to the stranger. Many a bully received a cracked head; some of the crusaders did not escape injury; but this selfish monopolising of shelters by small gangs came to an end.

The legendary wartime spirit fortified these city dwellers in crisis. But under such stress friction was inevitable.

Drunks, quarrelsome people, dirty people, people incapable of keeping any rules. The standard of behaviour during the war years in many parts of Liverpool, just as in other large cities, was often pitiably low. The housing conditions in which some people, who used our premises, had lived for many years were truly appalling, add to this the strain of loss of sleep and constant dread, and one easily gets a situation in which the worst in people can so readily gain control.

In the shelter diary, Mr Piper recorded typical examples:

Men fighting in bunks, several instances of gross dishonesty ie
people coming in for tea and beating it before the collection is
taken.

The church raised money to buy materials, and the shelterers themselves
built bunks, so the Hamilton Road shelter managed to accommodate
500 people at the height of the Blitz. Many of the users were elderly, and
most lived in or near badly damaged houses, while others were taken in
after an emergency.

One Sunday at 2am, twenty people were sent to us; they were
dazed, shocked survivors from a large public shelter which had
received a direct hit.

Kathleen Church-Bliss and her friend Elsie Whiteman had given up their
thatched Elizabethan cottage and country teashop to volunteer for work in
a Croydon munitions factory. After sleepless nights running up and down
stairs from their rooms to the basement shelter, they decided to try a public
shelter in Duppas Hill, Surrey.

We find our trench is occupied exclusively with the highly middle
class owners from Duppas Hill. It is very amusing to hear all the
various families arriving and bedding themselves out. Torches
and hurricane lamps light up the gloom, and husbands and wives
argue and fuss according to temperament, and the chorus of
snores! Noises of children and fish and chip parties come from
the adjoining trenches.

Despite raids, the pair managed a restful night's sleep and started to use the
shelter regularly. But class is no barrier to friction in stressful times.

Last night there was the most almighty row in our shelter. Mr
and Mrs Bellwood returned from their week's annual holiday
to find that one of their bunks had been given away to another
man by Mr Harvey (in charge of the shelter). They naturally felt
rather aggrieved about this – as Mr Harvey had told them before
they left that it would be quite all right – and now all he would

say – was that the Bellwood family must separate and one of them go into the upper shelter. Altogether there was a row royal and high words on all sides.

The 'trespassers' were a bombed-out family, who saved the situation by giving up the cherished bunk.

Teacher and voluntary social worker Phyllis Warner recorded in her diary the trauma of going on a London bus when the sirens went.

> We all fell flat on the floor of the bus. I remember thinking, 'My God, what did I come here for. I'm going to be blown to bits with this lousy crowd of strangers, and I haven't even got an identity disc on.' Then the bomb dropped a few streets away, but we still had to remain with our faces amongst other people's feet until the plane was a suitable distance away. I shall always detest the smell of shoe polish now.

Department stores had shelters for customers. Peg Cotton, the American, still living in London, found the John Lewis shelter in Oxford Street a delight.

> I was buying some cretonne when the Banshee howl drove me into the sub-basement. There in the shelter below Oxford Street were hundreds of people, mostly women shoppers, crowded on wooden benches set back to back in close rows across the basement rooms. I found a place among them and settled down to read. Almost everyone carries a book nowadays as well as a gas mask. Certain of the store staff wore armbands reading Head of Personnel, Shelter Warden or First Aid. Salesgirls circulated through the rooms selling candy, biscuits, soft drinks, small sixpenny books, embroidery patterns and silks and even offering free wool in navy, khaki and Air Force blue, complete with needles and directions. 'Won't you please knit for the forces at John Lewis' expense?' Music was furnished by gramophone and, every so often, an attendant sprayed the air with disinfectant. An hour and a half spent thus is not too bad. But still it is an aggravation and a waste of time. I got a perm

a few days ago. One less thing to bother with if one's hair is manageable. Of course the sirens went while I was still crowned with wet hair-pinned snails! I had plenty of company – lots of other women in various states of presentableness or rather, unpresentableness. I can see that inhibitions will soon be 'Gone with the Wind' – or the bombs!

One thoughtful daughter bought her ageing mother a dressing gown to throw over her nightclothes as she scurried to the shelter. No one wanted to be caught in the bath, or scantily clad, during a raid.

Mrs Cotton, whose husband ran a munitions factory on the outskirts of London, had her daughters, her baby granddaughter Penny and other family members sheltering in the flat during raids. The nightly journey down several flights of stairs to the basement proved too arduous with a baby in tow, so the family barricaded themselves in the flat.

Penny's basket and stand are behind the headboard of nurse's bed in a corner. We have pushed the wardrobe up before the window. And when the sirens go, the bedroom door is opened. According to Government pamphlets, this is supposed to mitigate any blast! Our dining room with mattresses all over the floor, now has the air of a very select, or posh, flop house, these bombing nights. The dining table, chairs piled on top of it, is up against the window. I try to think of this arrangement as some sort of real protection against bombs, as I am more terrified by what I am told than by what we have so far experienced – of how a batch of people were crowded in a public shelter, and all killed from the blast alone, a sort of vicious and deadly vacuum having rushed into the shelter, and pulled the people apart – eviscerated them.

Survivors who emerged into the streets found familiar landmarks had disappeared and saw gaping holes where neighbours' houses had stood the day before. Lylie Eldergill was a garment-machinist living in the East End of London. She found the noise of screaming planes, whining sirens and crashing bombs nerve-racking, as she wrote to her cousin in America.

I don't think the American people can realise how lucky they are.

I often wish I was miles away from here, but like the rest of the Londoners have just got to bear it till the end.

Lylie's husband, Tom, had been blind since the age of six, and his handicap brought added danger.

Tom and I don't go to a shelter. We have never been to one. We stay in the flat and chance it. If I had my way I should have gone to a shelter, but Tom didn't want to go. He was afraid of panic if a bomb hit the place. What I am afraid of is being buried alive underneath these buildings.

Tom's fears were justified. In March 1943, 178 people lost their lives in a tube station. They were crushed and suffocated in the entrance stairs after a woman had stumbled and fallen. Thousands sought refuge in the underground. Phyllis Warner described going home by tube in October 1940.

A subway journey through London these evenings is an awful experience. Men, women and children are packed into every inch of space, sleeping three deep on the platforms, cramming the doorways, the corridors, the stairs, the escalators; sleeping on a mattress, or a blanket or two, or newspapers, or the bare stones, with a bundle of clothing for a pillow. It is a mercy that the London subways are so deep and spacious, nevertheless the ventilation and sanitary conditions are appalling. Competition for the best places – against a wall – is fierce. Last week people were mounting guard over their bedding all day through. Traffic was so dislocated that now everybody is ordered out from 7am to 4pm when those who have been standing in line make a rush for their favourite pitch. Thousands are spending fifteen hours of the 24 in the subway stations, sleeping cheek to jowl, not taking their clothes off for weeks together. This is certainly a new low in city living. The danger of infection below ground must be a hundred times greater than that of bombs above.

People emerged into a world of dust and grime but baths became a luxury.

Damaged gas mains meant that the hot water supply was unreliable, and if there was a lull during the air raids it might not be long enough to take a bath. There were many reports of air-raid victims discovered in the bath. So hygiene had to take second place to survival. Ethel Mattison was one of those women who went to the hairdresser for a solution to the problem of 'shelter hair'.

> For a couple of months I have had a 'Liberty Cut', which was created to stem the epidemic of lousy heads caused by abnormal living conditions in crowded shelters etc. I think permanent waving is the biggest cause myself, because people go to get their hair washed and set and then leave it for weeks without washing, and in some cases almost without brushing or combing, for fear of spoiling the wave. Needless to say I didn't have the cut for that reason. It is very easy to manage, dries in a few minutes and is getting quite wavey. You probably know the cut, tapered all over so that it wisps.

Londoners regarded the underground as a place of safety. But on 11 March 1941 the Bank underground station was hit, killing 68 people. Mea Allan, the ambitious journalist on the *Daily Herald*, was the first reporter on the scene. In a letter to a close friend, she wrote an account that would not have got past the censor and on to the pages of her newspaper.

> One usually verbally measures bomb craters by the number of buses they would accommodate: but this one would take a depot. It stretches from pavement to pavement across the length and width of the roads. When I saw it, it was a jumble of thousands of tons of roadway, twisted steel girders and huge chunks of concrete. Beneath were dead shelterers whose bodies were one by one being brought out. The High Explosive had fallen through the roadway, exploded underneath, thrown the whole thing up, and then it had all dropped back again. The blast was as bad as the actual bombing. You know the terrific gale that can be caused by the ordinary approach of a tube train – multiply that gale by a terrific and horrible velocity – so that people were picked up like pieces of paper and hurled along passages and on to the

An elderly couple survey the mangled wreckage of one of the streets shattered during the Luftwaffe's attempt to destroy the port of Liverpool with seven consecutive nights of bombing in May 1941. The raids left 1,400 people dead, 1,000 seriously injured and 7,500 homeless.

line – every bone in their body smashed. By the time I got there, four forty-foot cranes were on the job, and yellow dredgers with caterpillar heels were scooping up walloping lengths of stone and piling it on the pavements. The crater swarmed with men – Pioneer Corps, ARP rescue squads – green mass-produced stretchers were waiting. I went down to the platforms, by way of steps plentifully covered with sawdust. Blood, brown and slippery was still oozing through. Talked to the 'regulars' who were taking up their positions for the night in passages that had not been damaged. They told me – 'the worst thing was getting breath, we were choked with fumes and dust'. A shaft of grey daylight pouring down from the shattered ceiling, a barrier up, and beyond it the machine gun roar of dozens of drills breaking up the debris. Chaos noise and death – and amid it all the regulars are sitting down to sleep – not thinking they are brave, just Londoners carrying on in the good old wartime style. A doctor told me how he'd got onto the platform and moved past two people standing at the mouth of the exit passage. They were killed. He was the only doctor on the platform and worked until he was exhausted. Women tore up their blouses and underclothes for bandages, and men tore up their shirts.

Mea had a lucky escape from her local street shelter in October 1940.

I don't know how we got out alive but none of us in the shelter were killed. It was ten past ten when we suddenly found ourselves sliddering about the floor as if it was the deck of a storm tossed ship, with the most frightful crashing like the end of everything. Dust and rubble and glass came flying along the passage and through the open shelter door. Most of the folk in the shelter either threw themselves on the floor or clutched their heads under their arms. All I could do was stare, so that I got a nice mouthful of dust. I can't get the smell of being bombed out of me. It's soot, plus old dust of plaster and brick, plus fire, plus mouldering fire hose water – so desolate no matter how many baths I take.

Cardboard coffins had been stockpiled by local authorities in preparation for war. They were intended for unidentified bomb victims. But Mea Allan was more terrified of lying in an unmarked grave than of being killed.

If it's a direct hit, be sure to have one's handbag near one – containing my identity card: my body shall *not* go in one of those ghastly cardboard boxes in which civilians, unclaimed, are dumped.

While many civilians took cover underground, a network of civil defence workers above ground coped with the aftermath. Frank Hurd, London firefighter, volunteered for the Auxiliary Fire Service in April 1939 and was called up in September. He wrote an account of the massive raid on 7 September 1940, when his unit was called to Becton Gasworks.

> Chaos met our eyes. Gasometers were punctured and were blazing away, a power house had been struck, rendering useless the hydraulic hydrant supply – the only source of water there. And then over head we heard Jerry. The searchlights were searching the sky in a vain attempt to locate him. Guns started firing, and then I had my first experience of a bomb explosion. A weird whistling sound and I ducked beside the pump. Then a weird flash of flame, a column of earth and debris flying into the air, and the ground heaved. I was thrown violently against the side of the appliance.

Despite being on duty for over 14 hours himself, his praise goes to the backroom staff.

> They are the people to thank for getting fires attended as soon as they break out. When a big raid is in progress they are hard at it, often all night, under pretty tough conditions. At Burdett Road [his station], their sole illumination is a candle beside each telephone operator.

Out on the streets, the blackout posed an added danger for firefighters.

> It's no joke finding your way about in a vehicle during the blackout through back streets in a district you or your driver have never been in before! As we were now some distance away from the fires, and jerry being overhead, we were proceeding without lights – except side lights, which are so dimmed as to be useless for illuminating the road. The pump in front of us had turned round a corner. We followed and suddenly the tender bumped, lurched and went along with two wheels on the pavement. We had only just missed dropping into a crater about twenty feet across by 10 to 15 feet deep. The first pump had swerved the other way from us and was stuck with its nose in a heap of debris.

Reaching an alleyway only 20 feet wide, lined with warehouses, Frank confronted every fireman's worst nightmare: a fractured gas main was on fire.

> The flames issued from wide cracks in the road surface. Gas main fires must not be put out, as this would leave escaping gas with great risk of explosion. We were working with our backs against one side of the street, aiming our jets into the warehouse, with the street alight in front of us. The top floor of the building against which we had our backs, kept bursting into flame. On top of this, we were warned not to let our jets strike the brickwork of the warehouse wall, as this was very shaky and the impact would probably cause it to fall. An eighty foot high wall collapsing into a twenty foot road – not a pleasant prospect.

A fortnight later, Frank Hurd was one of 14 firefighters killed during the great City of London raid on the night of 29 December 1940. Records show that he was off duty and probably on his way home.

Shortly after that massive raid on the City, journalist Mea Allan visited the remains of the Square Mile.

> *Ruins.* It was like the knocked up remains of a film set. It was like a child's mess of sandcastle after the child has kicked the sand city to pieces again. Hardly, in all that square mile, a building that was whole. And most of them razed to the ground. An occasional half building still standing – but windowless, burnt out, gaunt, empty as a skull. In my mind I still see the litter of yellow bricks, millions and millions and millions of them lying in tumbled heaps, and stretching out and beyond the bare desert of bricks, those dead windowless shells of buildings where big city business was done in a din of tapping typewriters and phone calls and a whirring traffic of messengers, lorries, vans, cars and *people*.

Many Londoners recalled making a similar pilgrimage to view the devastation, where St Paul's Cathedral rose defiantly amidst the smoking rubble. Mea also visited the East End after two months of the Blitz.

> Am feeling very cheery tonight. The visit to the East End was

not so depressing as one might imagine. Many houses down, of course, but after 8 weeks you'd think there'd be hardly any left standing. That is the reason I am cheered. The 6 o'clock news gave out that today's bombing was 'ineffective'. It seems to me that sums up the whole Blitz. They bomb houses; they bomb factories; they bomb railway lines. The houses – not nearly the number of people have been killed that was estimated. I understand the borough authorities reckoned 3,000 dead a day. At the worst it has been 300. The factories – you read the other day that ¼ of 1% damage has been done, and of course repairs are instantly put in hand. One factory I heard of in London, quite badly damaged, was in running order again in 24 hours. Railway lines are constantly being repaired.

Railway lines were targets for bombers on both sides, as their positions were conveniently marked on pre-war maps. Edna Morris was on her way from Sevenoaks to London by train on the night of the ferocious raid on the City of London on 29 December 1940. She described the experience in a letter to her mother six days later.

I can tell you I thought my last day had come. My train stopped on the line between London Bridge and Charing Cross Stations; it was shaking every few minutes and I could hear the bombs whistling by like shelled peas. I was alone in the compartment and was lying on the floor, expecting the carriage any moment to collapse and bury me. After a few minutes the guard came, opened the doors, and said that as there was a fire on the line immediately in front, the train could not go on, and we would have to walk to Cannon Street Station along the line. By this time I can tell you, I was like a jelly in a hot sun.

Leaving the shelter of her blacked-out compartment, Edna shakily stepped out on to the tracks to be greeted by an unforgettable sight.

The whole of the city in this part was as bright as day, and St Pauls was immediately to our right. I thought the fire was there, and when you see the news film of it you will understand that

Firefighters share a cup of tea for the camera during the London Blitz in the autumn of 1940. Frank Hurd (third from right) was killed on 29 December 1940, at the age of 24. During World War II, 793 firemen and 25 firewomen died and some 7,000 were seriously injured.

only a miracle preserved it. We could hear the planes overhead. A soldier took charge of me; otherwise I am afraid I would have panicked, and we had to go flat on the line about half a dozen times before we got to the shelter, which I suppose took us about five minutes or ten, and seemed like ten hours. I wouldn't go through it again for £100, and that is the truth. When the all clear went, I walked through the city escorted by two soldiers, because I wanted to get to the shelter where John [her husband] was waiting for me, as I knew he would be frantic. And the fires! If the weather had not prevented further attack, the centre of London would have been destroyed. Well I must close now. I am writing in a hurry to let you know we are still alright. If I wait for time, I will never write and I have not been feeling too fit since last Sunday, I suppose it is nervous reaction.

It is hardly surprising that diarists and letter writers record nervous breakdowns as people endured air raids night after night: raids that often went on for five or six hours. Earplugs were issued to 60 per cent of the population in the Suffolk port of Felixstowe, to give some respite from the constant noise during raids. For as they took refuge in cellars and garden shelters, people used to a world much quieter than it is today were bombarded with noise. Their eardrums were assaulted by the siren's wail, the screech of enemy fighters and the roar of explosions as bombs detonated, interspersed with the booming response from anti-aircraft batteries.

Air-raid survival was a lottery, and while air-raid shelters may have made the population feel safer there were many instances of direct hits, even outside London. The police logbook in Felixstowe, Suffolk, records how, on the evening of 25 August 1942, a semi-armour-piercing High Explosive landed directly on the Anderson shelter in the back garden of a house in Nacton Road. A mother and her eight children, who had taken refuge inside, were killed, but the father, who was standing nearby, survived, albeit seriously injured.

Bill Regan had been a builder in peacetime, but 'for the duration' was a member of a Heavy Rescue Squad on the Isle of Dogs in East London. These men dug through bombed-out buildings with sticks and hands, searching for survivors. On 18 September, 1940, they were still searching through the debris that had been Saunderness School, which had been bombed three months earlier. As Bill recorded at the time:

What a bloody mess, the whole guts blown away, only the two
end flanks standing. There were more than forty people stationed
here. The victims were fire brigade personnel, ambulance men,
and a complete mobile operating theatre, who were billeted
next to our depot in the swimming baths, and always left for
Saunderness when the sirens sounded. I had worked on the
building of the school, so I knew the general layout. After an
hour or so, George called me to help him with a doormat he had

found, but could not pull clear. It was black and of a thick curly texture, so I fished around for a while, loosening the packed rubble, then George came back with a length of iron rod to prise it out. I told him it was a bloke, and I knew who it was, Warden Herbie Martin.

Rescuers found the bodies of two girls, members of the Auxiliary Fire Service. Bill later discovered that the girls – Joan and Violet – shared the same names as his own daughters, who had been evacuated to Oxfordshire.

I know that none of us are very happy having to handle corpses and it shows. They have uncovered two young girls, about 18 years of age, quite unmarked, and they looked as if they were asleep. I looked around at the other men, and most of them looked shocked, and a bit sick; we had usually found bodies mutilated, and they were usually lifted out by hands and feet and quickly got away. Feeling a bit angry at the prospect of these girls being lugged out by their arms and legs, so I got down beside them, and they have obviously been in bed for the night. Dry weather we have had and the rubble packed round them had preserved them. Their limbs were not even rigid. They were lifelike; I could not let them be handled like the usual corpses.

Bill called for a stretcher and blankets.

Then I put my right arm under her shoulders, with her head resting against me, and the left arm under her knees, and so carried her up. I laid her on the stretcher, 'You'll be comfortable now my dear.' I did exactly the same for the other one.

Bill was equally traumatized by the necessary preparations for burial of the bodies. A senior member of the mortuary staff showed the Rescue Squad how it should be done.

The school playground had been screened off for the cleaning and shrouding; I never saw them coffined. It was fine warm weather, and the shed was wide open with the bodies lying on the asphalt.

He soon by order and example, had his men stripping off what clothing remained on the corpses. 'Now wash 'em off' he says, and the first one to try, had a water bucket and a sponge, and began to gently wash the face of one corpse with the sponge. The expert soon stopped that, he wasn't going to have a four hour job. He ordered two of his men to keep the buckets of water coming, and with a long-handled, well-wetted mop, gave the first corpse a good wash, front and back, showed his men how to wrap them in shrouds, label them, and stow them ready for final disposal. Each one took about three to four minutes, and he said, 'That's how it's done, you'll soon get the hang of it soon enough.' I don't think they ever did. We were all wandering around in small groups, feeling useless, wondering what tomorrow would be. We soon learned that tomorrow is never, now is what matters.

Many of the victims were his neighbours and friends. On his way to work early one morning Bill passed a crater.

Middle of the crater had been Bill Elderly's house. I knew him very well, so I had a look around but only found the remains of the shelter torn out of the ground. No trace of him and his two sisters, I felt depressed.

The two men had known each other since boyhood. Bill discovered that the night shift had been out to the incident and found no one.

I insisted that they must be somewhere about, maybe injured, so Major Brown came out with my squad to investigate. We gathered three bushel baskets of remains, I picked up two left feet. Eventually we found enough evidence for three people, so we came away.

Bill Regan was so dedicated to his work that on one occasion he worked for 76 hours without sleep.

Once rescue squads had pulled the survivors clear, first-aid workers helped the injured to casualty clearing stations. Constance Logan Wright described such a station at Great Ormond Street Hospital.

In the first room, the injuries are diagnosed by the doctor, and each patient is labelled according to his or her requirements. The staff work in absolute silence – a method found to be excellent since the first need, when rescued from the blazing shattered streets, was a sense of peace and quiet. They have a special device for keeping the patient warm if suffering from severe shock. It is a wooden cradle containing three very powerful electric bulbs, and the stretcher is put on top of this so that the patient is examined and kept warm at the same time. This casualty clearing station has an operating theatre specially prepared for the Blitz; it can be cut off from the London electricity and water mains and could be entirely self-providing for 24 hours in case of need. With gas proof ventilation, it is as well protected as is possible, and the architects say that it might even resist a direct hit.

While the London Blitz was in full swing, those in the provinces watched with admiration. In Cheshire, the teenager Brian Poole wrote to his young American penfriend on 20 September 1940:

Still alive and kicking. But greatly enraged at the brutal bombing by our swinish enemy of London. It's terrible to think of this beautiful city. I shall kill every Hun I can lay my hands on if they destroy the Tower of London, the Houses of Parliament or any building like that. I shall go raving mad. Just think if the Tower of London, built in 1088, nearly 900 years old, if it was destroyed, it would be terrible. It's buildings like these that the greatness of Empire has grown round. But the people of London will hold fast. It is their destiny to lead Britain to victory. The result of their endurance now will be glorious. If London holds fast, not only Britain and the peoples of the Empire are saved, but all the civilised peoples of the world.

A wartime song celebrated the fact that King George VI and his queen chose to stay in London during the war. Their visits to the bomb sites boosted the morale of beleaguered Londoners. Brian Poole was outraged when the first bomb hit Buckingham Palace, on 14 September 1940.

Then the dastardly attempts on the lives of our great King and Queen. They have proved themselves great and inspiring in our hour of trouble. The worst thing that has happened round here is the killing of twenty children ten miles away. They were having a pageant when the bomber dived out of the sun and dropped a bomb amongst them; one of our fighters shot it down later on.

Luftwaffe bombers did not just target London, they raided towns and cities across the country – from Cardiff to Canterbury, Newcastle to Norwich. The raid on Coventry and the destruction of its ancient cathedral on 14 November 1940 horrified the nation. PG Bridgstock, a former pupil of Kneller Boys School in Twickenham, wrote to one of his teachers afterwards.

Coventry looks a complete mess but the papers did not give a very good account of the damage done. The Town Centre was so unsafe that the military had to dynamite parts of it, and there is not a street in Coventry which hasn't at least one bomb crater in it. Austin Reed's Shop, where my father works, was very lucky and the only damage done was all the windows blown out. There is still no gas, electric or clean water, so we cook our food by fire, sit at night with candles and all the water must be boiled before using.

Attached to the letter is a diagram showing five bomb craters a few yards from his home. The morning after a particularly bad raid, anxious relatives jammed telephone exchanges, sending telegrams and booking long-distance calls to get news. Phyllis Warner waited 15 minutes for her long-distance trunk call to be put through to her family on the outskirts of Coventry. It had been a particularly clear night with a full moon, giving German bombers a grainy but clear picture of the landscape below. But it was *Londoners* who had been anticipating the resultant 'super blitz'.

It makes me sick to think of the devastation of the narrow bustling streets I have known since childhood; of the wreckage of that noble cathedral. True it was one of our smallest and simplest, but for me it has a hundred associations. The soaring spires of Coventry are mixed up with all sorts of idealism of childhood and adolescence. It is unbearable to think of them crashing down amidst such scenes of human agony. London people are profoundly shocked by Coventry's fate. In the subways and buses they were saying 'It's terrible, isn't it. Nothing they could do. You know, it's much better that the Jerries should come here, we're used to it, we're ready for it, so we can take it'. I completely agree with them in preferring that bombers should attack London. But I suppose that this is the London spirit that outsiders admire. We feel embarrassed by the news of praise that reaches us because we feel that it's just our job to stay here and stick it. Some of us have died and some of us are still alive to carry on – that's all.

The Coventry and Warwickshire Hospital suffered five direct hits in one raid, and patients had to be evacuated through a hail of bombs. Those who were bombed out were taken to rest centres - large public buildings (often schools) offering temporary accomodation, clothing and the essential cup of tea.

In October 1940 journalist Mea Allan, who spent her daylight hours reporting on the horrors of the Blitz, was bombed out herself. Anxious to recover her belongings, particularly the typescript of her first novel, she returned to what remained of her flat.

I'm quite sick with fatigue tonight. It was awful tramping through the flat, picking up an object, tapping the dirt and broken glass off it and then recognising it – 'Oh yes, that was the green cushion.' What filth, and dust and chaos. You could hardly believe blast could do such damage, but when I tell you it was a thousand pound heavy explosive, and an aerial torpedo – well, perhaps that accounts for it! The carpets are like earthy plots. You could have ploughed them. Inches of brick dust and lime, plus macaroni, flour, rice and the contents of my hall store cupboard, the side of which blew off and spewed the contents – including marmalade. It feels very queer having no home. I just don't know where to go! Someone suggests Kensington, and next day you hear of a landmine in the very vicinity one would have been in, and so it goes on.

As a Fleet Street journalist she could afford to stay in a hotel, albeit temporarily.

> I just can't sleep in bed listening to those bloody planes hovering overhead. Result of the discomfort was a nightmare in which I was being squeezed between two unrelenting walls. I woke myself screaming. I haven't started to look for rooms yet. The shelter problem is worrying me. Just can't bear the thought of sleeping in a public one along with a lot of drunks and prostitutes and worse than that – snorers.

Phyllis Warner also had to move out in October 1940, because of an unexploded bomb. It was part of the ARP warden's job to record the whereabouts of unexploded bombs, and evacuate nearby houses. A small suitcase stood ready at the door in every home for just such an emergency. Phyllis Warner heard 'her' bomb land one Tuesday evening.

> The door bell rang at 9.30 last night. The police, to say that the bang we had just heard was a time bomb in the garden next door but one, and would we please evacuate. We hastily picked up the thick coats and the suitcases we had brought to the shelter every night for just this emergency. It was an unpleasant walk through the streets, with the guns thudding and an occasional piece of shrapnel coming down with a terrific whang – in fact we finished at a sharp run. We were taken to a Government shelter beneath many floors of reinforced concrete, where noises came faintly, and we settled down to a real night's slumber, feeling secure at last.
>
> It was bewildering to wake up in that bare stone room, amongst a crowd of strangers, and to remember what had happened, and to realise that we couldn't go home to bath or change. We adjourned to a neighbouring hotel where we took a couple of rooms between a dozen of us to use for leaving our suitcases dressing etc, and then we had breakfast. It's no good taking rooms to sleep in, because we couldn't use them for that purpose anyway, and as long as we're 'time bombed' we shall be able to use the Government shelter.

During the war lapel buttons were produced saying 'I'm not interested in your bomb'. For Phyllis Warner 'her' bomb dominated the next few days.

> The bomb – which governs our lives – is still there, but they have sandbagged it, or frozen it or something, so we are allowed brief visits to the house today to collect a few possessions. I scuttled round the debris of my bedroom, collecting a few precious clean clothes from my scarred and pitted cupboards. But how blessed that cupboard and clothes are still present. The last few days have vividly strengthened my sympathy for other people who are evacuated by bombs, exploded or otherwise. I am fortunate enough to be able to command hotel meals, a room to leave my clothes, a place in a good and convenient shelter and somewhat elastic working hours; even so it takes me all my time to struggle from the shelter to work, from there to a meal, and back to the shelter before the night raid starts at 6.30.

As well as her day job as a teacher, Phyllis worked as a volunteer at a feeding centre in the mornings, where she encountered some of those less fortunate than herself.

> We had about 700 of the homeless poor crowding out the Feeding Centre this morning. We worked madly from the time the All Clear went at six, until after ten. I could have wept, as I put mugs of tea and slices of bread and butter into the trembling hands of old men dug out of the debris in their nightshirts, old women with blood on their white hair, little children covered with the dust of falling homes, fathers whose children are still beneath the ruins. It's their pathetic gratitude for the little we do that gets me by the throat.

Light was another enemy of those on the ground, and a friend to enemy bombers. ARP wardens patrolled the streets looking for chinks showing through the blackout. They are famously remembered for the phrase 'Put Out That Light!' Every factory and office had teams of fire-watchers perched on the roof to raise the alarm when incendiary bombs sparked fires. Equipped with stirrup pumps, ARP wardens worked to put out these fires, which lit up the streets and enabled the next wave of bombers to pinpoint targets on which to drop high explosives (HE).

Charity Bick was a 15-year-old bicycle messenger during the first major raid on West Bromwich, in the Midlands. Her father was an ARP warden and her mother a Red Cross nurse. Charity told the local newspaper:

> I was out on my bike, when I was blown off into the gutter by a bomb. I got up and carried on. Then I saw an incendiary drop on the roof of a pawnbroker's shop. I climbed up and put it out.

What the newspaper did not recount was cited in her recommendation for the George Medal.

> The occupier's stirrup pump proved to be out of order, but they were able to extinguish the bomb by splashing water onto it with their hands. Mr Bick turned to make for the entrance to the roof, but put his foot through the false ceiling. He turned to warn his daughter and as he did so, she fell through the ceiling into the bedroom below.

Injured, Charity went back to the Warden's Post.

> A High Explosive bomb fell immediately opposite the Warden's Post at which she was doing duty and she was instructed to take a message to the Control Room asking for assistance. The girl borrowed a bicycle and started off but on five occasions she had to get off and lie in the gutter because of bombs falling near her. She was the only despatch rider to this Post, and therefore the only means of communicating with the Control Room. She made three journeys from her Post to the Control Room, a distance of one and a quarter miles during the height of the raid. The town was lit up by four very large fires, and she had to pass in close vicinity to all these fires on her way to the control room. There was a continual rain of High Explosive bombs and shrapnel and anyone out of doors was incurring a very serious risk of injury.

By the end of the war 2,379 civil defence workers had been killed in the line of duty and 4,459 seriously injured. Joan Strange was a civil defence volunteer at the Report Centre in Worthing, one of the south coast towns that was a frequent target.

> We were all laughing and making a noise when we heard what we thought was tapping at the window, but – it was bombs. We all shot out to the telephones and messages came in fast and furious – the gas works had been hit, houses in Park Road and Lyndhurst Road demolished, 5 people killed and several injured, some still feared trapped and so on. Later we found that a lone raider had appeared suddenly – dropped its load, and in flying off in a westerly direction, machine gunned people walking in the road.

Lone raiders could wreak havoc. In another incident near Worthing, 28 children from a village school, and their headmaster, were killed. Mrs Paroutaud was at teacher training college in Bristol when Bath was bombed in 1942. This was one of the Baedeker raids, so called because the targets were historic or culturally important cities listed in the famous Baedeker guide books. Mrs Paroutaud volunteered as a bicycle courier taking telegrams to city homes from anxious relatives.

> In the case of Bath it was a systematic terror raid to break morale. It was totally unexpected, no military targets only cultural ones. I saw Bath the next day. We were taken over on a bus with our bicycles so that we could act as emergency message carriers. Bath was inundated with telegrams and who could deliver them? Call out the students. We cycled all over Bath carrying messages and bringing back reports. It was heartbreaking. We would go to one address only to find that it wasn't there any more. I shall never forget the streets of Bath all crunchy with broken glass and rubble. The shocked, tense faces of the people, and this stiff upper lip thing that kept them from crying and raging over the loss and the desolation. Why didn't they weep and mourn and lament? It would have been much better for everybody. I got to one address and found the lady of the house in labour. The husband 'in the military' had sent a telegram asking for news and hoping to get compassionate leave.

Near Christmas, 1940, Bill Regan, the Heavy Rescue worker, who had seen friends and neighbours killed on the Isle of Dogs, recorded the second raid on Bath in his diary with a degree of bitterness.

> Bath raided again last night. Hear they are asking for volunteers to help them. I can feel no sympathy for Bath. They did not rush to help us in our time of need, neither did they show any feeling. I have spoken with several people who all express the same opinion.

Norwich was another of the targets taken from the Baedeker guides.

> Norwich bombed again last night. Why all the fuss about 'ancient Monuments', when we know of the aerodromes, and factories round the city? Bomb the workers, as well as factories, then neither can produce. It's a civilian's war, and anyway, we are doing the same to Germany (I hope).

German bombers launched a massive attack on factories on Glasgow's Clydebank on Thursday 13 March 1941. As Director of Education for Dumbartonshire, Dr JP McHutchison toured the damage with the local MP.

> In the bus in the morning I heard that Clydebank 'was in ruins', though I was inclined to doubt that, since from our house no sign of conflagration was visible. A visit to Clydebank proved there was not much overstatement in the remark. Not a single school escaped, so thoroughly had HE and incendiary bombs been showered all over the town, and it was a heartbreak to see as gaunt ruins splendid buildings which the same week I had visited to discuss fire-watching. But the real tragedy of the indiscriminate bombing was the gutted tenements, and ruined and blasted council houses, in the poorest working class areas – in which streets the miles of four storey tenements had been completely gutted by fire. Some parts were still blazing and hundreds of the tenants watching from piles of saved furniture the holocaust of their homes. Long queues of now homeless folks awaited the buses

that would take them away, and Drumry Road was black with men women and children waiting at the Church Rest Centre for food and guidance.

On Friday 14 March, continuous waves of German bombers bombarded the town for another 5½ hours.

> Houses that had escaped on Thursday night did not escape this time, and over all the huge columns of black smoke from the oil tanks which were on fire. It was a great mercy that the weather was fair and fine, as otherwise the appalling situation, with practically the whole town homeless would have been unbearable.

The targets of these raids – three factories, including the Royal Ordnance Factory – came off relatively lightly, and early the following week people were starting to trickle back to their jobs, and to homes that were less severely damaged. More than a thousand people died in those two nights, and 90 per cent of the Clydebank population was made homeless. Survivors were billeted in surrounding rural districts, often in school buildings.

Some lucky Londoners, including those in the fire and rescue services, were given relief from the Blitz: rest homes in the countryside offered them a chance to recuperate from the stress and sleepless nights. Joan Strange arranged short holidays for elderly Londoners who were homeless and traumatized.

> I called on Mrs Read (the Londoner sent for a 14-day holiday by Kit) and she's spent four days in bed trying to make up her sleep and get stronger from the shock of having her daughter and son-in-law killed by bombs. The daughter could not be found and poor Mrs Read had to go round various mortuaries looking at poor dead girls. She never saw her, but eventually identified her from a photograph.

Sixty thousand British civilians were killed, and 85,000 seriously injured, during the German bombing of the British mainland in World War II.

6
SOLDIERING ON

Much is said about medals for troops, but I'm sure most housewives have
earned a row of 'em. Theirs is a job and a half, and when there is an
outside job to do in addition, it's very hard going.
(Ernie Britton, October 1940)

Ernie Britton summed up the lot of British women as they soldiered on
through the war. Women went out to work to release men for the Forces, just
as their mothers had done during World War I. They worked in factories and
in the London underground; they became postwomen and bus conductors.
Normal domestic life was completely disrupted during the Blitz, but washing
still had to be done in an era when few had washing machines. Long queues
formed outside shops rumoured to have a supply of precious oranges, or
some other rarity. Cooking meals required ingenuity, and clothes were
mended and altered to last longer. On top of all this, women in the ranks of
the Women's Institute and the Women's Voluntary Service collected salvage,
helped to billet evacuees and collected hedgerow fruits to make jam. If they
were not already exhausted by the daily grind they worked at feeding centres,
or made munitions in their 'spare time', and dug for victory in gardens and
allotments to supplement the family's rations.

Ernie Britton's wife May took great pride in her home, and combined
housework with her job as shop assistant in a North London department
store, where he felt conditions were less than ideal.

> Having to have her lunch at 11.30 and nothing to eat or
> drink until six in the evening (after she has got it ready!)
> it's much too long a spell especially as she works very hard
> while she is there.

In October 1940, a stray bomb landed 80 yards from their house.

> May and I were in the kitchen, making tea before the next lot
> of planes, and May was just leaving the kitchen with the tray,
> when the front door and kitchen door blew open and for what
> seemed minutes there was nothing but falling bricks, tiles,
> glass and the Lord knows what. May didn't drop the tray! We
> both laughed at our safety and she said 'Drink this tea I've just
> made!' So we did.

Leaving their blitzed home, Ernie and May took the car and ventured out
into the night, to find temporary shelter with friends.

> We couldn't go left so we went right. That was a bit troublesome
> owing to various fires, with roads stopped but we got there
> amid a few more bombs and gunfire. We didn't care a damn
> anyway.

After a sleepless night the couple returned to assess the damage.

> May worked on the inside cleaning up plaster and glass. May has
> always been such a one for her home, it was a sad day for her to
> have everything so upset. The affair shook her up badly.

With their home declared unsafe by a surveyor, Ernie found lodgings in
London, while May stayed with her mother in Dorset.

> Try as I will, I cannot get anywhere to live together. As you know
> May is such a home bird and her greatest joy in life has dropped
> right out. She is very bitter about it sometimes and although fairly
> frequent visitings helps things along it is far from satisfactory
> for either of us. I feel the loss very much and try to make light
> of it, but sometimes that only aggravates. As keenly as I feel the
> emptiness of things I know May feels it much more acutely.

Ernie's concerns for his wife, voiced in letters to his sister Florrie Elkus in
the United States, are echoed by another sibling, Ethel Mattison.

It is very rotten for them to be parted again this winter and to have their nice home wrecked. They were so proud of their home. We have most of the furniture here. Still they have each other, which is more than a good many. I do hope that it will all soon come to a peaceful end. It isn't natural for all these families to be parted. I know I wouldn't like to go away and be parted from Jack.

But her turn was to come when husband Jack was called up in January 1941. She wrote to her sister five days after he left.

He was called up at ten days notice. I managed to get five days off and so did Jack so we had that time together. We didn't go away because the weather has been so lousy and it's difficult to find accommodation now in the country on account of evacuees. Of course I felt desperate at first, but I have been toning myself up with Adexolin and Sanatogen and have kept myself fully occupied, so I am getting past the stage when I feel a terrible surge every time I think of him, though I feel pretty bad writing this.

Ethel found the separation hard, but even harder was her first visit to Jack, now Gunner Mattison.

I was nearly sick with excitement. I felt full of beans right up until the train got to around Salisbury, which is about two-thirds of the way and then suddenly I knew that I was going to be terribly upset by seeing him. I was furious with myself because the one thing I wanted was to look happy. I had been preparing myself for the shock of the uniform all the way in the train, but it was a shock all the same. The hat was the worst part. You know he's never worn any sort of hat since I've known him, and there he was in this cap with practically a convict's crop. I just didn't feel he was the same person until I saw him in pyjamas and a dressing gown.

She was lucky to be seeing Jack once a week, and wrote to him at least every other day. Mrs E Innes-Kerr wrote to her husband Tam once a week during her lunch hour at the BBC. Tam had been captured when the Japanese took Singapore, and was a prisoner of war.

> It was often baffling to know what to say in case the conditions
> in which the letter was received were so awful that what I wrote
> jarred with Tam's feelings at the time, still I enjoyed my quiet half
> hour of communing with him.

After her own escape from the Far East, it was 18 months before she heard that he was alive – on a postcard that reached her on 14 July 1943.

> It was little enough, just a few words written twelve months ago,
> but I cannot find the words to describe what it meant to me.
> The news spread round the office and people kept popping their
> heads round my door and saying how pleased they were that I had
> news at last.

Her boss gave her the afternoon off and she and a girlfriend went off to celebrate.

> We walked on air, the short distance to DH Evans for lunch and
> a celebratory drink, the latter being a most unusual indulgence.
> I left the card with Tam's mother, so that she would feel she had
> something from him. It may sound daft, but I felt this was a real
> sacrifice on my part.

Separation was just one of many wartime hardships, and with it the nagging doubt that it could so easily become permanent. Couples poured out their emotions to each via the Royal Mail. Two hours after saying goodbye to her husband, Mavis Bunyan wrote in October 1943:

> It was awful seeing you as just a number amongst all those
> boys, knowing you had to go, and there was nothing we could
> do about it. To them just a number, but to me, my whole life
> and happiness. I just feel right now that I can't face it. I know
> I will get by though. It is awful to think of the months without

you. I would not mind so much if I could hear from you every day like I used to, but maybe having to wait months for letters makes it seem worse.

Like many other wartime couples, Mavis and Gerald made a date to think of each other when the nine o'clock pips sounded on the BBC, but this didn't ease the frustration they fely, that the war meant they had lost control over their own lives.

Oh darling, I just cannot do without you, I feel I will go mad. To have to go round doing everyday things, outwardly normal, when all the time I feel dead and lifeless inside me. Reading some of your letters this morning, something hit me rather. All your letters are full of hatred at being away from me, as I know mine are too. When will we be left to live our lives together with no more wretched partings?

At 20, Mavis was bringing up their daughter Lesley on her own.

You ask, darling, if Lesley Ann recognises your photo as Daddy. She is always saying Dad-da but I am afraid she does not know you.

Mavis got a job as a bus conductor in her home town Torquay, to 'help the days go a little quicker', working 56 hours a week.

I was wanting to write you a letter this evening [instead of an airgraph, which was far shorter] but I am so tired. Heavens, what a day it has been. I carried just on 1500 passengers, full buses all the while and leaving loads behind. It makes us wonder where all the people come from. I had to hang out of the bus whenever possible to let the rush of wind cool me off. It is wonderful to lie in bed and rest my weary, weary bones. All next week I have a single decker on a comparatively easy route so I shall be able to recuperate. It is a late turn, 1.35 to 9.35.

Despite long hours, she still had to find time to 'make do and mend', especially when elastic became scarce in February 1944 (the major source of Britain's rubber had been cut off after the Japanese had invaded Malaya).

> If you could possibly send me some elastic I will love you for ever more. The elastic question has reached such a stage that I will have to buy panties just to get the elastic!

Seven months later she received a letter, which she opened with great excitement.

> I love you I adore you I worship you. This morning I had the airmail containing the elastic and poppers. Poor Lesley is running around with her trousers at her knees most of the time, me, with mine kept up by will-power. So thank you kind sir! It is very nice elastic and has arrived just in time to save me from probable, in fact certain embarrassment. Not your daughter I'm afraid, because she has already lost her trousers several times.

She was not alone. Anne Lee Michell was in London helping to evacuate children from the danger of doodlebugs in 1944.

> Lady V, another and I were station marshalls at St Pancras, not very auspicious as one child evacuee was lost, the water and biscuits were late arriving and I had to keep phoning from the station master's office; and as I raced down the platform with a precious spoon for the babies food I lost my pants: loud cheers from all beholders!!

In Devon, Mavis Bunyan longed for another baby, an impossible desire to fulfil with her husband overseas. In London, Ethel Mattison longed for a baby too, but she postponed starting a family because of the daily dangers and uncertainties of wartime life. There was also the prospect of bringing up a baby in Nazi-occupied Britain. On New Year's Day 1940 she wrote to her sister Florrie in America:

> I can't get a job for love nor money. If it wasn't for this bloody

war it would make all the difference between having a baby and not having one I guess, but in the circumstances that's unthinkable. Apart from considerations as to the eventual outcome of the war you would never be sure that you could go on giving it the proper food or anything. I always envy anybody I hear is going to have a baby almost instinctively, but my God what an awful responsibility.

In the spring of 1941, shortly after her husband Jack had been called up, she wrote:

Perhaps the war will be over next year and I'll be able to have a baby in April 1943, only two years later than I had planned. Two years isn't long in a lifetime, but I feel I shall burst.

Ethel kept her spirits up by doing physical training to the radio every morning for ten minutes. In April 1943, the month she had hoped to be a mother, the war news was better, but her desire was still unfulfilled.

I wasn't at all convinced in the early stages that we shall win the war, but now I am, to the extent that if Jack is still in this country in June I will start to have a baby. The desire is becoming an obsession like wanting a lover when you're adolescent, and it isn't made easier by the fact that since I've been in my present job, four women have left to have babies and two of them in my room. They bring all the things up to show us.

Ethel had found work in the Food Office, though she was a qualified nurse. Hospitals would not take on married women, because nurses were expected to 'live in', but her nursing skills made her in demand nonetheless.

A friend of Eileen's whom I know slightly, tried to get an abortion. She went to someone on Saturday afternoon, was up all night taking castor oil, and in pain all the next day and night. Eileen asked me to go so, although there was absolutely nothing I could do, I just had to stay there, and missed two nights sleep. On Monday morning I sent for my doctor and explained the whole thing and she got her to hospital, where apparently it came off fairly soon and she's OK.

Hasty wartime marriages, infidelity and lack of money forced women to such solutions, with sometimes tragic results. On 28 November 1941 Ethel told Florrie about a colleague.

> I feel awfully sorry for her. She's only twenty-one and has been married a year today. Her husband's in the army and she's never lived with him, except for brief leave periods when he has joined her at her mother's as they have never 'set up home'. She tried all the useless methods of producing an abortion, but without success. She only produced a prolapsed uterus. I tried to give her some tentative advice, but she is frightfully ignorant and has a mistaken sense of morality. So here she is with her life ended as it were, at twenty-one.

The uncertainty of what the morrow might bring had made many couples leap into these wartime marriages, snatching at happiness (however temporary). Ethel wrote to her sister about the impact on her own gunner husband.

> The pay bombardier has just left to return to his civilian job for six months, so Jack has stepped into his shoes. This bloke was a solicitor's clerk, and the number of divorces have reached such proportions that the firm can't cope without him!

In Chester, Frank Forster and his young wife Lyn had been told they were unable to have children. With an engineering job he was in a reserved occupation, and they were keen to offer a home to an unwanted child. His sister-in-law, Bessie, was one of many women whose husbands were in a prisoner-of-war (POW) camp.

> Lyn's sister Bessie is pregnant and cannot have very long to go before delivery – the child's father is probably a soldier whom Bessie has been going round with. Bessie is in a very bad way, she takes no interest in life, takes no interest in her personal appearance which in a young woman, is a bad sign.

In January 1943, Bessie went to a maternity home in Chepstow. Frank commented acidly in his diary:

> I presume that she has gone so that she can give birth to her child away from home and prevent scandal – it is to be regretted that she had begun such a life while her husband Colin is in a German concentration camp – she cannot bear him much love.

The baby was born, but Bessie was reluctant to give her up. Eventually she confessed her infidelity in a letter to her husband far away in a German POW camp. Devastated as he was by the news, he said he would rear the child as his own.

Those who had babies during the war often had to go through labour without pain relief, as nitrous oxide was in short supply. Dolly Howard's stepdaughter, May, worked in a Liverpool hospital.

> May is doing six months maternity work at the hospital, and gives us many a laugh over her experiences. She has been on night duty. The alert seems to send all the mothers into labour. During one night she said the babies were all born during the first alert, were being washed during the second and were registered in the third.

As the prospect of victory seemed more likely, Ethel Mattison finally achieved her dream and gave birth to a daughter, Patricia, in 1944. Her sister Florrie Elkus sent her nappies from America, and Ethel made a pram cover from a fur coat sent across the Atlantic at the beginning of the war – a rarity in England as many women had donated their furs to the Finns in the winter of 1939–40. Her ingenuity was helped by a sewing machine, which she bought at auction in October 1944.

> Already I've done lots of odd jobs, like making oven cloths out of old nurses aprons, hemming towel ends, making a sleeping bag for Patricia out of an old blanket-cloth dressing gown – things that I could never have tackled by hand.

Devon bus conductor Mavis Bunyan was also a canny needlewoman and made clothes for her daughter. When she went Christmas shopping in Torquay in 1944 she was outraged at the prices.

> I bought a tablecloth for George and Lillian, it was £2.18.10 and
> the pre-war price was 22s 6d. It is heartbreaking to go shopping,
> especially now it is Christmas. A box of four hankies that was
> 1s 11d is now 6s 10½d. Some binding that was 3d now costs
> 1s 8d. Second hand jewellery is fetching atrocious prices. One
> necklace marked £6 was awful, honestly I have seen better in
> Woolworths for 6d.

Clothes rationing was introduced in June 1941, and even the humble hankie was on the ration (this is the era before the use of tissues). By 1944 hankies were 'priceless'. Florrie Elkus in California sent over scores of handkerchiefs to her friends and family during the war. She was a one-woman transatlantic supply line, sending a warm coat for her father (which he wore for fire-watching) and a powder compact and underwear for her sister Ethel.

> I must thank you for that beautiful slip-and-knicker set you
> sent me, which must have been nearly new. I was urgently in
> need of a slip, but the coupon situation had prevented me from
> lashing out on one so far. If I had bought one it wouldn't have
> been nearly so beautiful and would certainly have been too
> long, whereas this one is just right. I couldn't have had a more
> delightful surprise.

In July 1942 Mrs E Walsh (Miss Williams had by now married Kenneth Walsh) wrote optimistically to her brother Ellis Williams in British Somaliland, hoping for similar bounty.

> By the way everyone seems to be getting silk stockings sent them
> by their relations in the Dominions. I suppose you couldn't do
> anything in that line. It's an absolutely crying need. The stockings
> are now all rayon and don't cling (you wouldn't know but this is
> an essential) to the legs. They look horrid and undermine one's
> self confidence.

Mrs E Innes-Ker had plenty of silk in her wardrobe, brought with her when she had escaped from the Far East as the Japanese invaded. As she shivered in the severe wartime winters, she and her mother, Maw, applied for extra clothing coupons.

> The Board of Trade informed us that from the items listed in our applications it would appear that we had quite an adequate amount of clothing, and they were therefore unable to issue us with any extra coupons. This was a bitter blow as we had made a point of underlining the fact that all our clothes were 'of tropical weight' only.

Maw went to the Board of Trade to force a change of mind.

> When I got home she was triumphantly waving the extra coupons she had induced them to fork out. Just before leaving home she had been visited by an inspiration and had stuffed a pair of my pants into her pocket. These were delicate Chinese silk knickers which I had happened to be wearing the day we left Singapore, and with the effort of heaving our baggage around, and the fact that they had stuck to me because I was so hot and sweaty, they had split down the back. I had mended the tears but the knickers were a deplorable sight. Maw met resistance at first at the Board of Trade. The official who dealt with her produced our forms and reiterated that it would appear we had sufficient clothing, quite ignoring our note about tropical weight only. That was when Maw produced my knickers, waved them in the startled official's face and asked indignantly, 'How would you like to go through an English winter with nothing more than that?'

The pair also went to the Red Cross Headquarters, and picked out jumpers that had been sent in the US 'Bundles for Britain' scheme.

> We laboriously undid them, washed the wool to take the kinks out, and then knitted it up to suit ourselves.

It was no accident that the postwar New Look featured feminine skirts flowing with an abundance of material. By 1943, even turn-ups on men's trousers were banned, in a drive to simplify garments and use less material. Monica McMurray, a girl in the Women's Timber Corps, was one of thousands who donned 'utility' clothing.

> Today is Home Guard celebrations. Lovely sunny day and quite warm so I wore my new Jaegar Utility blue thin herringbone price £4.12.11. Apparently all makers are forced to make a certain amount of Utility clothes. Utility clothes only allow a certain amount of pure wool and in specified colours, but there are heaps of these colours, but not as many shades.

How women came to hate the word utility! In 1943, when Mrs Innes Kerr received her first postcard from her POW husband Tam and knew at last that he was alive, she optimistically bought a secondhand armchair to await him on his return. It was comfortable but shabby.

> Then one day prowling round DH Evans after lunch I discovered they were selling, unrationed, what they called mattress covers. To support this myth these covers had a metal eyelet hole in each corner, but each was in fact a sizeable piece of natural coloured artificial linen, which would be purchased without clothing coupons.

These she ingenuously transformed into chair covers, stamped with some large floral transfers, and embroidered with bits of leftover wool.

Shoes were another scarce commodity. Crêpe-soled shoes became popular, because the soles lasted longer, and wooden soles were introduced. People made shoes last by strengthening them with pieces of cardboard. Physiotherapist Joan Strange in Worthing reported the drastic impact of rationing on the growing feet of children.

> Saw Miss Goldsmith's demonstrations of treatment, by splints and strapping, of children's foot deformities. She says she gets many more children with deformed toes since shoes were rationed. The kids wear their shoes too long (or rather too short).

Women painted lines down the backs of their bare legs in imitation of stocking seams; they remodelled clothes by adding new buttons and changing the cut; and they bought what clothes were available with the limited supply of coupons. Some items were not rationed: bib-and-brace boiler suits, for example, were off the ration, but hardly fitted the feminine ideal of the 1940s. Joan Strange made a list of the many items that were scarce by the middle of the war.

> Other things which are difficult are all things to do with hairdressing – setting lotion, hair nets, hair pins, kirby grips, permanent waving appertenances etc. Oranges are to be had for children under 6 only. Dog meat is very erratic – Mike [her dog] goes off every day somewhere (probably to the soldiers' billets) and comes back licking his chops! Jewellers are finding stock difficult, so are ironmongers. There is a great shortage of paper and the public is urged to save it as much as possible. We are urged to use as little fuel as possible too.

Newspapers were thin because paper was scarce, so the shortage described by American Peg Cotton (by then living in Devon) is remembered by many. It was the hot topic of conversation at a drinks party in early 1945.

> Making small talk over glasses of sherry, Mrs Russell suddenly said, 'Have you been able to buy any toilet paper, Mrs Cotton? I haven't. There doesn't seem to be a roll, or packet, in all Devon!' As a topic of conversation this may seem odd to the uninitiated – and the unrationed. But to the housewife in Britain, this sixth year of War, it was simply the introduction to a serious discussion of a very urgent problem. Just another 'one of those things' that have added to the intricacies of wartime life.

Peg Cotton had bought several dozen rolls of toilet paper at the beginning of the war on the advice of a friendly London grocer, but this had run out by 1944. She had been forced to buy blocks of writing paper and this was also in short supply.

> Until an article becomes very scarce, and later quite

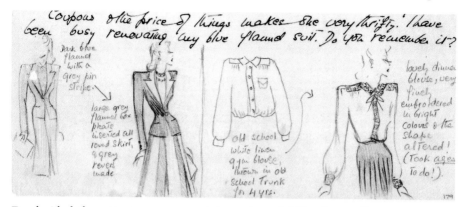

Coupons & the price of things makes she very thrifty. I have been busy renovating my blue flannel suit. Do you remember it?

Dark blue flannel with a grey pin stripe.

large grey flannel box pleate inserted all round Skirt, 9 grey revers made

old school white linen gym blouse, thrown in old School Trunk for 4 yrs.

lovely dinner blouse, very finely embroidered in bright colours & the shape altered! (Took ages To do!).

Faced with clothes rationing, one woman's ingenuity and skill with a needle turns an old school gym shirt into a evening blouse and refashions a coat and skirt. Maureen Bolster drew this fashion plate for her fiancé Eric, to show how she had learned to 'make do and mend'.

unobtainable, one rarely attaches a full value to it. Before the summer of 1944, TP was no particular problem, and certainly one never spoke of it in ordinary conversation. TP was one of those things found only upon household lists, or on the shelves of Grocer's and Chemist's Shops, or quite unobtrusively displayed in its proper habitat in homes, Hotels, [rail road] Stations, etc. TP was an uncounted blessing that one accepted without thought or thanks. But suddenly, in mid-1944, the British Public became 'TP-conscious' and began to realize how very unappreciative it had been of TP's important contribution to the Nation's comfort and morale. At first the shortage of TP merely meant searching from shop to shop. When I was fortunate enough to locate a few rolls the Clerk would brusquely say, 'Only two rolls to a customer, Moddam!' and would plunk the two rolls down upon the counter with an expression that seemed to imply that I had just tried to bribe her into selling me the crown jewels! I had no qualms whatever about putting them unwrapped (wrapping being forbidden anyway) into my mesh shopping bag and allowing the world to see the spoils of my day's shopping.

Thousands of women joined the Women's Voluntary Service, which was started in 1938. The WVS provided essential household services for women who had been bombed out. Children were kitted out from their clothing exchange; pots and pans, china and glass were available. All these practical items helped women to maintain some semblance of normal life. Anne Lee Michell was a stalwart of the WVS in the West Country. Her diary sparkles with vitality as she milks goats, tends house and hens, and learns to type. In August 1942 she was engaged in the WVS Herb Drive. Her branch was expected to gather 200 tons of dried nettles every month.

> This morning I finished off stripping nettles in the loft, and put in half-hours practise on the typewriter at the WVS office. Have now advanced to hash hash hash, lesson 6. Lois and a party of WVS came fox-gloving after lunch, we found a perfect place at the top of Ford St, and picked an immense load between storms of rain; I hope they will make enough to send off and we can then put our energies into hips and chestnut collecting. Stuart and Betty came along, most timely as I was milking, and again helped by holding Miranda, who behaves very fiddily when milked out doors.

The drug digitalis was harvested from foxgloves, and nettles could be used as a form of animal fodder. Anne also worked at a munitions factory, checking glass ampoules supplied to the RAF. She was not used to the tedium of factory work and constantly records the strain of checking ampoules for faults.

> Another depressing day of ampoules, ampoules, ampoules!

Anne was often brought low by the enormity of the tasks she had to fit into her day.

> Depressing day of rain and gales and rain again. Did a huge mound of washing and hung it out to dry, it ballooned and flapped valiantly on the line, then had to be brought in as the rain lashed down. A pouring wet afternoon and only 3 mothers ventured to the clinic, two being brought from Bathealton by a

fat lusty district nurse. Very depressed by my afternoon in the huge empty rooms, smelling of stale smoke and sweat from the factory-workers who'd been recreating there. It was 'doctor's day' and Cecilia depressed me further by her blunt assumption that all evacuees are cadgers and out to do you down – couldn't even enlist her sympathies for poor little Mrs Neeves. Took the latter her baby's food and found her very poorly and with a virulent rash all over her face. She has decided to stay on here but hates the thought of another interview with Mrs Ashplant about a billet.

The WVS offered a washing service in bombed areas, but evacuees, and many men and women in the Forces, sent their washing home to Mum. Mrs E Walsh recorded the somewhat pungent contents of a parcel sent by her husband Kenneth, a naval officer.

17 July 1940 – Yesterday the first of Kenneth's washing arrived. Mother opened the parcel before I arrived and washed it. You can imagine what hard work this was, bearing in mind he has been at sea for almost two months and there were only four or five shirts. I am to iron it on Monday evening.

Those in the Forces had one advantage over the ordinary population: better and more abundant food. Letters and diaries are packed with references to food. Londoner Phyllis Warner summed it up in her diary in August 1941.

We all think and talk about food eternally, not because we are hungry, but because our meals are boring and expensive and difficult to come by. How browned off I am with vegetable pie and savoury butter and inferior sausage and boiled potatoes, what wouldn't I give for orange juice or steak and onions or chocolate or apples or cream! People take most aspects of rationing philosophically but the great egg muddle makes them vitriolic. In London I haven't seen an egg for months, but many parts of the country had a reasonable supply until the control scheme came in a few weeks ago. Since then millions

Gas, electricity and water were frequently cut off during the Blitz, but the WVS stepped in to provide a hot meal. By 1940 half-a-million women were members. Makeshift kitchens were set up amid the debris and mobile laundries took care of the weekly wash.

of eggs have been immobilised in packing stations until they have gone rotten. Poultry keepers forced to yield up every one of their own supply, have been allowed to buy two or three Canadian eggs which also turn out to have been held up until they are rotten.

Anne Lee Michell kept hens on an allotment in Somerset. In May 1942 she had a mishap.

> Dropped all of my egg ration on to the back-path! Scraped them up into a bowl and we shall have to live on scrambled eggs.

Scrambled eggs could also be made using dried egg powder. In 1943 the Women's Institute gave useful tips on the 'essentials for success in making scrambled eggs with dried eggs – thorough blending of dried egg and water and slow cooking'. Leaflets were produced encouraging people to use a hay box – a box insulated with hay for cooking casseroles slowly, thus saving fuel.

Rationing had been planned in 1936, and ration books were issued in January 1940. The postwar consensus is that the wartime population was healthier as a result of a diet rich in vegetables and low in sugar and dairy products (a familiar regime today). Lord Woolton was the much maligned Minister of Food. After five years of war, Londoner Ernie Britton was filled with admiration for him.

> Lord Woolton and his staff make a good job of rationing and nobody goes hungry. Naturally we don't consume the amount of dairy produce we did before the war and we lack the infinite variety of pre-war days. Perhaps we lived too well before 1939.

Writing in the same year, as victory looked likely, Peg Cotton commented on the effect of the British wartime diet on the population.

> Although the English people have had enough to eat in quantity, throughout this war, the nutritional value of food has been so reduced that the average diet here has undermined people's vitality.

People were urged to eat things that were normally alien to the British diet (soya-link sausages are remembered with horror by many). Recipe tips were published in an article in a *Daily Telegraph* column, 'Women in Wartime'. Joan Strange, living in Worthing with her elderly mother, recorded in her wartime diary the government's attempt to persuade people to eat salt-cod.

> I thought I would mention food today, it is the most talked about subject now that Hess is stale! I actually brought Mother some salt-cod from Godalming, but she wasn't very keen. I was lucky today and bought ½lb of currants quite by chance. I had posted a parcel of flowers to one of Kit's bombed tenants and the man who also has a grocer's shop asked if I'd care to have some! I was lucky last Sunday too as Frammie gave me 6 ripe tomatoes, and they are about 5/- a lb in the shops.

Transport problems often made the supply of food unreliable, even goods 'on the ration'. In 1941 Worthing featured in the national newspapers because the town was so short of meat. Later that year, Joan Strange recorded how inventive wartime cooks had to be.

> Although our food position is remarkably good considering all things, yet Mother finds it difficult thinking out meals – our meat ration is still 1s 2d worth each per week (we're sure we had horse last week) and it's difficult to get any offal. We did have half a calf's head last week, which made some excellent brawn. Milk is rationed now and we get one quart a day. Sugar is 6oz per week, butter 2oz and margarine 4oz, cheese 4oz, 3 eggs a *month*! It's very difficult thinking out puddings or having visitors in to meals.

Wartime scarcities did not prevent Joan and her mother using all their ingenuity and contacts to raise money for charity. In the summer of 1941:

> Mother and I gave a bridge drive today for Council of Social Service and raised £7 7s 0d. Eight tables and tea and raffles. For raffles we had strawberries (a terrific treat given by

Mrs Claff from her father's nurseries). Two lots of eggs and a *rubber* hot water bottle! For tea we had *white* bread and *butter* (mother had saved some white flour). The butter came from Canada last Christmas. Tea from Australia and we saved milk from the ration.

No purely white bread was allowed after the spring of 1943. Even the sugar coating on pills was stopped that year. Wartime recipes were broadcast on the wireless, so that people could sample the delights of 'mock goose' and 'Victory sponge' (which capitalized on the natural sweetness of carrots instead of using sugar) and there was that wartime staple, 'Woolton Pie'. Mrs E Walsh wrote to her brother Ellis wondering if he had sampled this novelty, named after Lord Woolton and comprising root vegetables, cauliflower, onions, parsley and oatmeal, topped with mashed potato sprinkled with grated cheese.

> Have you had a Woolton Pie? They are for the pig pail. Nothing is wasted nowadays. Have you seen all the Ministry of Food appeals – jam out of the jar, cut don't break your bread, jam straight on to the bread and not on the plate etc.

Lack of variety, and an endless diet of swede and turnip, irked people. Bill Regan, living on the Isle of Dogs, summed up the joy of tracking down wartime rarities.

> Bought a jar of mustard pickle on the way home, they are very scarce now. They are good, no carrot or turnip to spoil it. The war-time abortion contains about 50% carrot and turnip. Horrible concoction. Winkles for tea, a great change, not had them for about a year.

Those lucky enough to have relatives and friends in Canada or the USA received frequent food parcels. Florrie Elkus sent delicacies from her California home to her family and friends: California raisins, tinned butter, tinned cheese and even cakes and cookies made their way across the Atlantic. People had been encouraged to dig up their gardens to grow fruit and vegetables. Dolly Howard described with pleasure the abundant produce that she bartered with her neighbours in Liverpool.

> Food is dearer, but we are fortunate in having a vegetable and
> fruit garden, besides a small allotment. The swedes are like huge
> footballs and the carrots yards in length. We also had a bumper
> crop of raspberries besides black and red currants so I was able to
> claim extra sugar for jam.

Hedgerows were plundered for blackberries. Rosehips were gathered to
make a syrup rich in Vitamin C for children. But as the war drew on, more
and more foodstuffs were rationed. In March 1941 Phyllis Warner wrote:

> A nasty shock today. Jam including marmalade treacle etc is
> to be rationed at half a pound a month, starting tomorrow.
> We're going to mind this meagre allowance more than any
> rationing yet. They must have let the stocks get very low to
> be so drastic.

No wonder she was upset. Jam had pepped up that wartime staple, bread
and margarine – a combination that was anathema to the British, with
their love of butter. American flyer Bob Raymond had joined the RAF,
abandoning plentiful food in the United States, for the wartime fare on
offer in Britain. He wrote in his diary in November 1941:

> Food situation – very plain and tasteless, but sufficient. Too
> much cold corn beef. No wonder the English are so fond of using
> spiced sauces for their meals. It's the only way to change the taste
> of this diet.

In fact, 'bully beef', as it was known, seems to have been reserved for troops.
Bob Raymond left the RAF to join the US Air Force in 1943. The food
enjoyed by the American forces was legendary. Peg Cotton's daughter Alix
got a job with the American Red Cross.

> Alix took a job as Liason Officer (Red Cross) at Fremington
> Hospital – one of the many such American hospitals scattered
> about the British Isles. Alix likes the job and makes our eyes

pop and our mouths water with accounts of the food to be
had there. According to Alix, our countrymen and women
– although far from home – are stuffed with the most wonderful
stuff! Tomato juice – orange juice – quarts! Chicken all the
time. (We almost *pray* over *our* fowls here – just to get an egg! As
for eating them – the fowls! It would be killing the goose that
laid the golden egg!) One and a half pounds of meat a day per
man! (Our whole family ration is less than that a week!) And
ice-cream – always ice-cream – the manufacture of which is now
forbidden to the English. As for the American coffee – it is really
coffee, pure coffee, not coffee essence.

Ice cream was a particular treat, as production was stopped in 1942 – a
date noted in many diaries. The Cotton family had moved to Instow on the
North Devon coast.

Here we live by the sea, and for days there is only chopped skate
to be had, red gurnet and bowls of laver, a gummy seaweed-like
mass of marine life that Devonians love when fried in blobs.

Fresh fish could only be bought if you took some newspaper in which to
wrap it, but newspapers had few pages and were essential for lighting the
fire. Oranges were prized not just for their rarity, but for the tissue paper in
which they were wrapped. As an American, Peg Cotton found it difficult to
understand the English devotion to one precious staple: tea. She noted its
particular importance on journeys by train.

After some time in England, I came to the conclusion that the
English when thirsty think in terms of tea, not water. Tea is
what the Englishman drinks, consistently and in quantity as
we Americans drink water. This 8:30am train from Instow to
London makes two 'long' stops – Exeter Central, and Salisbury.
At these stations practically every compartment door bangs
open, and figures, male and female, leap out upon the platform
and hurriedly zig-zag through the traffic of people and porters
milling about there. The platform tea-trolley or the Station
Buffet is the objective of this race. The prize – mugs of hot tea.

The return from this sortie for refreshment is like a triumphal
procession. With a large white china mug of steaming tea
in either hand, or a mug of tea in one hand and a couple of
saffron colored buns in the other, the returning contingent
surges back in groups – one eye on the slopping tea, the other
on the open door of a particular compartment, both ears
cocked for the Guard's whistle. At its shrill screech there is
a frantic dash of late stragglers. Cups in hand they leap into
the nearest open door on the train. Bang – clap – bang – clap!
Here in the compartment, is a fresh stir, a lively bit of chat, a
stimulus in the air. Tea! Opposite me sit four people – with
four mugs of tea. Two of the people cuddle the mugs in both
hands, as though the mugs were brandy inhalers. But each of
the four faces above those four mugs of tea has the serene,
concentrated expression of the connoisseur of fine wine. Tea!
It satisfies and stimulates.

Peg Cotton led a relatively privileged existence, with a large home and a
'daily'. Up in the Highlands of Scotland, May Chalmers was another of the
privileged class. It was not until 1942 that she felt the necessity for some
wartime economy.

Got really busy yesterday and put our house on a war footing.
Sacked the garden boy and two maids and shut up the morning
room. That leaves the library and my business room to sit in.
Also shut up the dining room and we are having our meals in the
pantry. The animals think it great fun.

With her privileged life, in a large house with servants, and her husband
Archie's status as the Sheriff of Oban, May Chalmers had not had to cook.

Archie says I've been threatening to cook for 20 years and it
has taken a war to make me! But I am finding it fun and am
getting to know how to work the Triplex and am on very matey
terms with three Primus stoves. Cooked bacon and eggs on one
last night. I find that the rations – salt butter, margarine etc
are ample. In fact last week I put coffee butter icing on a cake

to use it up and had to dispose of 4 ounces of bacon, and the Sunday roast lasted for the whole week! I'm only getting half ration of cheese, as we simply can't use it.

Her husband augmented their rations with a spot of shooting for the pot.

We did rather well 'off the land' last week as we had nothing from either butcher or fishmonger having lived on twelve rabbits (sure I'm growing a wee white tail!) and this week should be equally good as there is a whole roe deer hanging in the larder. I gather that we are worse off for food here as the convoys requisition just what they want. If things go on like this and the forces can get what they like from the Naafi there will be a revolution. The munition workers will say either Naafi for us too or no munitions. After all the Naafi was only intended to supply an army abroad and certainly not in the home country.

The Naafi (Navy, Army, Air Force Institute – a supermarket for the British Forces) was the source of many luxuries. In May 1942, an old friend in London sent May Chalmers a wartime treat.

Goodness where did you get the sherry? I haven't tasted it for over a year. The only drink I have now is Bass and it is most unsatisfactory and very loosening to the bowels. We are allowed one bottle of whisky per week, which is gone after one visit from the Home Guard forces, so I never get any.

Food shortages were not a nationwide problem. Phyllis Warner was shocked when she spent a weekend with friends in Hampshire in October 1941.

My hosts have a large garden and their own shoot, so there's no shortage of pheasant, partridge, vegetables and fruit, nor for that matter of wines and liquor. I went out with the guns today, not a pastime I particularly approve, but it does mean that you see parts of the country you would never reach normally. It was heart-achingly beautiful today with the leaves just yellowing under a washed blue sky. The evening mist drifted across countryside unchanged, except that there was no nostalgic sound of church bells lingering over the fields. The lives of these people haven't changed either – it's quite a shock to find how little some of us have been affected by the war.

In Rickmansworth, Hertfordshire, Mrs E Walsh's position as private secretary to the Chairman of the London Midland Scottish Railway (a post she had also held before her marriage to Kenneth) gave her access to supplies that would have been the envy of many.

My Chief continues to supply me with small but very welcome and regular quantities of eggs and butter. Your 'Sherlock Holmesing' regarding our food position is amusing. The day your letter arrived we were wolfing quantities. Quite honestly we eat far more and have far more variety nowadays than in peacetime for the simple reason that we don't take food for granted and if anything is going we feel we must have it. Mrs Walsh [her mother-in-law] gave a farewell supper to Kenneth on Wednesday evening and we had immense plates of ham, tomatoes, beetroot, radishes, and then quantities of chocolate blancmange and strawberries. We had previously had strawberries for Sunday morning breakfast and admittedly we didn't have castor sugar and cream but they were none the less good for all that.

One activity that every woman, regardless of class and age, started once war was declared was knitting. Telephone operators knitted at slack moments on their shift; shelterers in the Blitz kept their needles clicking away; when their housework, war work and vegetable garden had been attended to, women sat down to listen to the wireless with their knitting. At Christmas in 1942 Mrs Walsh unpicked old jumpers to remake as Christmas presents for her family. In 1939 she had been

... knitting clothes for evacuees and poor children at the moment, but must knit something for the minesweeping men, now that they are extending this service.

Petrol was rationed from the early weeks of war, to ensure a supply for those in essential jobs or on war work (some people took to cutting lawns and even tennis courts with shears). The use of private cars was later banned, and cars were stored in garages on blocks, but other vehicles, reminiscent of more peaceful times, were rolled out of outbuildings and stables. Rickmansworth was a far more rural spot then than it is today. Nevertheless, Mrs Walsh was still amazed at the action of one of her neighbours.

> To counter the petrol shortage Mr Needham has bought Mrs
> Needham a pony and trap. Brian is driving it up from Dorset
> this coming week and I suppose we shall see it next weekend.
> It should cause quite a stir at first. More trouble than it's worth
> I should imagine.

As the women of Britain soldiered on, they also had to cope with the loss of loved ones. Louie White, whose husband Jack was a gunner in the RAF, was a first aider at the munitions factory where she worked in Leeds. Her husband often came home on leave at short notice, and her sympathetic employers gave her the week off when he unexpectedly turned up in June 1943. The couple went to Scarborough for a week. On 21 June he went missing during a raid over the industrial city of Krefeld. Two days later she wrote in her diary:

> *June 23rd* – At 10.00 Mother brought a telegram to say that Jack
> was missing. I got a pass out and went up to his mothers. Came
> home for my dinner and then went back to work. Rather be doing
> something than think.

There followed several weeks of uncertainty as Louie filed her husband's details with the Red Cross, in case he had been taken prisoner. Air crews were known to reappear months after being listed as missing, making their way back to Britain via the Resistance in occupied countries, and so there was hope. But her war work had to carry on.

> Got up at 4 and sat in the garden. Went early to work as it was
> First Aid. Was a very depressing night, I felt awful and kept
> having fits of weeping.

A Home Guard instructor, wearing medals probably won in World War I, trains two Watford women as sharp shooters. The Home Guard was opened to women in 1942, with the intention that they would defend their homes and families in the event of invasion.

At the beginning of every subsequent week in her diary, Louie recorded the number of weeks that Jack had been missing. By 10 August he had been missing for six weeks.

> Got a letter today from Carol. She says that Mr Quigly has received a letter from Dick who is a prisoner. In it he says that Jack along with Reg and Johnny had been killed. I don't know what to think! So far however I have not had official confirmation. Went to work but was very depressed.

Two months after he went missing, the telegram came.

> *Aug 24* – Cold. Usual all day. Stayed for First Aid. Was very depressed. Got home at 9.00 and found a telegram to say that Jack

is believed to have lost his life. It upset me very much and I went
to bed immediately

Aug 25 – Showers. Did not go to work as I didn't feel I could stand
it. Went into town with Mother, then went to see Jack's mother.
We had a chat then I came home. Spent the afternoon knitting.
After tea I had to go out so I went to the Astoria.

She was back at work the next day. Louie White found some solace when
she joined the Home Guard (women had been allowed to join in 1942).

On exercise today with the Home Guard. I was detailed off with
Judd and Neville to go with a platoon. We went in a bus and got
off up King Lane. The rest was Battle Craft. Through the streets,
me with my Red X on my sleeve. Did a lot of crawling through
ditches and across fields. We eventually reached and captured the
farm through a smoke screen. Came home in a lorry. It was great!
Just like the real thing.

Louie turned out to be a crack shot, beating many of the men at target
practice. Even at the end of May, she was reluctant to believe that her
husband was dead – until she received an eyewitness account.

A letter from Richard Quigley, Jack's pilot. He tells me everything
that had happened on that night of June 21st–22nd 1943. There is
no doubt that *Jack was killed in his gun turret, at approx 1.30am June
22nd 1943.* Today I have been so heartbroken. I cannot think that
I shall never see Jack again – not on this earth anyway.

War memorials and cemeteries at home and abroad bear the names of those
who died. But the forbearance of the population who bore those losses is
not commemorated.

7
DARK DAYS

Theft of two 7lb tins of Palm slab toffee. Two 10-year-old boys interviewed.
Larceny of clothing coupons, money and gold Albert which she had pawned.
Theft of sheets, clothes etc while owner was away –
pawned by tenant to pay debts.
(PC Walter Atkins, October 1942)

The notebook of PC Walter Atkins, a Sheffield beat bobby, gives a snapshot of wartime petty crime. His notes refer largely to teenagers stealing food, including immense tins of molasses. Youth clubs, which had kept many teenagers entertained before the war, were closed, and parents were preoccupied with war work.

Some of the crime committed was peculiar to a nation in a state of wartime emergency: looting and the black market. Contemporary references to the black market in diaries and letters are veiled – hints that silk stockings might be obtained from a certain market stall, or extra meat slipped into a favoured shopper's bag by the butcher. Some took to petty crime to pay off their debts, breaking into factories, robbing tills in pubs, breaking into empty homes whose occupants were on war work elsewhere. Deserted streets without street lighting were ideal cover for such criminal activity. This was not behaviour that fitted the picture of the great British nation pulling together to win the war, but the population was starved of luxuries and in debt. For a minority this led to disaffection, with the result that they turned to crime. There was also some industrial unrest as the Government pushed workers to increase productivity for the 'war effort'. But financial worries were not purely the province of the working class. Joan Strange wrote in her diary in January 1940:

Mother heard that her money, which used to bring in 5% then 3½% is now 2%! Everyone is grumbling about their drop in income, and no wonder and for what? Other direct effects of war are the rationing of food and petrol; increase of cost of living (it's gone up 12½% at least); unemployment among certain trades, especially among building and flower growing concerns in Worthing. Then we hear of the Russians dying of cold by the hundreds; sailors being mined, torpedoed; airmen suffering big casualties. Many people are yearning for a just and lasting peace and are endeavouring to keep bitterness out of their minds at all cost.

Income tax reached 50 per cent during the war years. Frank Forster lived in a depressed area of Chester, and although he had a job in an engineering works he found it hard to make ends meet. In 1943 he wrote:

Life for us has become a terrific battle for existence. We struggle to pay our way on the few pounds which we receive, aiming all the time at keeping some semblance of decency – we try our best to feed ourselves and those dependent on us with food which is good for them – though this latter is becoming more and more difficult.

By January 1944 Frank was dreaming up money-making ideas.

For some days now I have been thinking of ideas which could be put to practical use of making a little money – handy ideas, such as floral sprays made out of dried milk tins, gloves knitted and so on – the few pounds which the idea would bring in would be very useful.

The scarcity of certain commodities was exacerbated by high prices.

We get more and more hard up. Our wages stay the same, yet the price of food, clothes and other things take up an increasing amount of them. The few entertainments, such as cinemas, are having prices increased.

As workers struggled to make ends meet, there was industrial unrest. Frank Forster records strikes in March 1943.

> In various parts of the north of England there are [a] number
> of strikes occurring over the recent wage increase awards to the
> Engineering trade – in some instances only a few have been given
> the increase – a delay has been manoeuvred by the employers who
> say that the necessary alterations in the pay sheets will take some
> time – chaos has been created in the clerical part of the work
> because of shortness of clerical staff.

Munitions workers often relied on buses to get to work, and many factories laid on special buses during these strikes. A month later Frank wrote:

> Strikes are becoming more frequent – the employers won't
> change their way of living and of making money – they are of
> the opinion that we workers should suffer and this won't do in
> wartime, especially when we are fighting for our lives. Since the
> beginning of this present war many fresh burdens and causes
> of irritation have been added to our lives – our work in the
> factories is telling on us more than it used to. There is evidence
> that the excessive time worked leads to tiredness, fatigue and
> the consequent train of minor things, which if left to develop
> make life a bugbear – yet we are supposed to carry on in the
> same way, we are expected to pull our weight, to obey all
> Government instructions, in short we have to put up with the
> added inconveniences without anyone giving us a helping
> hand – such as holidays with pay, visits to state sanatoria, free
> medical advice etc – no wonder the war effort is hindered.

Frank Forster was unaware that a Labour government would be elected in 1945, bringing in a National Health Service. But as he was writing, in 1943, the wartime Government was already looking at the issue of postwar housing, and the Beveridge Report on social reform was published.

> If one ever passes the remark at work that things after this war
> will be different than after the last; and if one happens to say

that a holiday would be welcomed, then one of them is bound to say that we are bound to have quite a long holiday then, on the Dole – the attitude of most workers (in this district at least) is the same as in peace time – the same fear of the boss, the shifty glance (expecting the boss along) at work, – all this interferes with the war effort – the only thing that has not altered yet, is the addition of burdens on our shoulders, more inconveniences – a 100% War Effort is impossible when people regard their jobs in such a cynical light – they never know when they'll lose their jobs.

Frank Forster's Communist sympathies had been honed during the depression, during which millions were unemployed. Journalist C Jory was horrified at 'the Communist-inspired strikes'. In the fifth year of war he wrote in his diary:

Mining strike in Yorkshire spread and shipyard and engineering apprentices in north east yards and works came out, on a very dubious excuse arising out of the miners' ballot. There is no doubt that this strike at least is organised by outsiders – an ex-communist organisation whose leaders should be put against a wall and shot without delay, as would long ago have happened in any other country.

A week later, while he was rejoicing at Russian successes as they encircled Odessa on the Black Sea, he wrote:

Coal strikes lost us over a million tons at this most vital time – same precious miners who had only a few weeks ago accepted an award which gave them better terms all round than they had ever had and which their leaders had been very pleased to get.

But he corroborates Frank Forster's views on the general lack of patriotism in the workforce.

I am more and more convinced that there is very little love of country in the average 'toiler', it is all self.

In April 1944 the country was anticipating a second front, with the invasion of France. Although the exact location and date were a closely guarded secret, speculation stalked the streets, as Jory noted.

> More obvious every day that we are at least very near the great invasion day. Possibly it will be in a week's time, it can hardly be much later. Everywhere one sees indications that zero hour is very near. Every day the Germans are telling their people the attack will come at any hour. There is restlessness that is akin to fever. To safeguard secret, the Government took unprecedented step of banning use of code in wires or letters to Ambassadors (Russia and US excepted). Bombing of Germany and occupied territories (aerodromes and communications mostly) went on day and night – at times over 2,000 planes a day took part. Venice docks were bombed for the first time. And while all this went on, London busmen and Manchester gas workers struck work for some trivial reason. With more firmness and promptitude than usual, the Government acted. Troops drove buses and troops manned gasworks, and strikes collapsed.

Cities darkened by blackout, and streets empty of people as they sheltered from raids, brought out opportunist looters. When Mea Allan was bombed out in October 1940, she returned to her flat to check on her belongings.

> Did I lose any cash? Nope. Had handbag with me in the shelter. Oh yes, I lost 2/6 outstanding to Gas, Light and Coke Company! But probably it's buying a pint for some thirsty looter – they're a beastly lot: they actually wait about at night for houses to be bombed and then dash in and muckrake round for what they can find. I hope his beer chokes him.

Opportunist looting was also recorded by Revd Markham, a parish priest in Walworth, South London, where he was chief ARP warden. In particular he wrote about one fire-fighting party.

> Most of them were youths centred on a café run by a gorilla-like ex wrestler, whom I suspected of being a fence, and who

A policeman stands guard beside the remains of a terraced house somewhere in the Southeast, following a raid in February 1943. A sign on the window warns that looting carried the death penalty, but this did not deter thieves, who took advantage of the blackout.

used his fire-guards for other purposes besides the fighting of fires. The Town Hall provided them with steel helmets, and armbands identifying them as members of a Fire Party. During gunfire they would patrol in pairs down the Walworth Road. If no one was about they would heave a brick through a shop window, and dash round the next corner. Another pair would follow and if the coast was clear, empty the shop window, and disappear with their loot to the café. On several occasions I chased them off if I saw this happening. I never reported anybody to the police, who during the air raids, except for the occasional war Reserve members of the Force, were conspicuously absent from the scene. The policy was that regular police reported to their station, when the warning went, and only went out, when incidents called for their presence. My job, both as a parish priest and as a warden would have been impossible, if I had been known to tell tales to the police. I probably owed my immunity to attack to the fact that my attitude was known. Looting did (still) occur of course.

The protection of an ARP warden's badge and identity card gave 'villains' licence to be on the streets when others were running for shelter.

I remember refusing to enrol one man, who, early on in the raids, wanted to join our [ARP] post. He said 'I am always first on the scene of any incident. I have a small van and can be on the spot without delay.' I made a few discreet inquiries, and found that he was a burglar, that his van was full of tools, and that he made a point of driving all over the borough, particularly to business premises, when they were hit, and diving straight into the ruins to find the safe.

This South London priest made a point of rescuing people's personal belongings from bombed buildings as quickly as possible. Even then he was sometimes too late.

It may seem that I was exaggerating the risk. But a family from one of the blasted flats came to collect their furniture, and found that a piano had been taken from the upstairs flat. Two other relatives came to ask me if they could enter their old mother's flat in Merrow Street, which had been blasted and made unsafe, and when I took them there, they found that all her trinkets, including her son's First World War medals, were gone. In fact, the very morning of the raid, the Borough Treasurer's men came down to empty the gas and electric meters in the blasted flats, only to find that every one had been broken open and rifled. That was only six hours after the bomb had exploded.

Rescue workers showed immense compassion in risking their lives to salvage precious keepsakes from ruined homes.

I always felt that these little salvage efforts were worthwhile. It is hard to realise that it was these small things that made such a difference to the morale of so many people. I suppose the secret of it lies in the fact that we showed someone cared about the loss of their homes. It was important that there should be some visible link with that home as they took refuge in the bare, amorphous surroundings of the schools, which acted as Rest Centres for the bombed-out. Nothing helped their recovery more than the knowledge that their personal treasures were safe.

But nothing was sacred.

When we recovered dead bodies, as soon as we found them, I had to put them in an empty room under the guard of two wardens, until the stretcher party could remove them to the mortuary. Otherwise their clothing would be rifled, there in the midst of the darkness and dust, and falling bombs. I often said that it was a good thing that I was not armed with a pistol or gun: I would probably have shot those whom I suspected of this kind of activity. It used to make me very angry.

Bill Regan, the Heavy Rescue worker on the Isle of Dogs in London's East

End, also salvaged people's belongings from bombed houses. In the winter of 1940 he had his eye on known scoundrels from his rescue squad.

> Saw Ringshaw with three of his men enter a house, after a while an old lady came out, looking lost, so George Jillings and I took her along to some ladies who had come from a Rest Centre, very capable and calm who took over. We went back to the house, but no furniture or anything had been brought out. I have a nasty suspicious mind where Ringshaw and Co are concerned. I said to George: 'Let's see what is going on.' We went in and listened. They were upstairs, so I quietly said to George, 'When you're ready upstairs quick.' We pelted up the stairs, and surprised them. Alf B and Ernie H have got some of the drawers out of a chest of drawers, and they are pawing over quite a big heap of what I think is cheap jewellery and trinkets, but they evidently think it real. Ringshaw is smart and quick. He says: 'Take all the drawers out, it will make it easier to get downstairs.' Me and George are blocking the doorway, so having little room to move, we fall for the empty chest.

Bill reported the men but unfortunately did not report the outcome in his diary. Two years later he reported another incident.

> A policeman told me of an incident where rescue men went to Little Stewart St to salvage money from flooded basement. The money was not found, although [ARP] warden had been able to feel the tin containing the money, but could not get it. Some days later the water was pumped out, but no money-box was found. The four rescue men were afterwards seen by this policeman, wearing new clothes. He says they also had a week's holiday. The missing money amounted to about £50.

After a night at work digging through rubble, he came home to his wife Vi, and the effects of that night's bombing on their own home.

> Found only one room habitable, shelter still flooded, so Vi has decided to sleep – no, *shelter* in the front room, with the table

pushed against the fireplace, and mattress and blankets under the table. The window is now heavily boarded, and Vi is confident that she will be safe.

At Christmas 1940, with an unexploded bomb on the other side of the street and his home in ruins, he was accosted by Lew Smith, a neighbour who lived a few doors away.

Lew Smith is the agent of our landlord and he said: 'You haven't paid any rent for some time now Bill, what are you going to do about it?' I said: 'I've got one room with a boarded up window, two doors that have to be propped up and the rest of the house uninhabitable, so out of 15/6 [77 pence] for the whole house, what would a fair rent be for the one room.' He could think of nothing suitable to say, except that I couldn't stay without paying something. I said I would look for another place to live, and in the meantime, I would act as unpaid caretaker of our one room. He didn't see it that way, but reluctantly agreed. Anyway he has a book full of empty, or wrecked houses, so he has problems and I have problems more worrying than he.

With wind and snow whistling through gaps in boarded-up windows, and with record low temperatures in many of those wartime winters, it is not surprising that Bill Regan was diagnosed with pleurisy.

In her job as a reporter for the *Daily Herald*, Mea Allan wrote an account of an interview with someone in the same rent predicament as Bill.

Some London landlords are demanding rent for houses rendered uninhabitable by bombing. One business girl received a rent notice two days after blast from a High Explosive bomb had shattered the block of flats where she lives. It was a very heavy calibre bomb and fell less than 9 yards away. She told me yesterday: 'My flat is quite unliveable-in. The windows have been wrenched out, frames and all and there are holes in the walls. There isn't a door in the place. My front door, opening off the stair landing has been splintered into pieces as if it had been a piece of brittle toffee. There is no gas, no electricity and no water. The gas company have collected the meter-box, so evidently they don't expect the place to be lived in any more. The outside of the building has big cracks in it, and there's a crack running up one of my walls inside. When I leased the flat my side of the bargain was to pay rent, the landlord's to provide a flat to live in. I paid a month in advance and I reckon I owe two days rent from the expiry of the last month's up till the time I was bombed. But he has asked me for the whole of the next month's rent. A neighbour who had paid three months in advance up till Christmas went to the landlords and asked them for a rebate. They laughed at her and told her the place was not uninhabitable – she could still go on living there. Her place is even worse knocked about than mine – we had a fire in the building as well and the weight of water from the hoses is bringing down the ceilings. I think this is one of the most unpatriotic things I've heard of. Not just because it's happened to me, but because I've heard it's happened to people all over London, even to poor people in the East End. I bet if I asked my landlords to dinner, they wouldn't even cross the threshold – they'd be so scared the building would topple down any minute.'

When there was a lull in bombing Bill Regan went back to ad hoc labouring jobs, as money troubles continued to bite. But in January 1942 it was again bitterly cold.

Layer of snow outside. Work tomorrow – unlikely. That means no pay. What an existence.

The next morning the weather was worse.

Up at 6.30am. Thick snow. No work. Signed on at Labour Exchange, given a grey card, to go to Glaucas St, was given a broom to do snow sweeping.

At the end of the month the postman called with three letters.

Received letter saying I owe £44.6.0 cost of the children's evacuation [to an Oxfordshire village]. Letter from Miller's

Identity cards had to be carried at all times: Mea Allan, was terrified of losing hers in a raid and being buried as an unidentified victim in a mass grave. She became the first woman journalist accredited to the British forces, covering the Nuremberg trials.

> Hospital, they want 10/6 X-ray charge for my left foot, done last August, when I smashed my cycle in a crash with a car. Letter from income tax people. What a day.

Phyllis Warner, after a visit to a London school, recorded the effects of bombing on the education of the new generation.

> The all clear of the previous night had not sounded until 3am, so that many of the children were looking heavy eyed. Education is suffering badly from the raids. On this particular day with a school working from nine till four, lessons were only possible for two hours – the rest of the day passed wearyingly in the shelters, for whatever other people do children must take shelter.

Evacuated children missed their homes, and despite conditions in London, the family ties in close-knit communities were a stronger pull than safety.

> I have pleaded with many parents, who replied, 'Well, if I'm

killed, I want to take my Tommy and Alice with me – I don't want them to be left homeless in the world.' So strong is this feeling that parents will take their children to spend night after night on draughty subway platforms or in the foul air of vast overcrowded shelters rather than send them to the pure air and safety of the countryside. This evening I went up to a big London County Council housing estate, made up of vast blocks of flats for ex-slum dwellers, who were shifted here just before the war started. The flats themselves are super, but placed in a remote district, badly served with buses, and excepting the pubs, without a single entertainment facility. The children were mostly evacuated when war started, but soon came back and have been running wild ever since. In spite of two years with no schooling, the older ones have been able to pick up war jobs, which put plenty of cash in their pockets. They're a tough crowd, whose parents virtually ignore them, and they're all running around in the blackout with nothing to do but mischief. During the summer Joan has started an evening club for them – a heroic one man job. The London County Council has let her have a hall, but nothing else. She has about a hundred young toughs there each night the club's open. Tonight John, Jack and I went up to see if we could get a discussion group started. I chose 'the Evacuation of Children should be compulsory' as a subject. Jack said it was a cold chestnut but I knew better. Every man-jack of them was granite hard against evacuation.

Joan Strange, whose sister Kit lived in London, came up from Worthing and visited flats in Kentish Town in 1940.

The caretaker seems worried over the fact that in the blackout each night hooligan boys come round breaking windows – stealing bricks being used for the air raid shelter in the process of construction and so on.

Fuel was also in short supply, as munitions factories were given priority. In 1942 the Government urged people not to use their central heating, or light fires until November. Kindly Bill Regan volunteered to help to deliver the limited supplies.

Myself, Herbert and Robinson, went to Quebec and Montreal buildings, to deliver coal to the people living there. There has been a grave shortage this winter, and when the coalman has some coal, he supplies the people living downstairs but is too lazy to carry it upstairs, so that they have been without for weeks at a time. We deliver it to them now. Had a jolly time, but I nearly had trouble with some of the people. One old lady crawled from the top floor to ask for some, and I sympathetically carried 1 hundred-weight to her flat, and I'm nearly beat when I get there. Entering I find a robust fellow, and bigger than I, sprawled on the sofa. Granny can crawl down, I can lug it up, he sits round the fire. Another person had a cupboard full of coal, and wants more, while neighbours are without. 'If you can't get it in mate put it on the floor.' I do, all over it. One woman with three kids, borrows the money from another for ½cwt. I bung a 1cwt in, and skip out.

8
WORKING FOR THE WAR EFFORT

We are both quite convinced that in spite of the dirt, the long tiring hours, the noise, and the annoyance of working for rather unhuman employers – and the general austerity of our life, we are much happier than we should have been if we had remained at Benacre where we were continually wondering whether we were doing essential work. Now at any rate we are doing what the Government has asked women to do – and find the war doesn't get on our minds nearly as much as it did.
(*Kathleen Church Bliss, July 1942*)

Thousands of women responded to the Government's call to take on war work. A population accustomed to living, working and marrying in the same community became far more mobile. In the ranks of the Women's Land Army, factory girls from industrial cities rubbed shoulders with young ladies from the Home Counties. The workforce became a glorious mix of accents, ages and attitudes, and the results were not always harmonious. Class barriers did not break down; they were merely temporarily breached. The status quo would be restored after the war. But these wartime jobs did give new and unforgettable working experiences.

War created work peculiar to the needs of the war machine, such as the job of billeting officer. Those who remained in their peacetime jobs had to work under wartime conditions, with the added pressure that this entailed.

Kathleen Church Bliss and Elsie Whiteman lived in the village of Milford, where they ran a teashop. Both in their forties, they were two of the thousands of women who responded to Government calls for more women to take up full-time war work. Family and friends tried to interest them

Elsie Whiteman and Kathleen Church Bliss, pictured with a customer at their teashop early in the war, never regretted the decision to give up this quiet life for the noise and dirt of an aircraft factory. Thousands of women donned overalls suits to become munitions workers.

in joining the WRNS or running hostels for the Land Army or Timber Corps, but these did not appeal. Visiting an Engineering Training Centre in Croydon changed their lives.

> The machine shop was fascinating. We saw centre lathes, capstan lathes, shapers, planers, mills and automatics all roaring away amidst a deafening clatter from the overhead shafting. Everyone appeared to be very expert and we watched with great interest. The centre lathes especially took our fancy, as the work needed constant care and attention, and we were told that this machine needed the most skill to work successfully.

Fired by this challenge, the two women enrolled on an engineering course.

On a snowy February day they arrived in Croydon and, after training, started at Morrison's aircraft factory. It was a culture shock.

> The factory building is really a disgrace. Broken windows let in the howling draught, the roof leaks and great puddles collect on the floor, the walls are splashed with oil and grease and the whole place is incredibly dirty and littered with filthy bits of equipment not at the moment in use. It is a frightful sight. These dirty conditions are made worse by the complete absence of hot water in the 8 washbasins and lavatories provided for 300 girls.

Both these middle-class women joined the union, and Kathleen whiled away the 11-hour days brooding on the wrongs of the workers and dreaming up reforms to working conditions.

> We are now members of a Trades Union. We are not quite certain of its name – but it's the Municipal and Something Workers. We joined in a most hole and corner way – and pushed our subscription over to the assistant shop steward – who looked furtive and said she had to be careful! She evidently lives in fear of the firm's Gestapo!

After five months they felt like old hands.

> We no longer suffer from the acute nervous dread we did when we first came to Morrisons. Els, during our first fortnight here felt as though she were fielding bent double in the slips in a very important cricket match – poised on her toes ready for a movement in any direction and her hands darting from handle to handle. It was a very long cricket match and exhausting.
> Now she has long been able to straighten her back and relax and turn the handle with calm and detachment. In fact she is much put to it, in the mechanical jobs that crop up, to know how to while away the time – *A Midsummer Night's Dream* which she learnt by heart at the age of 16 has been a tremendous help to her. 'Now fair Hippolyta,' she declaims in a loud shout – as

she retracts the drill – and so on scene after scene to the
end. This talking aloud is evidently sound engineering practice
as it seems to be pretty general – for looking round the shop
one sees everyone's mouth is moving – though no sound can
be heard.

The work was fiddly and exacting and great care was taken not to waste
precious raw materials by making mistakes. It was worthy – but tedious.

We nearly die of boredom. The hours drag interminably, the clock
never advances and Sunday seems a long way off. We think that
we might petition for a radio to relieve the tedium – which must
be worse for those who are always doing the mechanical jobs –
but doubt whether a radio would make itself heard above the
awful noise. Looking round the huge workshop it seems to us
that the hundreds of workers, though only separated from each
other by a few feet, are each shut away in an impenetrable box of
noise – and live their separate lives for 11 hours a day hardly able
to communicate with each other.

In May 1942 there was a heatwave. Combined with the pressures of air raids
and poor working conditions, tempers were frayed at Morrison's.

May 31st – Today Hilda was so hot – & so enraged with the
Management for not trying to improve the ventilation that she
threw a spanner through one of the windows in a temper! The
resulting hole was a great improvement.

Kathleen and Elsie cycled to their wartime jobs. The bicycle was a much-
prized form of transport in cities, enabling riders to swerve easily round
craters, though the rubber shortage meant that tyres were scarce. Phyllis
Warner summed up the worth of a bicycle.

Even duchesses are riding bicycles nowadays; their value is more
than a Rolls Royce.

Despite the disruption of routine daily life by air raids work went on;

Phyllis was impressed by the conscientiousness of people she encountered in her voluntary job at a feeding centre at the height of the 1940 Blitz.

> At the Feeding Centre today one of the things I notice most about the people who have just been bombed, is their anxiety about getting to work on time. You don't expect people who have just seen their home crash in rubble and have lost nearly all their possessions to be worrying about whether they'll be late for work, but in fact they do. Perhaps, because their jobs represent the one normal thing that is left, the only sober reality in a world turned to nightmare, and they just have to keep hold on what is sane and familiar. The whole tempo of London life has adjusted itself to this change. The rush hour has moved forward to half past four, and everybody leaving work makes an immediate and purposeful dash for the homeward bus or train – by six the streets are almost deserted. Home is no longer a place to live, it's somewhere to dump one's things and wash and change en route for the shelter, whether that is the cellar, the Anderson [a small prefabricated shelter] or the subway station. To many Londoners the chief irritation is having to transfer their dinner hour from eight pm to five thirty.

Dr JP McHutchison, Director of Education in Dumbartonshire, noticed the same phenomenon in Glasgow in 1939.

> One quite noticeable feature of life in these early war days, is the smartness folks display to get their buses at night; from 5 to 6 o'clock, business people are more businesslike in getting to the bus stations and making sure of getting out of Glasgow before a possible alert holds them up. Even in this part of the country where real air raiding has not begun, there is a sort of 'rounded off' feeling at the close of the day – 'Well that's one more day over in peace and comfort'. We are quite content to live one day at a time, for we all realise a long and hard road lies ahead.

After Ernie Britton and his wife May had been bombed out in October

At the top of a ladder a firefighter is still dousing flames from last night's raid as workers make their way as usual to offices in the City. This photograph of Farringdon Street and Great Bride Street was taken after the heaviest raid of the entire Blitz, on 10 May 1941.

1940, May had gone to Dorset to live with her mother. Ernie found digs in Harpenden, Hertfordshire.

> I'm in the office now having swapped my London job with a colleague whose home was and still is in London. He used to travel out and back each day, occupying three hours daily.

A three-hour commute was just as much a consideration in wartime as it is today. Buses had to deviate from established routes because of bomb craters or piles of rubble. Trains travelled at 15 miles an hour as a precaution, since railway lines were an easy target for bombers and there were sometimes craters on the line. Phyllis Warner noted:

> One of the oddest things about our present life is its mixture of

ruthless horror and everyday routine. I pick my way to work past the bomb craters and the shattered glass, and sit at my desk in a room with a hole in the roof – a block of paving stone came right through it.

As if the dust and dirt of the streets weren't enough to put up with, there were vermin too. Mrs E Walsh worked at Rickmansworth in Hertfordshire, a few miles out of London.

You will have gathered that our wartime office quarters aren't of the most civilised. Yesterday one of the older women was typing with concentration when she noticed a bump on her thigh. She tried to smooth it away but it was soft. On investigating it turned out to be a baby mouse. She had not felt it arriving there. Horrible experience. Miss Payne often has mice running over her feet in her room. We have each been issued with a gilt badge, depicting an engine, to wear during air raid alarms so that the wardens will allow us to go to work. Can't see that my bit of typing is necessary when bombs are dropping, but apparently the Powers that Be think so.

As in other areas of the workforce, women stepped into office jobs to release men for the armed forces. Office talk inevitably dwelt on husbands, fathers, brothers and fiancés who were away. Phyllis Warner had a loved one in the Far East.

Women do indeed get the rough end of war – whatever hell men may endure in the fight, they at least have the consolation of action and responsibility. They don't sit at home drinking tea and wearing their hearts out. What would we give for absorbing action and a conviction that we were playing a vital responsible part in the struggle – not sitting in dead alive offices.

As well as dealing with the uncertainties of war, people had to do their jobs under heavy blackout, as Ernie Britton described.

In the factories it's not possible to have such a big scale

shuttering so it's always blackout and artificial light – not so good and not so healthy, never to see a bit of daylight except perhaps a snatch at midday break. During the last few weeks we've had flourescent lighting (daylight) in our office and it makes a world of difference. As I had to be there Saturday and Sunday the first two weeks of its installation I thought it grand!

Seventeen-year-old Monica McMurray was not enjoying her working conditions at Laycock Engineering in Sheffield in 1941.

This eternal smell of oil combined with next-to-no ventilation and artificial light at work is suffocating, I think I shall have to try to get on the land.

As the engines of the British war machine, factories were especially at risk in air raids. Louie White was a milling inspector at the Blackburn Aircraft Factory, Roundhay, Leeds, during a heatwave in August 1942.

Very hot. About 12.40 the guns and sirens went. It was awful we all put on our tin hats and coats and went on working in them. Two pieces of shrapnel came through the roof, which is very thin. Jack Brand said it was raining shrapnel all over the place outside. We heard that it was Kirkstall Forge that had been hit.

Down in Croydon, Kathleen Church Bliss and Elsie Whiteman recorded how air raids disrupted their work.

When we got to work we found the night shift had been in the shelters most of the night – & 48 bombs had fallen. Lily arrived rather late & very much shaken as all the windows of the train had been broken by blast & some of the passengers had been cut.

We learnt that Kath Weaver was in hospital. Her house was hit – & she & her father injured & her mother was killed. She is a nice girl from Inspection – whose husband is a prisoner of war. Everyone is dreadfully sorry for her. Jim Sawyer went

to see her in hospital & found her cut about the face and a
tummy wound – but taking it all very bravely.

We hadn't been in the place more than a few minutes before
the alert went – & we started rushing to the shelters. Luckily
it was some distance off. During the day various people were
fetched away because their homes had been demolished – &
Costello went off to enquire about his brother who had had a
bomb in his road.

A good many interruptions during the morning – but after
that there was a lull – A quiet afternoon but the alert went
just before pay-time – & twice the queue had to break up &
everyone scuttled to the shelters before all were paid.

People could lose their jobs overnight thanks to the raids. Martha Cotton
lost her job at the Welbeck Clinic in London. Her mother Peg Cotton wrote
in her diary:

The Clinic 'went' the other night! The Jerries are using land
mines in the air raids. Like prize packages, these monstrous High
Explosives are dropped now and then. And, when they fall, it
is like a miniature end-of-the-world! These land mines explode
above the ground, and blast buildings and people over wide areas.

Because of one of these land mines, Martha had to walk most
of the way to the Clinic the other morning – the streets being
impassable to traffic, with litter and rubble scattered about.
Martha's soles were cut to ribbons with shattered glass – and her
soul torn to bits with the sight of the people being excavated.
When she arrived at the Clinic, the Out Patient Department
was quite gutted by an oil bomb. Rescue work had ended, but
drugs and instruments were being salvaged. So Martha stayed to
help. One nurse was killed. There were no casualties among the
patients. What a miracle! And what a horror! Of course, Martha
cannot get her degree now. There'll be no more lectures. She is
deeply disappointed. One can not plan a thing these days! You
just live, strictly in the present.

In London's East End, Lylie Eldergill was on short time because the garment factory where she worked had been blitzed. As she wrote to her cousin, the newspaper and printing industry was hit particularly badly.

> As you know already the Air Raids have been simply terrifying, and the damage whichever way you go is appalling. Uncle Will's firm has been raised to the ground, two large buildings. Uncle went round Finsbury way the other day and the sight that met his eye was so shocking he was afraid to go further on or even turn back. So of course he is now out of work. There are now 37 printer and Newspaper firms done in.

Chronic paper shortages had also affected newspapers and printing firms. Doreen Manwaring's husband Len had been working a four-day week since the beginning of the war.

> Len's job at the *Evening News* is a bit rocky. They are having trouble to get the paper. I suppose we must think ourselves lucky that he has been able to keep his job. It's no good grumbling though our troubles are by no means exceptional. Everybody seems to be hit in some way. Men are losing jobs they have held for years, little businesses break down, the youth of the country is merged into the machinery of war, and our children have been out of homes for nearly a year now.

Melville P Troy, an American, ran a prestigious business importing cigars. He was 62 when war broke out and kept in constant touch with his family in the United States. On 28 December 1939 he described the devastating effects of war on his business.

> At the office we have been discussing the business situation. We can get no cigars from Havana, as it is not permitted to send any money out of the country to pay for them. The cigar business will soon dry up unless this is changed, and the same will apply in time to cigarette tobacco, except that it may be easier to find a substitute for cigarette tobacco. The restriction does not apply to Rhodesian, Indian or other Empire leaf, or in

the last resort some other vegetable product might be doctored up and used for tobacco.

By June 1940, as cigar stocks disappeared from the market, Melville trudged round London selling cigarettes to customers.

My own income from B & H is gradually disappearing with Havana cigars, and I am devoting myself to general cigarette sales. The commission is very small and the increase slow, but like the caterpillars and the mulberry tree, after sufficient time a little progress can be detected. I have just reached 50 accounts which in fact average nearly £20 a month on account of a few of them being large ones, but they are not found very often. The work is among small restaurants, clubs and ARP canteens. Our business being in articles of luxury we are hard hit both by the necessity for economy on the part of buyers and the intention of the Government to stop all spending that does not help win the war. So my income has been cut down fifty per cent since the war started and will no doubt fade out entirely in this line.

To ensure some future income, Melville went to work for a tobacconist . . .

. . . who distributes the popular lines of cigarettes and tobacco, which are not considered luxuries but one of the prime necessities of the working man and soldier.

Just as Melville P Troy found a new outlet for his wares, many people retrained or discovered new skills to fulfil the needs of troops or war workers. Ethel Mattison's sister Jenny joined a factory canteen.

Jenny started work today, training for canteen management. She's awfully excited about it but tired out of course and has blistered hands from cutting up pounds of stewing beef! They don't have a meat meal every day of course, but all the same they get a good big well-cooked and well-served two-course meal for 9d. They do about 300 lunches a day. The pupils take it in turns to have their food and have the same as the workers and with them.

Britain's need for food had never been greater. The convoys were bringing in vital supplies, but the country needed to produce more of its own food. Fit young agricultural workers were needed for the Forces, so the Women's Land Army provided land girls. Ernie Britton had married a farmer's daughter from Dorset and in 1940 his in-laws were struggling.

> Their one and only remaining man has been called up and they have only got a young girl of the women's Land Army. She's a town lass, but I expect she pulls her weight although perhaps not like the old time country girl. This week they have a boy of 16½ starting. Theirs is a pretty hard life. Like most civil occupations, it's done by the old and the young.

While many had volunteered for war work, single women – and married women without children – were conscripted in March 1942. For some this offered an ideal opportunity to get away from an office job. Monica McMurray could not wait to join the Women's Land Army and loved her new job, as she wrote in her diary:

> Oh! How strange everything in Stoughton seems, I wish I'd been here a few weeks. Home Farm is a lovely place, swimming pool, and tennis court. We seem to have a nice family of girls.
> Gosh! But are milk pails heavy!!! My poor muscles. We have spent a hard first day emptying three railway carts full of salt, one potash of salt and two white salt. I seem to be getting an appetite. I think I shall sleep tonight.

Monica was not a country girl, but she threw herself into the daily routine of agricultural life, getting up early, milking, hedging and ditching, planting and weeding.

> I have for the first time seen a birth! One of the cows in Hayle's Yard very graciously allowed me to see her son born. Unfortunately nearly all bull calves are killed on the following

Wednesday. The work seems to be getting too heavy for me, I hate to say it, but I'm always short of that bit of extra energy needed, it's not that I'm lazy, I just get fagged and I did think I was getting tough.

Monica transferred to the Women's Timber Corps, an offshoot of the Women's Land Army. She was issued with the regulation breeches, pullover, two shirts, three pairs of army socks, two pairs of dungarees, hat and arm badge. What she did not know was that she would have to share a bed with another girl at her billet in Cumbria.

30th September 1941 – Find to my horror that we are without any water system or electric light. We have to wash in about a pint of water at which two have to join apparently. My first day of tree peeling – didn't last long, it poured.

Tree peeling was a particularly messy job as sap got on her clothes. Women in the Timber Corps were plagued by insects in summer, and snow and bitter winds in winter. Forestry work was extremely dangerous in high winds, and involved heavy machinery. Monica was eventually forced to leave after an injury to her foot.

The last two years have been on the whole the happiest and brightest of any I have ever spent, yes even remembering the long walk to heavy work at Kirkhampton, cold and thick snow of the Ratlingate winter and the dreadful wood bugs. It's a sad, sad business this packing up and uprooting again, especially as my future now lies in the hands of The National Service Officer who can direct me into whatever he chooses.

The country was in the grip of war, and the civilian workforce was subject to state control.

28th July – Kept my ordered appointment at the Labour Exchange. The only jobs I can choose from are, bus conductress (which I couldn't do because of my foot), hospital nurse which is ruled out for the same reason, factory trainee or unskilled factory hand – and I asked for a vacancy in AID [Aeronautical Inspection Division], the officer said I could have a try, so along I went to the AID office in the big bank buildings. What questions I had to answer, triganometry, decimals, fractions, also all about my inspection and testing work.

Two months later she entered the ranks of the AID based at Armstrong Whitworth's aircraft factory.

Louie White, at Blackburn's Aircraft Factory, was working alternate weeks of days and nights. An ardent reader and socialist, she recorded regularly in her diary the shortage of work.

> Had so little to do all night, that I actually read one book before I went home next morning. I can't understand why we are doing nothing at work, an aircraft factory – while the Russians are fighting like mad. What can one expect with our government?

Engineering was a reserved occupation, and men working in the industry were not immediately liable to call-up for the armed forces. The part of Chester in which Frank Forster lived and worked was a depressed area. Like Louie White, he could not understand how there could be slack times when an all-out war effort had been called for. In January 1943 he wrote:

> For the past week or so in the . . . shop at Brookhurst [Engineering], we have been doing almost nothing but sit around and stand around – now a large number of us have had to report to the Labour Exchange this evening – transferred to other factories.

Frank Forster had been at Brookhurst Engineering for three years. He and two workmates were sent to another firm.

> The job Bill Thomas and Jack Brown are on, is a labouring job outside – they are sometimes mixing concrete, sorting scrap wood, sorting scrap iron. This is so different from the

settled job at Brookhurst. Makes one feel so very unsettled, uncertain.

In contrast to these periods of short time and inactivity, in April 1943 Frank was employed on an urgent job – thanks to someone's inefficiency.

> So far this week I have worked on two occasions until 20.00 hours and now tonight until 21.00 hours. Our holidays have been cancelled until later – orders have been received from the War Ministry that a particular job is to be completed by Sunday night – we have been told that there are no definite hours to work to (that is, one can work as long as one likes, providing sufficient people are in work). The job in question is one of re-packing vehicles which were packed at the Ford factory and have been standing in their boxes for over 12 months – many of them are covered with rust.

Some factories had to relocate, thanks to the accuracy of German bombers. American Dick Cotton, husband of Peg, ran a factory making essential de-icing equipment for the RAF. During the Blitz in 1940, the whole family had to move, as Peg recorded.

> The factory nearly went up in smoke the other night so it is being rushed out of town piecemeal on lorries. Dick had to go along of course. So we all grabbed what we could take in the car – and drove clear across England. Things should be safe here – everything seems so peaceful.

The entire factory moved to Bideford in North Devon, uprooting hundreds of factory workers and their families from London and billeting them on the local population. The workforce, and their pets, travelled by train.

> The train was so crowded, like most wartime trains, that the people were standing jam-packed in the corridors and in solid wedges of humanity in the luggage vans. Poor Mrs Maynard was completely exhausted. She had not only stood the entire six hours of the trip, but had held the large and

restless black family cat all the way. And think of the mothers
with babies! And the poor youngsters being evacuated down
here from bombed areas! The train was very late. There had
been no restaurant car. So hunger was added to the travellers'
weariness. When Dick returned to the Inn at about three
o'clock in the morning he was quite worn out but enthusiastic
about the welcome that his workers and their families had
received. 'The town has been darned nice,' he said. 'The women
simply marvellous. No one went hungry. Those WVS workers –
I take my hat off to them! They managed beans, eggs, bread
and butter, cake, tea, etc. And the men helped in getting folks
to billets. We've come to the right place all right . . .'

The Women's Voluntary Service played a vital role on these occasions,
acting as volunteer drivers to get families to their billets. Many factories
had their own billeting officer which is another job created by the war.
Maureen Bolster was a billeting officer for an engineering factory. She
regarded it as an essential but thankless job, as she wrote to her fiancé
Eric Wells early in 1942.

Lord what a job this is. Extreme tact and patience is a
necessity. A. Bright cheerfulness (even if you're feeling as
cold as ice) is also necessity. B. Lastly but not leastly by any
means, comes sense of humour! That is vital. If I hadn't that
I wouldn't have lasted a week at Vokes. Also one must be
physically fit. One musn't mind getting soaked through, frost
bitten, blown about, or over tired. Yesterday was quite a typical
day in the Life of Billeting Lady – alarm goes off at 6.45 get up
dress come down to cereal coffee and toast by the kitchen fire.
Put on the old leather coat, sling Gertie gas mask round me,
grab my torch and out into the darkness. Wait about in the
cold for the bus and wish on my star if it's out. Clamber into
the luxury coach hired by the firm, and endure nasty pipes,
coughing noise and screeching factory girls.

This mixing of classes and accents was regarded as an opportunity
by some. Former teashop owners Elsie Whiteman and Kathleen

Church Bliss were now clad in scarves and overalls as factory girls.

> We have very much enjoyed the opportunity we have had of mixing with working class people on absolutely equal terms.

Women of all classes, mobilized into war work, found themselves living in close proximity with others. It was not always a happy experience. Pamela Moore received her call-up papers in the summer of 1943 and joined the Women's Land Army. She found that many Land Girls, freed from the restrictions of home, threw themselves into a wild social life. She wrote to her fiancé after her first night at a Land Army camp at Yate, near Bristol.

> To start with had an awful night's sleep, two girls sneaked in very late 'slightly merry', another one was up and down all through the night sick, and not being used to sleeping on the floor on a palliass my shoulders ached. There are seven of us in this great big hut, besides Beryl, Irene and myself who have all cuddled together for warmth, there are two other girls, very nice, and you can guess what the other two are like. The greater part of the girls are pretty awful, quite a number coming from Birmingham, but we three keep together as much as possible. One very di-da-di-da girl hasn't been seen since Sunday afternoon, when she said she was going to the station to collect her luggage.
>
> Altogether there are 66 girls, charge of Lieutenant Colonel (can't remember his name for the minute) but of course affectionately known as – the Colonel. He really is a nice old stick, and tries to keep the girls who are friends with each other together. He calls us with his whistle at 6.15 each morning, breakfast is from 7–7.45, and the lorries depart straight after that.
>
> The lorry never came until 11 o'clock having been ditched, and we started work, picking spuds. The farmer was a very decent chap and works with us, probably to keep us on the job. We had a rotten lunch of rotten sandwiches, and when it started to rain at 4.30pm we packed up work. This wasn't too

bad for the day, sort of broke my back in. But we walked most of the way back, and then it started to *rain*. I got soaked to the skin. I've had a hot bath in a filthy bath, some half cold grub, can't find anywhere to hang my wet clothes they're here in the hut at the moment and it's not exactly a healthy state of air to sleep in. What a life!

The girls are all going to the shed that boasts a piano, but very few chairs, and they're all wooden, so picture Beryl and I lying on our stomachs on our divan-like beds with the smoke of the oil lamp our only light, getting up our noses, and the rain falling heavens hard on the tin roof, and I've already killed two spiders. Once again, what a life!

Veronica Owen, who had reluctantly been evacuated to Canada as a schoolgirl, returned home in 1942, keen to play her part in her country's war, and became a Wren. She wrote to her mother in May 1944 about a new addition to her watch in the Coding Room at Fort Southwick, Portsmouth.

Monica Newburn, a Canadian of 24, who is rather overbearing and always holds the floor with a penetrating voice, either talking about the numerous men who are in love with her and whom she is inclined to 'play' with – most of them Lt RNs, poor devils, or sex! She's staunch Roman Catholic, and lives with her sister married to a Lt RN. Well I've been very unkind and she sounds grim and really isn't nearly as bad as that – it's just that her talk is a bit much at times, but she is kind underneath and in some ways very amusing.

Veronica had been at boarding school, and was used to community life, but she still found living with some of her fellow Wrens a culture shock – particularly petty jealousies.

Gosh, there's been such a row in our room – it's a very silly thing – but about a fortnight ago Maxine and I went out for a walk together, and didn't ask Elise and I didn't tell her that I was going out – so for a fortnight we didn't speak to each

other – when I came in after the walk we had an almighty
thunderstorm and of course Rosemary burnt her boats
and joined in on my side and both of us have been not on
speaking terms with Elise since, until about yesterday when
she suddenly became quite friendly. Well about ten minutes
ago, I've just gone and done it again – because I said draw lots
for who to sleep in what beds etc and she happens to sleep in
the not so nice lot of beds and is in a furious temper about
it, because I should have said the new people to have them
anyhow, without any lots.

Some munitions workers lived in hostels. Miss Nora O'Connor ran the
Burghfield Residential Club in Berkshire, which housed 1,000 female
munitions workers. Eight hundred of the girls were Irish, and ages ranged
between 18 and 60. They were employed at a factory near Reading.

The making of munitions was hazardous in the extreme,
involving the use of TNT and, in spite of rigourously enforced
safety precautions, 'blows' did occur. Having refused one girl
permission to go to a dance, I was immensely saddened by
my next news of her – she had been killed by an explosion at
work. The fact that a worker had been killed on duty didn't
deter her companions; they showed neither fear nor hesitation
in carrying on. Lack of clothing coupons was a source of
frustration, but it nourished the initiative of a small group
who organised a flourishing Exchange and Mart in secondhand garments.

Kathleen Crawley toured village halls, military hospitals and Army and
Air Force bases as an actress with ENSA (Entertainments National Service
Association). On tour near Lincoln she stayed in a munitions hostel.

We didn't know quite what to expect yesterday, but it turned out
to be the hostel of a Clax factory here and nearly all the girls are
Irish. I suppose all munitions hostels are like this. The corridor
of bedrooms looks like a prison. All the rooms are tiny and two
of everything. The food seems alright though it's rather muckily

served, but I think we'll enjoy the week – it's a change anyhow. It has masses of bathrooms and the water is always boiling. What appealed to us were the laundry sinks, wringer and ironing room. The entire company has washed everything, and dried and ironed everything with one speck of dirt on it. It was such a novelty to have it all there when you wanted it. There's a games' room here with darts and ping pong which Betty Fuller and I intend to be proficient at by the end of the week. The only trouble is that it's such a noisy place and none of the factory girls even try to be quiet after 7 in the morning.

Dirty sheets in boarding houses, leaky roofs in the dressing rooms and an uncertain power supply are all described in her letters home to her mother in London. This was theatre under 'wartime conditions'.

Last night's venue was terrible. It was so unbelievably awful that we thought we were having an actor's nightmare – the not knowing your lines or having half a mile to run and being late for your cue.

Well, it was the village hall we found ourselves in – we've been playing many of these lately. There were no tabs [front curtains], the lighting was no better than 6 candle power – really it wasn't. The doors in the hall had to be opened to let light onto the stage! The stage was surrounded by camouflage netting – filthy dirty and smelly – which we had to remove. Anyway we could have borne with all this – they'd never had a play before. The Entertainments Officer didn't even know it was a play, and the whole audience sat the whole way through without a sound and without any applause till Eric told them the play had finished. Even the cat must have found it tiresome – she had four beautiful black kittens during the show.

On tour in Scotland in 1944 she wrote:

Tonight's show is too funny for words. Four times the lights have gone out & we've continued playing by torch light from the wings!

During the Scottish tour Kathleen's company visited an RAF base near Port Ellen.

> What a welcome we had on the quay. Everything but flags.
> Everyone was so nice and kind and a strange RAF 'grey' Maria
> was there to take us to our rooms. Last night's theatre was
> tiny but we'd have done anything, even been seasick again for
> the wonderful reception we had. They just lapped it up since
> they've had nothing but Variety for a year. They wouldn't even
> stop applauding for The King. Tonight we are invited to the
> Sergeants Dance!

Kathleen was horrified by some of the conditions in which those on war work had to live. Her brother Derek had joined the Forces and she thought him lucky by comparison with the Bevin Boys, after the company had performed at one of their camps. A chronic shortage of miners, coupled with severe wartime winters and the increasing needs of industry, led to drastic measures from Ernest Bevin, Minister of Labour. Many skilled miners had entered the Forces, and in December 1943 the Bevin Boys were called up to replace them in the mines. They were chosen by a random ballot to ensure that this form of conscription applied to all classes and backgrounds. John Whisson was working as a clerk at the Ministry of Supply in London, and had just qualified as an emergency motorcycle despatch rider. He had hoped to join the army when he was called up in February 1944. Instead he was sent to Moor Green Colliery, in Eastwood, where he moved in to the newly built Miners' Hostel.

> Unfortunately the Nissen huts which served as dormitories for
> groups of twelve were not heated. During the winter months it
> was not unusual to find, on waking up that the walls above our
> beds were covered with hoar frost.

The new miners spent a month training before going down the pits. Michael Banister wrote his experiences for his school magazine three months later.

> The lecturers were all mining men, and though they no doubt
> knew their jobs, some clearly had difficulty in imparting their

Coal was needed to cope with freezing winters as well as to fuel munitions factories. Thousands of young men were conscripted as miners, in a scheme devised by Ernest Bevin, Minister of Labour, but many Bevin Boys resented their lack of recognition.

knowledge to the trainees, who were in any case, for the most part truculent and in no mood to receive any information on the now abhorred subject of mining. During the whole of my period of training I never saw the coal face. Any knowledge I gained was derived almost entirely from the lecture room and hence was purely theoretical.

Writing his first letter home, Noel Humphrey described the training equipment.

We were given a helmet, boots, overalls and a pair of white gym shoes. The helmets are made of cardboard but it looks like black bakelite. The boots are studded and they have a metal toe-cap. I am billeted with a boy from London. It is very nice here with this miner and his wife. There is plenty of good food here. I have bought three bars of soap in Woolworths with the coupons George gave me.

In another letter home to his mother in Pulborough, Sussex, Noel described his first trip underground.

There is a funny feeling in one's stomach first, but it soon passes off. About half way down it feels as if you are going up again. On the way up it feels as if you are going down again before you reach the top. We all have electric lamps which weigh about six pounds. In some of the tunnels there are electric lights and you can walk with ease while in others you have to bend your head.

Among his fellow Bevin Boys was the future leader of the Liberal Party, David Steele. Another future MP, Geoffrey Finsberg, was a Bevin Boy, as were the entertainers Eric Morecambe and Jimmy Saville. David Jedwab was an idealistic 17-year-old in 1944, when he described a day at a pit in Lancashire.

When I am not in a particular hurry, I like to walk across those fifty yards of surface slowly, and sometimes – on nice fresh mornings – rather hesitatingly. This is all that separates me from the choking depths into which I shall descend shortly. I feel sorry to leave the fresh air and hear the wind rustling among the grass and hedges. My gaze turns up at the great tall chimney in front of me. Together with the pitshafts, with their clumsy looks, it makes a gruesome site in the dark. I take one last look at the sky that is gradually beginning to be filled with a pale light, and make my way to the lift cage.

The cage took David and his fellow miners down 1,000 feet.

Down here it is strangely quiet; only the dull thudding sound of our steps breaks the silence and the former garrulous chatter of the men has become a strained and tense silence.

Soon we are walking, supporting ourselves on our knees,
along four foot high passages and tunnels, now crawling on
all fours, now on our stomachs by drawing ourselves forward
with the elbows, and now climbing up brows as steep as Welsh
mountains.

Michael Banister trained at Doncaster and was posted to Bedlington
Colliery in Northumberland in February 1944. He was the first Bevin Boy
to be sent to this pit.

I was received with great kindness. I was something of a curiosity,
being the first of my species to arrive at Bedlington. My first
day was spent on a tour round the pit in action, and during it I
learnt more than four weeks of lectures and navvying had taught
me. I realised that much of my training in Yorkshire had been
wasted, for not only are the technical terms in Northumberland
quite different, but conditions and methods of working and
transporting the coal vary to a great extent in the two coalfields.

He was assigned to help a 17-year-old who had been down the pit for three
years, and the two teenagers managed a junction on the haulage roads.

It is not pleasant work, but it is far short of 'hard labour'. In
fact I have one of the best jobs in the pit. In comparison with
that of a member of the Forces, it has its merits and demerits. It
holds no glamour of uniform, no regular three monthly leaves,
and very slight chances of promotion. But we have a home life
with its undeniable advantages. We have regular and definite
hours of work, and weekends entirely free; and we have a longer
expectation of life!

Despite their increased life expectancy, many Bevin Boys resented losing
the chance to serve their country *above* ground. While military conscripts
were awarded campaign medals for serving their country abroad, the
young miners who had served their country at home did not have their
contribution officially recognized.

9
NEWS AND PROPAGANDA

Well, it certainly is a comical war! At least on the wireless:
our own short-wave transmitter broadcasting in a dozen or two
foreign languages, and every country frantically doing the same.
Everybody it seems is trying to lecture everybody else into doing what
the first everybody wants done – And then German broadcasts in
English! Can anything be more Gilbertian for example, than
the German announcer on 49.2m wave length wishing his listeners
a good night's rest after he has done his best to make sound sleep
for many people difficult to come by, with his harrowing accounts
of the result of Britain's continuance of the war: or his colleague
from Hamburg tonight concluding his 9–10pm 'news' – but really
militant propaganda – by saying: 'Since this is Sunday we will
conclude our broadcast with the hymn The Day Thou Gavest
Lord Is Ended.' Verily a mad world my masters.
(Dr JP McHutchison, October 1939)

As the light shone through the wireless dial into dimly lit and blacked-out homes, many could not resist twiddling the knob from the BBC Home Service across a myriad of tiny European stations to Berlin. The wireless was a new weapon in modern warfare. Great war correspondents such as Frank Gillard pre-recorded reports from the front line, to be heard hours later in British homes. War news in 1914–18 had been carried by the only means available: the newspapers. Limited filming had taken place in the trenches of the Great War, but in this new war the camera lens transferred images of battle straight to the retinas of cinemagoers. It was all subject to censorship, but the population was able to follow the progress of the Allied Armies as they had never been able to before.

Dr JP McHutchison (Director of Education for Dumbartonshire) found he could not resist tuning in to German radio stations.

> What a depressing 'nightcap' the German news broadcast in
> English is – one must really cease listening, but curiosity as to
> what new lies they are spreading is always strong.

Listening to these German broadcasts in English must have made the population recognize the reality of spies and a 'fifth column' (a phrase borrowed from the recent Spanish Civil War to describe enemy sympathizers), and the necessity for slogans luch as 'Careless Talk Costs Lives' and 'Be Like Dad, Keep Mum'. Examples of disturbingly accurate information, broadcast to shake the morale of the civilian population, were scattered throughout contemporary diaries. Dr McHutchison lived on the outskirts of Glasgow, which rated a mention in the German 'news' in English in late 1939.

> Last week local interest was created in a mention of Clydebank
> (Queen Elizabeth), Dumbarton (Blackburn Aircraft Works)
> and Alexandria (Torpedo Factory). The green painting of the
> Blackburn Works was noted.

Many were tuning in to the notorious William Joyce, an Englishman who broadcast Nazi propaganda throughout the war and was subsequently executed. He was known as Lord Haw Haw, because of the languid upper-class tones in which he drawled, 'Germany calling, Germany calling'. Joan Strange had been listening to him just before her summer holiday in August 1942.

> We've left Worthing just at the time of more evacuation owing
> to the possibility of more commando raids and possible
> invasion. Our road is lined with troop-carrying lorries and all
> roads with trees have numerous camouflaged tanks hiding
> beneath them. Lord Haw Haw has mentioned the fact on the
> wireless more than once!

The Germans were not averse to attempted interference with BBC programmes. In October 1942 Joan Strange cut out a story from her daily paper, and stuck it in her diary. She added her own ear-witness account of this bizarre attempt at German propaganda.

> Nazi radio voice butts in on BBC news. The voice has butted in for the last 3 days now. It's absolutely childish. He is not nearly quick enough and is devoid of all wit. Tonight all he could think to say was 'That's a lie' or 'Of course' then 'That's a lie' again, a most feeble effort!!

The mystery voice interrupted the BBC Forces programme with a running barrage of abuse of Winston Churchill and Foreign Secretary Anthony Eden. But the Germans were not alone in their use of the radio as a weapon of war. The BBC World Service, funded by the Foreign Office, started broadcasting in German after the Munich crisis in 1938. By the end of the war it was broadcasting in 45 languages. Messages were even sent to the Far East, where prisoners of war listened secretly in the camps. The BBC Home Service broadcast uplifting messages from evacuated children to their parents; the young Princess Elizabeth encouraged the children of the Empire; and Queen Elizabeth broadcast to the Women of America in 1941. Dr McHutchison and his mother were regular listeners to the Sunday service, which was broadcast by the BBC and was one instance of how simple propaganda could raise morale.

> Tonight's broadcast service was relayed from a shelter in London and was almost too poignantly pathetic in its setting. The hymns sung for the most part by folks now homeless and sheltering every night in the crypt of the church had a significance they never had before, and that their authors could never have imagined possible. It moved me, and it must have moved all the angels in heaven, to hear the voices of the grown ups and children singing, O God, our help in ages past; the King of Love My Shepherd is; Holy Father in Thy Mercy, Guide Me Oh Thou Great Jehovah and Abide With Me. One felt surer of our victory somehow after listening to such a service from such a place.

In rural areas many people were not connected to electricity, and went to great lengths to listen in to the wireless. Crystal sets were not uncommon, and a conventional wireless set could be powered by an accumulator – a cumbersome type of battery taken to a central depot for recharging.

Switching on the wireless in the evenings was how the British population got their war news, concerts and light entertainment in their own homes. Great literary names such as George Orwell and JB Priestley attracted large audiences. Prime Minister Winston Churchill used the radio to great effect, cajoling and encouraging unity on the Home Front. The wireless brought the news vividly to life for people far from the action – sometimes perhaps too vividly. Leonard Marsland Gander (who later became a war reporter) was the wireless correspondent for *The Daily Telegraph* during the early years of the war:

> *July 15th 1940* – There is great interest in the sensational running commentary (recorded) given by Charles Gardner on Sunday on an air fight he watched over the English Channel. He included such phrases as 'Oh boy, oh boy, this is the best thing I've seen', as young men were crashing to their death – it was strong meat for some listeners.

The wireless was a source of comfort, too. In Somerset, Ann Lee Michell found herself exhausted and often depressed about wartime events. But she would turn that button and, as the set warmed up, listen to the magic words 'It's That Man Again'.

> Very tired, had some supper on a tray by the fire and giggled weakly at the absurdities of ITMA on the wireless.

Mrs E Innes-Ker had worked for the Malaya Broadcasting Corporation in Singapore, and after escaping to England she joined the BBC in London.

> Sometime in the middle of 1943 the BBC's Engineering Division organised voluntary spare time munitions work in the evenings. When this was started most people in our department said they would willingly give up one evening a

week to munitions, but when it came to choosing an evening, everyone was adamant they could not do Thursday evening, because that was the evening for ITMA with Tommy Handley. Maw and I were regular listeners to this, but it quite surprised me how certain everyone was, even the intellectuals in the department, they were not going to miss Tommy Handley's programme. Honor and I elected to do our munitions work on Monday evenings, and we used to go straight from the office. We worked from 7–10pm making lamp sockets for aircraft. Probably about 30–40 of us in a big room. The radio was tuned to 'Music While You Work'.

Daphne Pearson was a guest on one of the hit wartime shows, as she wrote to her mother, swelling with pride, in February 1941.

Do you remember you saying I wonder whether you'll ever do 'In Town Tonight', well I was on the air last night and this morning. Only one had to say exactly what was written and not much choice. Odd words I was allowed to correct – we had five rehearsals and I got colder and colder and at 6.15 I could not stand it any more and said I must have a drink – this was hailed with great cheer. So into the nearest pub and I drank 3 brandies and ginger ales before I could warm up. During rehearsal they said we were very cold and lifeless. Most of the BBC having moved into a cinema without any heating, I'm not surprised.

In their sitting rooms, couples swayed to music played on the gramophone, and dance music played live, by the likes of Henry Hall and his orchestra, and broadcast via the wireless. In a letter to her sister in America in 1942, Ethel Mattison recorded censorship of the type of music broadcast by the BBC.

There has been a lot of discussions in the papers lately about the ban of 'slushy music' on the BBC. No doubt you have heard about it. According to The Sunday Times, Tinpan Alley are very upset about it and fear that their voice will not be heard this side of the Atlantic. Personally I think the loss will be all theirs.

If *you* can't go to the factory help the neighbour who *can*

How you can help

Arrange **now** with a neighbour to look after her children when she goes to her war-work—or give your name to

CARING FOR WAR WORKERS' CHILDREN IS A NATIONAL SERVICE

Although women were not conscripted until 1942, they were encouraged to take up war work. Caring for other people's children and offering your home as a billet were both seen as a national service. War workers could also take their children to Government nurseries.

Newspapers published tales of the courage and dedication of men in the forces, particularly the RAF. But listening to the voices of those airmen on the wireless was far more effective. In August 1941 Dr McHutchison was glued to his set.

> Some recent broadcast talks by airmen, pilots and gunners, have impressed and moved one by their quietly-spoken, calm and almost matter of fact tones, no bravado, no consciousness of bravery, but only a sort of quizzical modesty about their exploits, a kind of very boyish interest in deeds of superb skill and daring – the typical English sporting spirit.

Phyllis Warner went to see a similar production in her local London cinema in August 1941.

> Went to see *Target for Tonight*, the new film of a bombing raid in which all the actors are active members of the Bomber Command. It was slightly eerie to sit in that cinema after black out time, and watch on the screen all the sinister routine preparations for a raid and the planes humming nearer and nearer their goal, knowing that any minute the warning might shriek that German bombers were upon us here. My experiences of raids being exclusively that of the target, my sympathies drifted to the German AA gunners down below rather than to our side up in the plane – until they were on their lonely and perilous journey back, when something about their simple cheerfulness took hold of the imagination, and made those minutes painfully tense. It is above all a memorable film, one presented in undertones, but which keeps recurring to the mind days later.

Not everyone agreed with these sentiments. Lucy Kemp spent much of the war waiting for her husband Teddie to return from his voyages to North America with the transatlantic convoys. While he was away from home in February 1942 she went to the cinema.

> The war news is so —, and I have been getting so keyed up

waiting for Teddie that on Saturday I thought I should
explode, so went to our village cinema for relaxation. We
led off with Donald Duck, which was very funny, then a
propaganda thing about 'more ships'. This consisted of a
man reciting some poem with fade-ins and fade-outs of
convoys, mostly being bombed! I thought 'Good Heavens',
and then settled down to Wuthering Heights.

Propaganda films were used to boost the morale and productivity of
factory workers. Elsie Whiteman and Kathleen Church Bliss were among
the workforce at Morrison's Aircraft Factory in Croydon.

At dinner time today the Ministry of Information film 'Let's
finish the job' was shown in the Canteen. The place was
crowded to suffocation as all the windows had to be shut
in order to put up the blackout – and every worker in the
place was there – including all the office. It was really a very
wonderful film – designed to show by illustration how every
excrescence however minute on the body of the plane sets up
resistance to its passage through the air – & in consequence
slows up the speed. It was very cleverly devised & must have
been planned by a skilled engineer. The right & wrong ways
of doing jobs was also shown in an amusing & narrative form.
The moral was, that how we finish the job is all important. Old
Els who has so often wondered whether her slow careful work
was justified, came away inwardly uplifted as obviously you
can't be too careful. They told us that rough finish can make a
difference of 25 mph to a plane's speed.

During 1940, when Germany controlled 50 per cent of the world's bauxite
(the raw material from which aluminium is smelted), an appeal was made
for aluminium utensils, which would be turned into Spitfires. Mea Allan
wrote this for the *Daily Herald*:

What happened to my frying pan, by Mea Allan
I bought it three weeks ago. A week later the appeal of Lord
Beaverbrook, Minister of Aircraft, went out to the housewives

of Britain, and I took it to the headquarters of the Women's Voluntary Services in Tothill Street. Yesterday it became part of a Spitfire.

I was sitting over breakfast reading the newspapers when my eye caught the following paragraph printed in italics – *We will turn your pots and pans into Spitfires and Hurricanes, Blenheims and Wellingtons. Give us your aluminium. The need is instant. The call is urgent. We want it new and old.* I didn't take any notice at first. After all I'd just bought it and it was useful, and it turned out the most delicious omelettes.

I went back to see what the rest of the news was and forgot that tantalising appeal. But the news only turned the appeal into a mute demand. There it was printed in huge black headlines: 200 Nazi planes attack. And then came the stirring account of the RAF – Spitfire and Hurricane pilots of the RAF yesterday inflicted the greatest damage on the German Air Force since bombing raids on this country began. I read on. All day long the RAF pilots' reports kept coming in. Always they told the same story – victory against odds. That decided me, as it was deciding thousands of other women all over the country.

When I got down to the WVS headquarters the place was already besieged by people dumping equally beloved frying pans and kettles and shoe-trees, meat covers, trays and teapots. The army lorry came and the hundreds of kettles, cake moulds, vacuum cleaners, coat hangers, pots and pans, coffee percolators and hot water bottles were shovelled up into it. It was taken to a London collection centre to be cleaned – its iron handle knocked off. Next it went to be sorted in another part of the yard. Was it 'allie' or 'dural'? It went into the allie sack with 1½cwt of other pots and pans.

The following day my frying pan went for another ride in another army lorry. It went to a London railway terminus and was there unloaded. That night a queer train slid out of the station. It was the first aluminium train, consisting of eight trucks full of pots and pans. My frying pan was bound for a place, which must be nameless, there to be turned into that magic sounding thing – an ingot. A lot had to happen to it before it became an ingot.

A builder's barrow is requisitioned to collect aluminium in the London Borough of Kensington. The WVS ran the collection in the summer of 1940; the RAF was suffering terrible casualties fighting the Battle of Britain, and new aeroplanes were desperately needed.

It found a temporary home in a smelting shop where it was put into an outsize pot and there melted down. This was an exciting stage in its career. All impurities were boiled out of it, in the form of glittering sparks which jumped out of the pot and shot roofwards. A giant fountain of fireworks.

It was at this stage that I said goodbye to my frying pan as a frying pan and began to think of it in terms of a Spitfire. For when it next appeared it was a shining pint of liquid aluminium among gallons of other pots and pans. It was then poured into a casting mould and left to cool off. It was now an ingot, this time mixed with alloys. In the alloys department it then found itself being boiled again and poured into another mould. It was now ready for the rolling mills. Perhaps that was the most trying stage in its career. It was popped into an electric furnace. It was drawn out into a bar. It was squeezed through rollers until it was flattened into a sheet of the required size and thickness. Only then was it ready for the aircraft factory. Almost a fortnight had passed since it had last cooked my bacon and egg. But now, a slim shining sheet, it was ready for stamping. What was it to become? Part of a wing surface, or a spar, or a bit of a Spitfire's fuselage? It was chosen to become part of a wing. Another few days and it would be cleaving the air, part of Britain's air fighting force, part of our final victory. It was stamped, the pattern tool cutting it into shape as neatly as an experienced dressmaker cuts cloth. Finally it went to the Assembly shop.

Fourteen days had passed, and now my frying pan was really part of a Spitfire. Bit by bit the lovely metal bird had been built, with careful unerring hands and clever tools. It was ready for testing, for flight, for the fight. Yesterday a new Spitfire took to the air. I'm proud to think my frying pan was part of it. I think it would be proud too, if it knew.

Factories, schools and villages adopted ships, planes and even whole squadrons, and were treated to visits and flypasts by the men whose work they were supporting. Salvage campaigns exhorted the population to 'keep a rag bag' (four old collars would make a new map for the RAF); food leftovers were collected in huge bins by the WVS to feed pigs; and paper was collected to make munitions (one propaganda photograph showed Queen Mary's secretary donating a huge pile of her old letters to this campaign). Joan Strange recorded some of the efforts in Worthing in November 1941.

We've ransacked the house and collected all sorts of old bills etc. there is a big national competition for paper with a £20,000 prize for the winning county. There were stacks of old forms all ready to be collected at the town hall.

Dustcarts pulled a separate salvage cart behind them for recyclable materials. In 1944 there was a book recovery and salvage drive for the Services, blitzed libraries and munitions.

School children are collecting the books, and we turned out 130 today which were removed triumphantly in two sacks – up to today about 50,000 have been received.

Three thousand disused slot machines from Britain's railway stations were recycled as part of a campaign for iron and steel scrap, as well as, infamously, the railings. Telephone boxes carried a poster declaring: 'I'm on war work, if you must use me be brief.' Some people gave up their home telephones as part of their war effort. On the underground, posters encouraged people with colds to keep their germs to themselves so as not to infect others and harm the war effort. The 'V for Victory' campaign even spawned a V for Victory hat, worn by one enterprising woman in London. The most productive campaign was 'Dig for Victory', which saw front gardens, bomb craters and public parks used to produce vegetables; the People's Park in Grimsby produced 15 tons of onions one year. In his school essay in September 1940, D Madge recorded the success of the allotments at the Kneller Boys School in Twickenham.

> Ever since war began the School's Field has been dug up into allotments 16 by 6 yards. All of them bear vegetables of some kind such as turnips, carrots, beetroot, cabbage, marrows, potatoes, Brussels Sprouts etc. They are all worked by the boys themselves. The ground is very dry and the things aren't growing so well but the weather is breaking now and looking more like rain. Boys could come up to their allotments during the holidays, which owing to the war were only a fortnight. Just before the holidays a boy in the school stole most of the fruit from the orchard, but it was not long before he was found out. A lot of the vegetables are now being sold to the school and the money which we get is given to the Red Cross. Boys are still doing their bit 'Digging for Victory'!

Joan Strange held an allotment in Worthing, and picked up tips on vegetable growing from her fellow allotment holders.

> *March* – Help! I've not written this old diary for nearly a week. It's the allotment's fault! The weather has been so good that I've gone up most evenings and got too tired digging to write the diary. The two oldish men on the next plot have helped me a bit as they are taking over a bit of Ken's plot, which is already dug. There is a very friendly spirit up there.

'Make do and mend' was a watchword for housewives. Sheets were turned 'sides to middle', and people were encouraged to save and re-use scraps of string and paper. Joan Strange and her mother used their needlework skills to raise hundreds of pounds for wartime causes.

> *January 24th 1944* – Mother is very busy making trolley cloths
> from a linen sheet given her by Miss Bridges marked 1882! It's
> an enormous sheet and will make dozens of such like things for
> sales. In this case it's for a Prisoner of War sale 'something new
> from something old'.

Despite the proximity of Fleet Street to the City of London, and wartime paper shortages, the papers were still published and were a vital source of news, propaganda campaigns, recipes and handy hints for 'making do'. Peg Cotton, as an American, was impressed when she described wartime newspapers in early 1945.

> For years these have been but two scant sheets of paper. Paper
> makes munitions. Yet these rationed newspapers have carried on
> throughout the war. Only when a severe Blitz has temporarily
> stopped printing or circulation, has this voice of the people failed
> to present its messages, heartening, or heart rending, every day, so
> surely as that day would dawn.

Talking to 'the press' in wartime had its risks. In January 1941 May Chalmers, whose husband Archie was the Sheriff of Oban on the west coast of Scotland, innocently recounted her local news in a *private* letter to a close friend, Mea Allan, who happened to be assistant news editor on a national newspaper, the *Daily Herald*. There were to be embarrassing consequences after May recounted the dramatic results of enemy bombing in Argyll.

> I'm still slightly sick when I think of the last visitation when
> they got the boat full of the Aga Khan's stable and only one
> poor horse got ashore and none of the greyhounds. Somehow
> the animals cause me more sorrow than the men who passed
> out, even more upset than the Sunderland which thought

the sea was twenty feet lower opposite Kilbowie and crashed scuppering the whole crew of twelve.

The two women kept up a chatty and frequent exchange of news in the early years of the war. Mea Allan wrote back a week later on 8 January:

> Today, on the desk, in comes a Press Association slip about the Aga Khan's bloodstock in France having been purloined by the Germans – and I am in charge. So being a conscientious Scot, I pen little notes to some of the items, and one of them is, 'It may interest you to know that one ship of a convoy bombed off Oban Argyll Scotland, had on board the Aga Khan's horses and hounds. Only one horse swam ashore. The rest were killed or drowned.'

Mea Allan was the first woman to be appointed to a Fleet Street newsdesk and was always delighted to beat her male colleagues to a story.

> Now how was I to know, when nobody told the innocent sweetheart of 50 rampin' stampin' newsmen – how could I know that for the past week every other journalist on every other paper in the kingdom had been trying to find out who that horse belonged to?? 'Where did you get this story and *how* did *you* get it?' they bellowed. If the Edinburgh office did ring you up I hope you weren't annoyed; they are very nice people. If we get an exclusive, tops!

But May Chalmers could not share her enthusiasm after a brush with the police, which revealed that all calls from journalists were monitored.

> You have got me properly in the soup – Oban Inspector of Police rang up yesterday and then the County Police from Lochgilphead. The only saving thing about it all is, though, they have been decent enough not to tell the Sheriff [her husband, Archie Chalmers]. If they had done so he would have certainly shot me or put me in the sea, so if our friendship is to continue, will you promise, honour bright, *never* to pass on anything I tell you? It is

rather a revelation to learn that the County Police listen in to any conversation on the telephone which *comes* from a reporter, and I was congratulated on the way I ticked off the Edinburgh man although being told off as well. Gosh to goodness if Archie knew! It's just too awful to contemplate and I'm completely sunk. You probably think it's a storm in a tea cup but it means a lot to me and apparently the AK episode was *terribly* secret.

Censorship of news, and of letters going abroad, was all part of the war machine, designed to prevent fifth columnists from discovering scraps of information useful to enemy agents. Blue pencil was used to delete words and place names deemed to give away vital information to the enemy. Newspapers had to submit stories to the Ministry of Information to be 'passed by censor'. Mea Allan described the procedure.

> One rings for A Boy. When A Boy comes, one says rapidly over one's shoulder: 'Ministry – at once!' If there's a raid on The Boy puts forward Union rules and won't go out. He will if the office car is at the door to take him. Later one of our men at the Ministry phones over corrections – copies have to be corrected and sent to subs [sub editors].

Contemporary diaries and letters summarized the war news every day. When the island of Pontillaria was finally taken in the Italian campaign, one British woman even named her daughter Pontillaria. The population was kept relatively well informed, despite the censor. Phyllis Warner had a shock when she opened her newspaper in February 1942.

> Started the day feeling cheerful, but was horrified at the lunch time headlines. Japs land in force at Singapore. The papers are cruel – they put the worst news in the biggest headlines, with no thought of those of us who suffer. I can't believe that this is true, that with all the defences of Singapore Island the Japs can land in thousands. But the radio holds out no promise of better news.

If the headlines appalled, pictures could be far worse.

> What is going to happen to all our men? There won't be a chance
> of evacuation. Are they all to be killed or taken prisoner? I do
> wish I hadn't seen those horrible *Picture Post* photographs of what
> the Japs do to their prisoners.

News of Russia's continued stand against invading German troops was
recorded day by day in many diaries. The British were inspired and heartened
by their Russian allies. Phyllis Warner went to a festival of Russian films in
London, and she could not help comparing Stalin's inspirational speeches
with the propaganda issued by the British Government.

> Where are our War Office nabobs and political boneheads who
> were convinced the Russians wouldn't last ten days? Sitting
> up and taking notes on how to fight a war tooth and nail and
> not by a series of gentlemanly retreats, I should hope. Stalin's
> call to the Russian people 'Rise to defend your land' . . . 'be
> ruthless' . . . 'create guerrilla bands' . . . 'make conditions
> unbearable for the enemy' . . . 'rise in your millions', is a pretty
> shaming contrast to our War Office instructions to the Home
> Guard that weapons and explosives must on no account be
> improvised, and the official invasion leaflet, which told us to
> hide in shelters till the fighting was over. I wonder if I would
> have the courage to sling a milk bottle at a parachutist: I hope
> to God I would.

Scrapbooks of newspaper cuttings show that by 1941 the British public was
aware of the extent of Jewish persecution. One article even predicted that
the number of Jewish victims of the 'final solution' would be six million.
Mea Allan mixed with other journalists and with Government officials
all day, and was privy to classified information. Her vivid description of a
German air raid, in a letter to a friend, included this in October 1940.

> If it's not High Explosives its landmines – our own if you please,
> wot the Germans pinched at Dunkirk!! If that's news to you
> swallow it and forget it!!

It was the job of the newspapers to provide morale-boosting stories too.

Daphne Pearson was splashed all over the newspapers in 1940. Daphne had been only a few hours short of gaining her pilot's licence at the outbreak of war, but she was turned down by the Women's Air Transport Service (whose ranks included Amy Johnson). Instead she joined the WAAF (Women's Auxiliary Air Force). At two o'clock on the morning of 31 May, Daphne was asleep in her bunk at an RAF Coastal Command Station in Kent. A noise stirred her from sleep and she was alarmed to hear the rattle of a plane's labouring engine and a terrible crash. Leaping out of bed, she rushed out and found a plane in flames. She pulled the injured pilot free and then, as an enormous bomb exploded in the fuselage, threw herself over him to protect him from the blast and shrapnel. Daphne was awarded the George Cross – the first member of the WAAF to be honoured for bravery. Three months later she wrote to her mother from Malvern:

> I am staying here until Wednesday – Dame Laura Knight is
> painting me – am full of conflictions because we are so busy on
> our station.

Dame Laura Knight, one of the official war artists, painted many extraordinary scenes of life on the Home Front, from women handling enormous barrage balloons to heroines such as Daphne.

> I am being painted in a tin helmet and holding a rifle – Air
> Ministry will be furious but Dame Laura says my helmet is rather
> like an effect on the back of my head and the rifle makes a good
> line – the WAAFs-are-not-to-carry-arms controversy is still
> waging and this will upset the apple cart. Dame Laura is adamant
> and firm.

Daphne was itching to carry a gun *officially*, particularly with the Germans poised for invasion on the other side of the English Channel.

> I say if Germans kill women and children in their homes and in
> the streets, machine gunning them, the women must be prepared
> to kill to protect their children. This war is near us, yet I go on,
> and never listen in to the wireless or bother with a paper. What is
> the good? The Germans may be here any moment so it's no use

worrying except I can't get a gun for love or money unless it is a large one and I can't cart that around with all my belongings.

In a modern war Daphne might well be put into more frontline duties. Instead she found herself being used as a feisty role model for the women of Britain, to garner new recruits. She travelled all over the country, often at very short notice.

Apparently, everyone hates recruiting, very few officers remain. It is very thankless and the department certainly gets more curses than thanks.

Daphne was soon disillusioned with her new role, as she wrote to a friend:

Am longing to smell fresh air and see clear skies. My eyes are glued to papers and innumerable forms, and all electric light. I long for a jersey and slacks and water and unspoilt grass.

In addition to her public relations and recruitment work, Daphne was sworn into the RAF CID (Criminal Investigation Department) to vet civilian workers for connections with fifth columnists, but her skills acquired in her pre-war career as a photographer were ignored.

I am terribly busy. Just by chance they have put me on to getting all the recruits photographed on arrival. I do sometimes 200 a day. An outside man, who is very hopeless takes them and I have to see all their descriptions tally and numbers. It's simply awful – I had to do [it] single handed until I couldn't, so a Sergeant helps me now, but even then we never finish before 9–10 pm every night.

Risking her life for that of an injured airman had brought her glory, but not job satisfaction. Her role in the propaganda machine did give her a chance to visit her mother and home on the Cornish coast at St Ives, a town filled with refugees and artists.

Am to do Cornish recruiting for 8 or 9 days as it is St Ives and Penzance War Weapons Week. I come down by train on the

Thursday 24th and look round and confirm arrangements of Friday. On Saturday be present at the opening of the War Weapons [Week] St Ives. In the evening attend a dinner and meeting and Boxing Match at St Ives.

Her public relations itinerary continued at St Just and Helston. This was a prestigious role, and Daphne had a corporal to drive her and another officer to accompany her. Her appearance at War Weapons Week parades was intended to act as a fundraising boost. In one week Liverpool raised £11,500,000 in voluntary contributions, and even small towns raised enormous sums of money in these regular events. But Phyllis Warner was surprised that War Weapons Week events did not capitalize on the glamour of men and women in uniform.

This war has been marked by a complete absence of military bands, processions or colourful uniforms. Much as I hate that kind of thing in peace time, I think that while we are at war we might as well get what fun we can out of it. Even this week there has been a very half-hearted attempt at it. A few dingy ARP processions, headed by a skeleton of a band, plus a tank and a Messerschmidt in Trafalgar Square. Nobody seems a bit interested in the Messerschmidt, but there are men and boys climbing over the tank all the time – another tank in Holborn is an equal attraction. When I was staying at Aston Tyrrold (a little village) in Berkshire they were having their War Weapons Week. They had an exhibition of all their local antiques and an auction sale at which a pound of butter fetched £10, and two chocolate bars another £10.

War Weapons Week at Twickenham on the outskirts of London had a different flavour. It was opened by Miss Chili Bouchier on 17 May 1941, featured a parade of bulldogs, a Wild West show, fan dancers and white mice, and was kicked off by a football match between Teddington Wanderers and the Free French Forces. Seven days of free entertainment followed, to encourage people to 'Lend Like Helen B Merry And to Hell With the Jerry'. The *Richmond and Twickenham Times* carried an exhortation from Jimmy Knode:

Lend all you can to your country. Remember it is not a bit of good hanging on to your 'cash', it will never win the war in your pocket, or hidden under the bed, or in the cupboard, the old iron pot, under the floor boards, behind the old man's picture on the wall. Some people are even crazy enough to string the money round their necks so that when 'Mr Hitler' calls to collect, he gets the lot. Now be sensible folks, take a bookmaker's tip and be on a sure winner. Lend all you can during the *War Weapons Week* for the sake of dear old Twickenham. Make up your mind today and get ready to part with your hidden treasure before old Nasty knocks the lid off the tin.

It obviously worked, as Twickenham raised £593,344 that year. The activities of one Twickenham secondary school give a snapshot of wartime fundraising. Living on the outskirts of the capital, boys from the Kneller Senior Boys School spent many happy hours picking up 'souvenirs from Jerry'. These pieces of shrapnel and bomb debris were sent to other towns to be put on display, raising money for Spitfire Funds. In his notes for assembly in October 1940, the headmaster recorded other fundraising efforts made by the boys that month.

> Air Raid Exhibition in Hall in aid of Red Cross. Wallis the organiser is worried at lack of support. Please announce the exhibition and the charge ½d.
>
> L Smith of Form 2PB has organised a show in his garden and has given me 4/6½ in aid of the Red Cross. Give him a public word and praise for his initiative.
>
> Ronald Whiting Form 2PA has collected by various means £1.4.6 for Red Cross and £2 for London Air Raid Distress Fund. He has received a personal letter from the Lord Mayor of London, thanking him.

Even family pets were drawn into fundraising for the war effort. Tinker, a Birmingham cat, deserves a special mention: she sold her kittens in exchange for donations to the Red Cross Penny-A-Week Fund.

10
HIGH DAYS AND HOLIDAYS

Farewell to theatres, movies, dances, dinner parties and such pleasures;
we pass our evenings in dug-outs, trying to read, write or talk or play
bridge, so far as the rattle of guns, the roar of planes and the crash of
bombs will allow.
(Phyllis Warner, September 1940)

In the midst of war, and the inevitable separation of family and friends, there was an added poignancy to parties and celebrations. Families toasted the photographs of dead sons and husbands. At Christmas, Wrens hung out socks for Father Christmas and then took turns to creep round in the dark and fill them. Women wrote to faraway husbands, describing tiny, precious objects gathered to poke into socks for their children. Women on the YMCA tea-car run filled stockings for men spending Christmas Day at anti-aircraft batteries and barrage balloon sites. Couples were married in the midst of air raids, babies were christened, and dance halls were thronged with swaying couples aware that this might be their last evening of happiness. Going out could be dangerous: several dance halls and cinemas were bombed. Many civilians felt guilty at the contrast between life on the Home Front and the life of men in the front line.

Phyllis Warner's gloomy prediction that the war signalled the end of social pleasures had a ring of truth. Cinemas and theatres had closed at the outset of war, though they subsequently reopened. But she soon found that shelterers, as they scuttled underground at night, made the most of this new opportunity to socialize. Two weeks later she wrote:

We really have quite good fun in our basement shelter. Last night

somebody brought a guitar, and we sang negro spirituals, sea shanties and part songs until lights out.

By December these shelter singsongs had developed into large social occasions.

Ten of us went to a singing party tonight to our nearest public shelter. It houses about 250. We sang John Brown's body, Genevieve, Under the Lilacs, Upidee, Juanita, Drink to me Only, Shenandoah, Sweet and Low and the Swanee River with the whole company joining in the easy ones. This shelter has a programme committee and I was interested to see this week's schedule. Monday – Keep Fit Class, Darts. Tuesday – Concert followed by a religious service. Wednesday – Musical Evening – contributions welcomed by members of the shelter. Thursday – religious service. Concert by Father Adams and Father Knight of the Parish Church. Friday – Whist Drive. Saturday – Keep Fit class. Religious Service followed by dancing. The shelter is lucky in having an excellent piano lent 'for the duration' but people think it is safer down there than in their own homes. The shelterers seem to be enjoying their social activities so much that I wondered if they would ever want to go back to their own family life again.

Phyllis lived in the Mary Ward Settlement in London, where young intellectuals and idealists, often university students, lived in the slums and did voluntary work there.

In our shelter, we have devised a programme which provides a different fixture for every night of the week. Chief limitation is the necessity for sleeping in the shelter nearly all the members who come to the classes. We have physical training on Mondays, choir on Tuesday, play reading and dramatics on Wednesday, organised games on Thursday, debates on Friday and dancing on Saturday – shelter dancing is strenuous as it has to be done on a concrete floor. Play reading and the debates are outstandingly successful, much livelier than they were in pre-Blitz days.

A war-weary population grabbed every opportunity for fun. There were trips to the pantomime, theatre and ballet; and above all there was the cinema, visited several times a week by many diarists. Many of the films were morale-boosting tales of courage and 'derring-do'. Phyllis went to see *Kipps* in 1941.

> At the beginning the trailing skirts, high collars, queer bicycles and so on made it seem as remote as the dark ages, but we were soon swept up in an entirely natural and believable love story. By the time it finished, that uncomplicated world seemed far more real than the world of shattered buildings and bits of charred paper from the last raid still blowing about the streets, into which we emerged.

Dr JP McHutchison, a veteran of World War I, was not a frequent cinemagoer but in 1940 he was at an evening show at The Picture House in Glasgow when the red 'Air Raid Warning' sign flashed up on the screen.

> The manager was clapped heartily after he made the announcement, and only two persons left (and they may have been ARP workers). In my desire to get back to Airdrie, I left in ¼ hour and was only the fourth person to leave. Such courage on the part of the large audience in such a vulnerable building, made one proud and confident of our ability to stand up to Nazi terrorism. Folks too on the street were quite nonchalant as I made my way (the warning still on) to the bus stand, and the all-clear went after 20 minutes, just as my bus was leaving the station.

Phyllis Warner had a similar experience of the 'British stiff upper lip'.

> Today I attended a Promenade Concert at the Queens Hall, where the entire ground-floor space is given up to standing-room. It was a Beethoven Concert, and although the warning had gone, the entire hall was packed with a mammoth audience. On to a theatre where a further warning had no effect on a big audience, and then to a restaurant jam-packed with jovial beings and home through streets whizzing with traffic under an impressive display

of searchlights. There is now lunchtime ballet at the Arts Theatre, and an enterprising manager has put on matinees of the little acted *All's Well That Ends Well* at the Vaudeville. (Has this play un-acted for seventy years been chosen for its title?) At the Ballet, we had a special performance from a dancer on brief military leave who explained he 'just had time to do Giselle for us before he must return to his gun'!

Going out held its own dangers, particularly in the blackout, as pedestrians picked their way past bomb craters and sandbags. Ernie and May Britton lived in the London suburbs.

> We used to go to the pictures on Saturdays but now May is working and gets so tired we don't go as she very much needs tea and generally we prefer not to be out o' nights. Getting home in the blackout is a bit of a burden and it takes the gilt off.

Double summer time had been introduced to benefit farmers, but it also benefited theatregoers like Phyllis Warner.

> The theatres are all packed out because everybody is having an orgy of play-going whilst the black out still permits. There aren't many shows to choose from, but just because there are so few, the casts are all-star and the acting super. This is particularly true of *Blithe Spirit*, Noel Coward's airy trifle of wild improbability which Margaret Rutherford, Cecil Parker, Fay Compton and Kay Hammond make appear positively credible. How like Noel Coward to concoct even now a comedy that is completely original and adroitly fitted to the times. I went to a matinee on a stuffy Turkish-Bath day of pouring rain, with an incipient headache and a sullen temper, and in no time was laughing delightedly at its utter nonsense.

Going for an evening out in the provinces was an even better experience, a rare indulgence for Phyllis in January 1942.

> Came down to Oxford to spend a weekend with Maisie. GR

took me to dinner at the Mitre, and to the theatre to see *Hedda Gabler*. I hadn't been to an evening theatre for six months so it was quite an occasion. Strangest sensation was walking home afterwards through streets thronged with people. In London after dark you only see wardens and policemen, and an occasional belated pedestrian tearing home. Sitting indoors you only hear footsteps at long intervals – the slow tread of the police or the hurried patter of an occasional passer-by – in Oxford you hear footsteps all the time, leisurely, carefree ones at that.

Mollie Dineen went to a New Year's Eve dance to see in the year 1942, while she was looking after evacuees in a tiny Welsh village. The number of male partners was boosted by men from the nearby RAF camp.

The floor was frightfully crowded, but who cares anyway. It was my first dance for over two years, and I was very nervous at first, but the boys were good and I danced with John, Bill, Harold and Ted and enjoyed every moment. Soon it is 12pm as the clock strikes, the band played the National Anthem and not a sound is heard; hundreds of men and women, many in uniform stand stiffly to attention, ready to stand and defend their land as the New Year dawns. Then cheers and kisses all round.

Pamela Higgins, a widow living in Cheshire, had cut down on her entertaining because of the war. But she wrote to her son Stephen:

Next Sunday I am having about 12 to 15 people to tea and the following Friday the 12th I am having a dinner party. Last week I felt so depressed I thought 'come, this will not do at all', so I telephoned to various friends that live near to ask them to come and to put on their prettiest frocks. I don't think the men will change. Everyone was delighted and thought it a marvellous idea. The meal will have to be very simple, soup, cold tongue and chicken and sweets.

In 1941 an anonymous diarist went to the President's Dinner, United

Kingdom Commercial Travellers Association (Grimsby branch). His fare was luxurious.

> For dinner we had Hors d'Oeuvres, oxtail soup, roast chicken, Brussels sprouts, roast and mashed potatoes, trifle, fruit tart, cheese and biscuits, celery and coffee. There was also a bar. Not so bad after two years and four months of war!

At times the contrast between life on the Home Front and life in the front line gave civilians a guilty conscience. But places of entertainment were not immune from the trappings of war. Phyllis Warner had a memorable night out at the Savoy Hotel in London.

> Tonight I had a delirious return to peacetime living – I put on formal clothes and went to the Savoy, where gaiety survives even in an air-raid. At 9pm we were driving in pitchy darkness through completely empty streets – with the guns thudding overhead and shrapnel pattering down on the sidewalks. I wasn't too happy about it, having seen a few cars with large shrapnel holes in their roofs, and was glad to find myself in the hotel Air Raid Shelter, where guests dine dance and sleep. The Savoy doesn't pretend that there isn't a war on. It makes no attempt to disguise the forest of girders which support the ceiling, nor the piles of sandbags that prop up the walls – beyond painting them red, white and blue that is. The Air Raid shelter used to be the Lincoln Room, and although Lincoln's statue has disappeared behind the boarding of the windows, the Stars and Stripes still decorate the walls. There were about three hundred people dining and dancing including Lord Beaverbrook, Minister of Aircraft Production, and Mr Herbert Morrison celebrating his new appointment as Home Secretary. An elaborate six-course meal was good testimony to the adequacy of our food supply, and evidently the bombs on each side of the hotel had had no effect on its cellars. As we danced to Carroll Gibbons Band the guns added unrehearsed effects, so that we had 'a nightingale – *bang* – sang in – *thud* – Berkeley Square – *crash*' and 'Franklin D – *woof* – Roosevelt

Jones – *smash*.' Nobody appeared to mind. But we were told that one night a bomb landed so close, that only Lieutenant Davies of the Bomb Disposal Squad that saved St Paul's was entirely unmoved! As the perils of the streets and the absence of taxis make it impossible to go home till daylight the hotel provides its dinner guests with mattresses and pillows in the safety of the basement. It is an experience to sleep in Evening dress on the floor of the Savoy! Hundreds of guests slumber side by side in this de luxe shelter. Its spacious first-aid room contained only three casualties, victims of the rain of shrapnel. Distinguished residents of the hotel were wandering around in dressing gowns. As we drove through the streets in the drizzly dawn, people were emerging from shelters to be greeted by the coffee-stalls and mobile canteens that are now so quickly on the streets at the All Clear.

While nightlife in the capital may have been dim but undaunted, things were somewhat different up in Shapinsay in the Orkney Islands. Teenager Bessie Skea was disgusted that the adults had seen fit to stop all forms of entertainment when war broke out.

There won't be any more fine times until this war is over. Shapinsay is too bad; they've stopped everything; dances, concerts, ploughing match, shows; practically everything that can be stopped. Of course we have a great many Terriers [Territorial Army] away, thirty five I think, and the older people believe it isn't right to have anything enjoyable – but what on earth is to hinder us having Red Cross concerts in aid of the troops? All the youngsters are complaining and longing for a dance – myself included – and I do think it's too bad. They won't even have a Farmer's Union Social! There is the SWRI, Women's Guild and Bible Class of course, but nothing else except knitting socks! The rest of Orkney is not cutting out anything – but it's no good grumbling.

Munitions worker Louie White recorded few parties in her diary. Her main forms of entertainment were trips to the cinema, but in January 1944 she went to a dance thrown by her firm, the Blackburn Aircraft Company, where she was currently working the night shift.

> Got up at 4pm and ironed my burgundy dress. After tea I got changed and went to Blackburns dance. Met Vivien who had brought a Polish soldier called Casmere. She introduced us and we all kept together. We went to work but I was too tired to do anything at all.

Social occasions were enlivened by the presence of glamorous foreigners. Dance halls were crowded with young men and women, often in uniform, far from home, clutching at an evening of escapism. Christmas rarely offered such respite, bringing as it did thoughts of those far from home. Three months after the start of the London Blitz, the nation celebrated Christmas – rather quietly in the case of Phyllis Warner's family.

> There was little present-giving except to the children, and little card-sending on account of the paper shortage. Everyone so faithfully obeyed the instruction to post early that in thousands of households the postman didn't call at all on Christmas Day.
> We entertained ourselves by showing the films we made in the days of peace, and a nostalgic display it was. Gendarmes in the Champs Elysées, the roofs of Moscow, Ascot Races, Henley Regatta, New York Harbour and the shining decks of the Empress of Britain – sights that seem to speak of some far off idyll. But no doubt when peace returns we shall look back half nostalgic for the excitements and endurances of the war.

A year later Christmas celebrations had become even more frugal. Like many others she spent Christmas Day in the office.

> This is a most un-Christmassy Christmas, Christmas cards are pretty well in abeyance because of scarcity of paper, and presents are very nearly out too because of the necessity to cut consumption. I've sent no cards at all and only three useful gift tokens. It will be a Christmas without chocolates, or fruit or nuts, and short of drinks and cigarettes; there are no Christmas

decorations, the stores look much as usual, and I haven't heard a single carol. Most un-Christmassy of all are the fantastic prices being charged for ordinary goods, holly at 6d a twig is typical of this racket. Everything is being done to discourage travel, by taking off trains and issuing warnings that passengers will be left standing on the platform. I'm going to stay in London and work at the office as usual on Christmas day, a dreary prospect. But I'm in no spirit for Christmas cheer while P is in danger in Malaya, and while Hong Kong faces its last agony with desperate, hopeless courage.

Newspaper and radio warnings urged the population not to travel at holiday time, as trains were already crowded with troops coming home on leave and parents of evacuees visiting their children. Long queues formed for tickets. Phyllis Warner delayed her journey back to her family in Warwickshire until after Christmas that year.

I went home on Saturday afternoon [28 December]. Coming back on Monday the trains were more crowded than I have ever known, for the first time I really did see throngs of passengers left behind on the platform.

Christmas trees, when they could be found, were decorated with coloured buttons and earrings. Ethel Mattison, with no children of her own, managed to find a tree for her sister's children.

Today I brought home a Christmas Tree and potted it and have put it in the scullery for a surprise. They probably won't see it for a day or two, because we never go into the scullery when the garden isn't used. We are collecting things piecemeal, such as quarters of sweets and odd bars of chocolate. Other things seem plentiful enough, I mean decorations, books and toys, but of course there is no fruit at all.

Toys were sold at inflated prices and rescue worker Bill Regan scavenged the bombsites of the Isle of Dogs to find presents for his daughters. Old toys and doll's prams were refurbished, and as toys became scarce people made wooden toys and toy animals. In Worthing, physiotherapist Joan Strange and her carol party still went carol singing.

> Our carol party gave its party to the ex-servicemen at Gifford House. The war has upset many of these men, and matron said several had died without putting up much of a struggle in consequence. They'd imagined they'd fought '14–18 to prevent this sort of thing happening again in a lifetime.

As a coastal town, Worthing was full of troops, and the carol singers brought them a little Christmas cheer, despite wartime conditions.

> We were usually over 20 strong and in spite of intense darkness, sirens (which necessitated very dim torches), rain and biting winds we made a record sum of £23. We went out 6 nights in all, including singing to the soldiers at the YMCA canteen and ARP and FAP [First Aid Post] at the Town Hall. One night half the party got lost in the blackout, but on the whole we managed very well and got asked in most nights for hot drinks etc.

On a visit to see her sister Kit in London in July 1941, Joan was astonished to see Londoners still enjoying some of the peacetime pleasures in Hyde Park.

> In Hyde Park there is a central dump for rubble etc – it's a young mountain with a road over it. I wonder how many houses have helped make it – thousands? Next to the mountain were the bowlers, playing hard! Hundreds were bathing in the Serpentine and allotments abound everywhere! I bought some tennis balls (they are *very scarce*) @ 19/6 a dozen! The orators very amusing. Hyde Park is also an anti-aircraft gun centre and ARP shelter centre, horrid. But the grown ups still sail boats on the pond.

Joan had been an avid pre-war tennis player, but did not find much time to play during the war; her free time was consumed by fundraising, digging her allotment and her work at the ARP control centre. In 1943 she finally picked up her racquet.

I had a game of tennis with Dutch and Christine and a young Canadian up at the club this afternoon. It was the first time I'd played there for three years. The place looked awful – only two courts are usable, weeds are everywhere, the ARP have two huts there, and allotments have been dug in the car park. The working men's club, which was bombed in the road, now use the pavilion. So it was tennis under wartime conditions, especially as the balls were awful and the net very bad.

After the retreat from Dunkirk in 1940, many people gave up their holidays to continue in war work. A year later Ethel Mattison, who worked at the Food Office, dealing with ration books, wrote to her sister in America:

> It has become official that we are to have only one week's holiday this year. I think this is plum crazy and very short sighted, especially for people working in conditions that prevail in our office – no natural light and a very inadequate 'conditioned air' system. I think it likely that most people will find it necessary to take a week off sick. However to make the most of the summer Eileen and I have decided to have weekends on the river such as we had last year. It won't be the same without the men of course, but it should do us good physically. It's a cheap way of spending a weekend and very restful and peaceful.

Holidaymakers found accommodation difficult to get, as boarding houses and hotels were full of troops and evacuees. Phyllis Warner stayed with friends when she spent a week in her favourite English county, Devon.

> The holiday has been heaven. Nothing much to it, a few bathes, some dancing, some tennis, some walking, a lot of lazy sitting in adorable little country pubs, bending the elbow and chatting idly, and occasionally laughing uproariously. I wonder if I ought to have enjoyed it so much in a world in which thousands are dying in man-made agony, millions losing their most cherished hopes and treasures, a world in which it is the best and most splendid who are falling in combat daily. This is the same guilty feeling I used to have in the year before the raids when the agony

Pubs were not the normal realm of women before the war, but the village inn offered war workers like these Land Army girls an opportunity to socialize, and to get away from cramped lodgings. Though bottled beer became increasingly scarce, draught was readily available.

was elsewhere. A winter of London blitz removed that trouble – I snatched at such pleasures as came my way without a pang. But now that life is placid here, I'm beginning to worry again.

Men in the Forces were sometimes given leave at short notice. Munitions worker Louie White spent a romantic week at the Yorkshire seaside resort of Scarborough in June 1943, when her husband Jack was given a week's leave from the RAF. They had been married a little over two years.

In the morning went in a canoe on the lake. It was grand better than rowing. Saw a bomber on the North Beach, one of ours that had come down during the night. It broke up later in the day. Saw another convoy complete with barrage balloons. Heard gunfire out at sea. Went in the pool after dinner, then in a canoe again after tea. Spent our last night on Castle Hill. The two bays were beautiful, and the sea was like silver.

A few days after that week of sparkling sea and sand, Jack was shot down and listed as missing, presumed dead.

Apart from the restrictions of travel and accommodation, holiday preparations in themselves were far from simple, as physiotherapist Joan Strange recorded in August 1942.

It was a great effort getting ready for a wartime holiday – in addition to the usual arrangements to be made about patients etc I had to fix up a deputy at the Report Centre, 2 canteens and fire watchers. Then we had to tell the Warden we should be away and tell him our key was at Mr Tyrers. We turned off water, gas and electricity and only half drew the curtains to enable ARP wardens to look inside in case of incendiary bomb trouble. I got 'emergency' food cards for two weeks and arranged for our paper (*Daily Telegraph*) to be delivered at the Shepherds. If you cancel its delivery altogether it's impossible to get it again on our return.

Joan and her sister Kit were among the thousands who responded to a Government campaign to take a working holiday on a farm. They cycled 60 miles to an agricultural camp.

We arrived soon after 7 o'clock and discovered it is a real camp of tents. I'd hoped it might be in a building. We'd been told to bring plates, cutlery and a tea cloth, and we had an evening meal straight away. We were given a ground sheet and blankets and a straw mattress! The camp is in a lovely situation there are between 250–300 people. To bed early and slept fairly well.

Aug 24th – Up at 6am and queued for breakfast at 7am. Then queued again for work. There seems some difficulty about work. The farmers send in lorries for so many people but usually there are more people than the farmers need. We were not lucky so took our bicycles and rode to Harpenden. It was a lovely day.

Aug 25 – Eleven of us went by lorry (with about 30 others – terrific pack) to Stranghams farm where we were met by a very nice foreman. We were shown how to stook wheat and we worked well all day. We had a meal at midday provided by the camp – bread and margarine, meat (dehydrated) pies and tea made at a neighbouring cottage. We all earned 5/10 and arrived back in the lorry at about 7.30. Most of the people are from London or the north and there are a few foreigners. Something is organised in the camp most evenings but Kit and I go to our hard and boney beds early.

The holiday was not an unmitigated success for these two middle-class ladies. Pouring rain turned the camp into a quagmire and so, as there seemed little work to do, they cycled up to London to stay with friends.

Allotments sprang up in bomb craters, roadsides and even in the Tower of London moat as part of the Dig for Victory campaign. Joan Strange spent many hours on her allotment, surrounded by the old boys who dug, weeded and planted to supplement their rations.

For newly widowed munitions worker Louie White, working on a farm far from her factory job in Leeds was an adventure and a delight. Her diary entries, which had become brief and monotonous after her husband had been shot down, suddenly sparked to life. He had been missing 54 weeks by July 1944, when she and a friend, Peg, travelled by train to Crayke Castle, near Alne in Northumbria.

> A lorry came to meet us, and what a laugh we had bundled together. The castle where we are spending a farming holiday at Crayke is lovely. Built on top of a hill with the village just below, it looks like a grim fortress, but looks much bigger and milder when you ride up the drive to the door. The window is a real castle one with bars and a very wide window sill.

Although she was staying in a fairytale castle, Louie shared a room with eight others. They worked hard and played hard.

> Went to Sparrows Field and weeded carrots, not bad at all. Finished at 5 came home in a lorry. At night went to a dance in Easingwold. Had a marvellous time.
>
> *July 6* – Weeding again.
> *July 7* – Last day at weeding. Went to a dance and rode back in the lorries under a lovely harvest moon. The sky was full of planes lit up.

School children were also asked to go and work on farms in their holidays, all as part of the nation's drive for more food.

The basic raw materials for celebrations were scarce, as Phyllis Warner described in her diary in April 1941.

> Went to Aunt Jennie's Golden wedding. There were many apologies for a meagre feast, but probably it compared favourably with 1891, when tomatoes and grapefruit and canned goods and other things we now lament were still unknown. But 1891 had its advantages, at least they had a chance to get married in peace, and not the way their youngest daughter

did last autumn, having to keep dashing into the church crypt during the ceremony, and into the coal cellar during the reception.

The romance of a couple's wedding day was heightened by the uncertainties of war. Peg Cotton's daughter Alix had a fairytale wedding when she was married to a naval flyer, Peter Dean, in October 1939.

The service was to be at four-thirty. Firstly, because English law prohibited such after six pm and secondly, because the blackout must be considered. In spite of the war, the 100-odd gas masks accompanying the guests, and Pete's orders to report back to his Naval Air Base on the very next day, nothing could detract from Alix's loveliness as she came down the aisle of that old English church on her father's arm in her pale blue costume, her Grandmother Cotton's tiny ermine hat and muff, and a corsage of pale pink roses and lilies-of-the-valley. Awaiting her stood Pete and his Best man, Rob D'Almaine, Lieutenant on a submarine. Resplendent in their Naval uniforms. They seemed young heroes of a new Crusade.

The new Mrs Dean soon discovered she was pregnant, but Pete Dean was never to meet his daughter: he was killed test-flying a new plane. On doctor's orders Peg Cotton had to keep the news from her daughter until the baby was born a few weeks later. Penelope Marianne Dean was christened on 11 September 1940. The Blitz had just begun its nightly tune as Peg Cotton wrote her diary that evening:

I am writing, with the tea trolley as desk, in the lower hall. The rest of the gang are asleep – apparently. There has been, and still is, an almost continuous roar of guns. The flat shivers and trembles with the impact of solid sound upon its walls. The top of the trolley vibrates beneath my arms. Well, it seems that, indeed, one can get used to anything! Besides, what else can one do save carry-on? Penny was to be christened this afternoon at 4:20, but at that hour the Jerrys and the RAF staged a dog-fight right over Regency Lodge. Shrapnel fell in the courtyard. Endeavouring to do as everyone else does – carry on as normally as possible – I continued to arrange the flowers, and chatted with the family and Dorothy and Tony, who had joined us about four o'clock, just before the Siren went. Well, the 'All Clear' finally went, shortly before 5 o'clock. So Dick drove us around to the church – St Paul's Church, Avenue Road, a block from our flat, the same little church in which Alix and dear Pete were married almost a year ago, on October 7th, 1939.

We were all grouped about the baptismal font, and Mr Malet, the Vicar, had just given baby her name, 'Penelope Marianne' and had baptized her for the third time, 'And of the Holy Ghost,' when the Sirens went, and the Devil was upon us again. 'Shall I proceed?' asked Mr Malet, 'Or do you care to go down to the shelter?' We elected to finish the ceremony. Then rushed Penny home in the car – the men following on foot, keeping under the trees as the AA guns were in action. Alas, none of the Godparents could attend the Christening, and only one friend, Hartley Davies, appeared – because of the darned raids. However, we (the family) and Dorothy, Tony, Hartley and Mr Malet assembled here afterwards in the flat, and drank dear little Penny's health in sherry and had a piece of Martha's fine fruit cake, iced, and decorated with pink and white ribbons. Elsie and Frank almost got to the Christening. But the 4 o'clock raid drove them into a roadside shelter, and the AA fire kept them under cover until too late. A shame!

Phyllis Warner went to a wedding in Cambridge in November 1940 and expressed the pleasure of leaving the Blitz behind and going to

> . . . simple functions at which one has friends rarely seen in wartime. This was a cheerful informal gathering and most of us seized the chance to stay overnight and sleep in a real bed. On a clear autumn morning the lovely pinnacles and towers of Cambridge looked more gracious and heart-lifting than ever. I got a lift back to London by automobile – a rare treat nowadays – we enjoyed the ride like ten year olds.

As the war entered its third year, Joan Strange went to a friend's wedding. By this time icing sugar was a rarity, and growers had planted vegetables in their greenhouses rather than flowers.

> I went to Betty Patching's wedding and to her wartime reception at Cranleigh Court afterwards. Really quite a 'do'! The 'iced' cake was very cleverly camouflaged – the white icing being some rice paper neatly placed on top and around. The inside was quite good. Almond icing is still allowed if you can get the almonds (which are usually peanuts!).

11
FRIENDLY ALIENS

God it's a disheartening business. Letters come every day from Vienna, imploring me to do something, to get visas, labour permits, temporary permits – anything, to go anywhere for friends.
(Isabelle Granger, 27 June 1938)

Refugees from the Nazi regime had been arriving in Britain long before war was declared on 3 September 1939. Those with friends in Germany and Austria were well aware of Hitler's hostility to the Jews, but appeasement of Herr Hitler was the watchword of the 1930s and the British Government was not keen to offer asylum to persecuted men and women. With hindsight the facts of the final solution are now known, and the persecution that preceded it. But concentration camps were a fact even before the outbreak of war – a fact that was also known to some Britons. Isabelle Granger, a schoolmistress, spent her holidays travelling on the Continent. She was passionate about the alpine meadows scattered with wild flowers, and equally passionately concerned about her many friends scattered through the countries that Hitler was eyeing greedily.

> The young Scheus, thank God, have got a job. Their baby is alas, with Herta's mother in Vienna, under police supervision, so all my good plans for fetching her are useless – her disappearance would coincide with Mrs Puegger's loss of pension, and her son's going to a concentration camp. The rest of my friends are trickling out or shooting themselves. Three months of ceaseless correspondence have resulted in three Jewish friends of mine getting jobs – one here, one in France, one in the United States and that's been my sole contribution to 'civilisation'. One of my best friends, a pacifist from the Wachau, disappeared, I got news

last week from a servant of his to say he was proud to say he'd denounced the 'infamous traitor'.

By the summer of 1939 her letters to a friend in British Columbia had become angry and bitter at the bureaucracy she was dealing with in her attempts to help refugees.

> We are conditioned by bolts from the blue, sudden phone calls,
> appeals that must be answered at once, an important feeling that
> if I don't act at once by ringing up a committee in London, or
> wiring a committee in Vienna, or standing in a queue in order
> personally to hand in some poor wretch's papers, then something
> will go badly wrong for someone, and that it will be my fault.
> It's like existing in a lunatic asylum, my head is crammed with
> shibboleths and rules.

Many with close friends and contacts in continental Europe had recognized the dangers of Hitler and his National Socialists long before war was declared. On 3 September millions of Britons listened to Chamberlain's historic announcement that 'this country is at war'. Isabelle Granger felt a sense of relief.

> That day for me has no war significance, quite on the contrary it
> signified a personal cessation of hostilities and a relegation of the
> struggle to other people – a calm and comforting conception.

Isabelle had already given a home to a German friend, Elisabeth Gruber, known as Lillibet, who with the advent of war was classified as an enemy alien. In May 1940, as Britain's continental neighbours were falling under Nazi rule, Isabelle wrote to British Columbia again.

> If you get this, and if you hear we're blown to atoms here, would
> you please do something for me: get in touch and make sure
> my executors give my remnants of fortune and life insurance to
> Lillibet. I feel as her nationality is still enemy she'll need a good
> deal of bolstering up, and she knows all my interests and what to
> do with all the people I've guaranteed lately.

Miss Granger was one of those sympathizers in England prepared to act as guarantor to refugees, by giving their names and bank account details to the Government. In Germany, Martha Ulrich had a stunning portrait taken of her and her son Klaus, which she hoped would appeal to an American sponsor. An aunt and her family had escaped to America in 1938, but in June 1939 Klaus was found a place on the *Kindertransport*. In later years he told his story.

> We were allowed one large case and one piece of hand luggage. It was all so exciting, I was going to England, though I had not the foggiest notion what to expect, or even where exactly in England I was going, and didn't care. Mother cried. She was not a crying sort of person, I just couldn't understand it.

This was not a trainload of excited modern children rushing from carriage to carriage making new friends.

> We were cowed, you have to remember what we had been used to.

On the journey through Holland, Dutch friends met the train with a bag of food for the hungry 12-year-old. But when he arrived at Liverpool Street station the reception was very different.

> We were taken to a nearby gymnasium and sat on benches round the wall. Strange people came, looking not at us, but at the labels round our necks.

Despite his limited English, on arrival in Britain Klaus Ulrich began to write his diary in his new adopted language. The scruffy pencil entries were very different from the neat Gothic script he had employed in Germany. He had been taken in by an Oxford don, Mr Moore, and his wife.

> Two or three years earlier I had been given a notebook, a rather elegant affair with a cloth binding and plain blank pages. There are entries for two 1938 periods in, for a ten-year-old, pretty good German writing. Then there is a gap until that Autumn of 1939, when I noted that I asked Mrs Moore to teach me to

Martha Ulrich and her son Klaus had this portrait taken at the beginning of 1939, hoping it would appeal to an American sponsor and allow them to escape from Germany. Klaus brought the photograph with him to Britain. Martha was to die in a concentration camp.

darn my socks, because I needed to be able to look after myself. The handwriting had changed from that of a neat well-ordered German ten-year-old's to that of a rather disturbed English child – tangible evidence of an inner turmoil.

Like Klaus Ulrich, many refugees were taken in by complete strangers. On 21 April, 1939, in the genteel seaside resort of Worthing, Joan Strange welcomed a family of Jewish refugees from Vienna: Mr and Mrs Beermann and their children Henry and two-year-old Elizabeth.

The Beermanns are impressed with English ways, for instance that we do not lock our front doors in the daytime – that our police are friendly – that they are allowed free entry to cinema etc. For months fear has reigned in their hearts, now – safety and self-confidence.

Easing them into their new life, Joan got Henry a library card and found him a bicycle, and within two days he was celebrating St George's Day at St Paul's with hundreds of other scouts. She and her elderly mother put up the Beermanns in their own home, but Joan was also preparing for their successors.

> *May 8th–May 17th 1939* – Missed writing diary because Mrs Lymes and I 'finished' the refugee house (72 Canterbury Road) and it took all my spare time. We got the stuff from all over Worthing and district and the finished product is really quite nice. Some people have been awfully generous, others have a very funny idea of refugees and quite a lot of stuff had to be burnt.

Although she was an active member of the town's refugee committee, Joan had used her own money to buy the house in Canterbury Road. In December she wrote in her diary:

> There are over 1,000 aliens in West Sussex and as Worthing is the only place with a committee, about 500 in Worthing.

As a physiotherapist and masseur, Joan also had refugees among her patients.

> *May 27th* – Had Dr Fleischman as a patient. A political refugee from Czechoslovakia – had been beaten by Nazis in a concentration camp and paralysed – a very nice man – a lawyer.

Joan acted as a taxi service, taking her protégés to register at the police station, giving the children days out at the seaside and taking families for drives into the surrounding countryside. After Poland's collapse, she recorded the impact on her new friends.

September 18th – Our refugees are depressed about it but they were cheered up on Saturday morning when Mr Ritter heard a most interesting broadcast from a German woman belonging to a secret anti-Nazi society, urging women to prevent more bloodshed. She hopes to broadcast again next Saturday. The end of her speech was jammed.

That anonymous broadcaster was not mentioned again. Mr Ritter, the avid listener, was one of many Jews who escaped and anglicized their names – in his case from Rittesheim. Just as many of these refugees took a decision to speak only English after their escape, this anglicization of names was common practice. Klaus Ulrich did the same, changing his forename and surname. He spent the summer of 1939 at Eastbourne, taken in by a young couple, until war was declared.

That made me into an 'enemy alien'. Though it was some time before that reality took hold, it was significant to me none-the-less. I had been an outcast so long, and during this lovely summer I had started to belong. Now it was back to being an outcast. All the people with whom I came into contact were as pleasant as ever they had been. But it is certain that, just as I felt outcast for being a beastly Jew, now I felt outcast again for being a beastly German.

Foreigners were classified as either friendly aliens or enemy aliens, with accompanying restrictions. The Cotton family in London, being Americans, were friendly aliens and had to conform to a midnight curfew. Joan Strange had both groups among her circle of Worthing refugees.

Friendly aliens can go outside the five mile limit from Worthing – not so the Beermans who are 'enemy aliens'! They may leave only with police permission.

In May 1940 Joan began to record the internment of the men and its impact on those living in her 'refugee house' at Canterbury Road.

May 23rd 1940 – We had all Canterbury Road to tea and

Mrs Schleichter and Peter too – nine of us! The women who've lost husbands are so sad and upset, almost as if they were dead. It's because the men aren't allowed to write and Mrs Thorneycroft telephones to me to say the men are being moved to —?

This secrecy and internment werre understandable precautions in time of war. Isabelle Granger felt the tension as her numerous refugee friends in London were sent to internment camps.

Every ring at the bell seemed to herald Lillibet's departure. It cluttered up our lives too, as well as making us nervous and apprehensive. I always came home to find babies screaming who had been left to spend the day while their young mothers trudged from the Home Office to Scotland Yard, trying to find out where their husbands had gone to; and old ladies who couldn't afford a phone and whose English was too shaky to warrant their using one so they sought information about sons and husbands – Lillibet has these to cope with all day and to feed and generally prop up. Now, thank God, enough dust has been raised against this disgraceful persecution of our allies, to put at least a temporary stop to the wholesale internment – though I shan't stop interfering till they let out Friedl Scheu, one of the best brains and most honest and lovable of all democratic Austrians.

Dr Enoch, a Jewish research chemist, had escaped from Germany in 1939. He had managed to establish himself in business, but as an alien had to appear at the tribunals set up to root out Nazi sympathizers.

We were interrogated very thoroughly. We were questioned not only about ourselves but about our families, our ancestors, our friends. Those who came out worst were interned immediately. For the others it was only a question of time, as the fear of spies, of 'Fifth columnists' became really grotesque. So I was visited one day, by two officers of Scotland Yard, who demanded to see the attic of our house. I had recently installed a small room into it, and for light a small roof window was put into the roof. Some people had intimated that this roof window had been made with the purpose of giving light signals to the enemy. One of the officers took a chair and looked out of the window. I don't know what he expected to see.

Dr Enoch's job at a pharmaceutical laboratory gave the police added 'grounds' for suspicion.

> Three officers came and asked me, what would happen if I would bring some of my typhus bacilli in to the water supply system. Apparently they thought I could do this by pouring them into the sink or flushing them down the toilet.

On 6 June 1940 his turn arrived for internment. Two officers from Scotland Yard came to fetch him.

> I was allowed to take with me only the most necessary things. I declared that I could not leave the laboratory, which contained dangerous bacteria, without control.

His escort allowed him to contact an assistant to put the laboratory in order, then he was whisked away. Two days later he was taken to the racecourse at Kempton Park, which had been surrounded with barbed wire for its new role as a holding point for internees.

> In the camp a group of pro German-minded Aryans was formed at once, led by an Austrian baron. This group sympathised quite openly with the Nazis.

None of the men was allowed newspapers or any form of war news.

> The separation from my mother, and the withholding of any news of her and the war was very tormenting. Only after strong pressure, were we allowed to send a printed postcard stating that we were well to our families, but they received these cards only many weeks later.

Friends did manage to track him down and send a basket of strawberries and chocolate, but on 13 June the internees were on the move again.

> We were led through an espalier of soldiers with fixed bayonets to a train, which brought us through the night to Liverpool. In the train to Liverpool I experienced the only sign of friendliness from our guards: A young soldier said: 'I am sorry for you boys.'

Under heavy guard the men arrived at Onchan on the Isle of Man, where enemy aliens aged 16 and over were interned.

> We were accommodated in a big block of boarding houses, which was surrounded by a double fence of wire netting. There were rooms for two to six people who had to sleep mostly in double beds.

Earlier arrivals had purloined furniture, cooking utensils and blankets, leaving the rooms ill equipped for newcomers. Dr Enoch found the food 'very bad and entirely insufficient'.

> Most tormenting was we did not receive news from our families nor of the war. At irregular intervals the camp commander issued some communications, which were hung at two places in the camp, but these were mostly entirely vague. As just at this time the big catastrophes happened in Holland, Belgium and France, a great nervousness developed, which was stirred up intentionally by the Nazi elements in the camp.
> Twice a week we were allowed to write letters of 24 lines each. In urgent cases we could also send telegrams. After more time we were also allowed to receive letters, these and those from us took about 12 days. After the postal connection had been established the mood improved considerably.

Gradually some of the men were transported to Canada, an option that Dr Enoch thought would give him a chance to carry on with his work.

> One day a long list of names of internees was issued. I was very unhappy that my name was not on the list, as I felt myself in

Onchan like being in a mousetrap and ready to be served on a salver to the Nazis in case of invasion.

Another internee offered to swap with him, so the two men went to the camp commander.

> He asked me how old I was, I said 36 years (in effect I was nearly 44 years old). Moved by our entreaties he intimated that I should take the place of the other man when his name would be called. We thanked him and I ran back to my house, packed my things in the greatest hurry and arrived at the gate. The roll call was already in full swing. Apparently the name, Rosenthal, had been called up already, but it was repeated once more at the end of the list. I called 'here' and passed the gate as the last one. I had not even had time to say goodbye to my friends who had stayed in Onchan.

They were packed on to a ship at the Isle of Man port of Douglas and arrived in Liverpool four hours later.

> There we were pressed literally into a shed. It was impossible to sit down. Those who tried to get near the door, were threatened by guards with their arms.

This chance to escape from internment in Britain had given Dr Enoch a sense of relief and optimism. But that mood changed as they were loaded on to the SS *Ettrick* of the P & O Line.

> We were led from the upper deck, deeper and deeper, until we had to pass a passage through barbed wire, which was so narrow we could pass it only in single file. This separated the under-the-water-line holds of the ship from the other parts, which were sealed off hermetically by the barbed wire well. We descended into this airless and lightless inferno. About 1,600 men were pressed into our dungeon. On top of us, but separated by the barbed wire, were 1,000 German prisoners of war. In addition there were very many guards on board the ship. Long rows of tables and benches

were in our quarter, furthermore many hammocks, but although these covered the whole available space, they were hardly sufficient for a third of the internees. The others had to sleep on or under the tables. At night time it was impossible to get from one place to another without crawling over rows of sleeping people. We had to eat, smoke and sleep in the same place, and in the same place were the toilet buckets.

In day time we had to queue for hours to reach the wash room, the toilets, the kitchen, the hospital, or a little space of fresh air in the outside board of the ship. Even the air here was contaminated by the many sea-sick persons who could relieve themselves only here outside the common quarters, and that only in day time. When I heard later that many drowned when the *Arandora Star* (another ship carrying internees) was torpedoed and sunk, I was convinced there had been similar conditions.

Miss Nora O'Connor was deputy commandant of an internment camp for women who had originally been interned on the Isle of Man before moving to the mainland.

The internees were sent to us for screening by M15, before being released to the United States or other neutral countries, where sponsors awaited them with open arms and open purses. They were mainly German and Austrian Jewesses. They came from all walks of life, intellectual, business, professional, and domestic service. The internee with the really dramatic background was Friedelinde Wagner, who bore a startling resemblance to her illustrious grandfather. Hitler's unbounded admiration for Grandpa's works and for all the ideology which the name Wagner implied, accounted for the presence of Friedelinde amongst us. After some months, and several interviews with MI5 she was released 'without a stain upon her character', to study music with Toscanini in South America, but not before she had caused me agonies of frustration trying to teach her to dance.

Nora had been a bridge hostess for troops on the south coast before she took up the post of deputy commandant. She organized fancy dress dances, indoor gymkhanas and bridge drives to entertain the women while they waited to be released. The next intake was 70 internees who were being repatriated to Germany as part of a prisoner exchange.

> I was warned 'They could be dangerous.' It appeared to the Establishment that anyone wishing to be returned to the Vaterland was a potential danger. This struck me as rather pessimistic. Many of the women in question had been interned because they happened to be within reach of Regulation 18b at the outbreak of war, possibly travelling in Allied ships or on holiday in Allied countries and naturally wished to return to their homes and families.

As the 'ragged RAF' was shooting down German planes in the south of England, it is not surprising that there was palpable unease about 'aliens'. Maureen Bolster was a billeting officer for an engineering works, finding accommodation for workers who were attached to the factory.

> The day before yesterday I billeted a man called Fingerhut. He was a foreigner of sorts taken on in the drawing office. Then yesterday I had a phone call from an irate landlord! Did I know I had landed them with a *German* born in Berlin, only just released from internment on the Isle of Man, and who had to report to the police every few days? Dear oh dear! I had to spend half yesterday afternoon trying to pacify the poor wife – apparently the man went there and said 'My name is Fingerhut – I am a *German*,' and demanded this that and the other – a fire in his room and special food etc. I think the poor little woman thought the invasion had begun!

Even Joan Strange, who had many friends among the refugee population, was nervous occasionally. Drivers were encouraged to pick up hitchhikers as one way of saving fuel.

> We picked up an Austrian refugee near Godalming – at least we hope he was! Jack said he might have been an escaped prisoner! Anyhow we only took him a couple of miles.

Isabelle Granger, who dedicated so many years to helping refugees from the Nazis, got the sack from the Foreign Office in 1940 because of these humanitarian activities.

> We were visited by a very pleasant CID man who said certain
> allegations had been made against us, and he named them – I
> was a Government official living with a German [her refugee
> friend Elisabeth Gruber]. We had been heard to criticise the
> Government, though as he explained, we had every right to do
> that, but the Alligators (a nice name for these useful servants
> of England) hadn't liked that. We had met casually in a foreign
> hotel (it reeks of suspicion doesn't it – if only it had been
> Bournemouth) and finally we were passing on information to
> Germany through America, which information, Lillibet told him,
> would be rather obsolete by the time it reached its destination
> in this Blitzkrieg. The detective was kind and stayed to supper
> where he met Margery and two other English women, and
> the tough fiancé of one of them and Friedl Scheu – who was
> horribly overawed at the presence of the police, it recalled raids in
> Larochegasse. He assured Lillibet and me that he was convinced
> the allegations had been made by spiteful people, and that there
> was no word of truth in them – he inferred that as such specific
> lies had been told, the Alligators were well known to us, and led
> us to believe that they might have been found on the staff [of her
> former school]. This doesn't altogether surprise us, as we knew
> one or two had strongly resented our being right about Hitler –
> you cannot imagine how big a crime it is to have known all along
> that he was a menace. He said we ought to hear no more about
> it. He came to tea a week later, and played with two Viennese
> children who were with us, and swopped stories of thief catching,
> for the children's Hitler atrocities, which they related freely.

The kindly sergeant's report led to no further action from Scotland Yard.

> However the Alligators hadn't had their pound of flesh and I
> suppose they got news that Lillibet wasn't interned and that I
> was at large in the Foreign Office. So they wrote to the FO and

pointed out the dangers of allowing a civil servant to live with a German. Unfortunately, in a war, any suspicion connected with Government Offices, is tackled not by the office in question, but by MI5, and so the FO was given the choice of keeping me and turning Lillibet into the street, or getting rid of me. We were both guiltless on all the charges, and we were shadowed and had our phone wires tapped, but when mud is thrown it sticks, and the Government officials have decided to wage war on Hitler now, so they begin by finding Fifth Columnists among the ranks of Hitler's old enemies. It's funny now, to think that, in extremis, when they even found Moseley was dangerous, they decided that my association with an Aryan who renounced her birthright four years ago, and has existed on £70 a year since – because she wouldn't go back to Germany and because she insisted on throwing in her lot with the exiles – was also a menace to the country. There was of course no choice: to turn Lillibet out would have been unwarranted criminal lunacy, and it wouldn't have ended here – next I expect I should have been requested to disassociate myself with aliens in general, so I didn't appease but said I'd go.

So Isabelle Granger went job hunting, finding work as a means test woman, a hated profession assessing the income of the poor for entitlement to welfare payments. Lillibet, who had worked in Germany as an engineer, supplemented their income with cleaning and needlework. But their unpaid work was still helping refugees. Despite her brush with MI5, Isabelle continued to be critical of the authorities.

The refugee population of London (enemy alien one) is very stricken now – they have not been interned wholesale, but forbidden areas have been devised which have served to drive these unhappy people about like a flock of sheep. Then the Home Office has arrested sometimes a whole category, and at others a few chosen sheep from another category. All this has served to create a defeatist and panicky atmosphere which is lamentable and dangerous. All day long we are besieged with people who are frightened, angry and puzzled – and always underfed and therefore lacking in any moral or physical resistance. At times we swear, in the privacy of our kitchen, that we must have a rest from the atmospheric Viennese weltschmertz, but these lapses are momentary and we always repent them at once. In our hearts we know we are fortunate to have the confidence of this neglected, lost population – it's a side of the persecution [of war] that has been insanely neglected and grossly badly treated by the authorities.

Many of her 'flock' found a permanent home in the United States after she had assisted in their battles with officialdom.

Today the Engels, he was a Vienna radio official, leave for the States. The Nazis took his leg off in Dachau, he was there for nine months. He has a heavy wooden peg to hop on now, and money has at last been raised to have a real false leg fitted. Until a day or two ago we were worried lest he wouldn't be allowed to export the money – a leg costs £90 – owing to currency restrictions, but it's arranged now, so the Engels will go to Los Angeles and buy a cork leg there.

After the fall of France in 1940, her Hampstead home soon began to fill with French refugees, too.

Perhaps they are the most unlucky as the men had to bolt leaving their wives and children, and they are in a state of bitter disillusionment at present, as there is still no organisation for absorbing them in the war effort.

Among them was Monsieur Mallard, owner of a wool factory,

... who said goodbye to his wife and five exquisite children of under ten years old in June – 'So that we can be reunited in the future we must be separated for the moment.' He had a wire from her on Friday imploring him to come back at once, but he knows it is a ruse and isn't even going to answer it – if he goes back the Nazis will shoot him and then torture his family, so they won't be any better off or worse if he stays here and they just torture his family. This decision wasn't taken easily or in cold blood – he came to see me with the wire on Friday and he and Lillibet and I discussed probable Nazi reactions to his return or his remaining here, and it was a vile thing to advise. As M Demenis and M Gueron had been independently to see us with similar entreaties on Thursday, it can only be a Nazi dodge to get back these technicians and scientists: how these men can face these decisions is more than I can understand. And to talk to them, to hammer out these things is an agonising priviledge that I shall always be thankful for.

The French were regarded as 'friendly aliens'. But just how friendly were they? This was a question that Nora O'Connor, promoted to Commandant of an Internment Camp, helped to answer.

The Friendly Aliens were men and women, many in underground movements, who had escaped from their occupied countries, enduring much hardship en route, and sought refuge in Britain. A number of them tried to impress us with, 'I am a personal friend of General de Gaulle.' The Croix de Guerre was prominently displayed on their bosoms, but MI5 required credentials more convincing than this pectoral show of patriotism before letting them loose. The various 'Comtesses' and 'amies personelles du General' took the dimmest view of the little iron bedsteads and the tiny lockers in between.

It wasn't just the London streets which thronged with exotic foreigners. Dr JP McHutchison wrote about the Glasgow area in August 1940:

What with Polish and French troops in the country, now learning English to be able the better to fight along with us, street advertisements in Polish for photographic supplies and facilities, a Scotch newly joined recruit in very drab if business-like battle-dress saluting a fancily attired Polish Officer in Sauchiehall Street, the Polish and French soldiers walking out young girls – these and many other features could never have been imagined even as remotely possible eleven months ago, or indeed even three months ago.

In Cheshire, in letters to his American penfriend, 17-year-old schoolboy Brian Poole recorded the fascination aroused by the Poles.

> The Royal Air Force are distinctly puzzled. For years they have had no rivalry – met no serious competition in matters of the fair sex. But now the Poles. No one quite knows what it is about the Poles. The girls are not very helpful about it. They just make silly cooing noises and go all goofy when you ask them 'Oo! They're too wonderful!' is about all you get. It is all very mysterious and galling for the Don Juans of England.

Grace Dennithorne was another of those anxious to help friends in occupied Europe, but without success. She used a friend in Berkeley, California, as a conduit for notes and news prior to the US engagement in the war in December 1941.

> One of the things that has grieved me very much is that I had a very dear friend in Salzburg (now Germany – once Austria) and of course I cannot send to or hear from her. Also a young girl (19 or 20 years) has been writing to me from Czechoslovakia and I was trying to get her into a hospital in England for training as a nurse. Again we cannot correspond. I wondered whether you could write a little note to them, to let them know that the present upheaval makes no difference to my outlook and feelings and that someday I hope to be able to write again as before – give them my very best wishes and love. I should be most grateful if you could do this giving your address so that a message may some day get back.

A message did get back from Germany with the news that her friend Maria remembered her happy days with Grace Dennithorne.

At the outbreak of war, aliens working in Britain found themselves marooned. In addition to her job and campaigning activities, Isabelle Granger helped to entertain them.

I went to sing at a hostel for Germans and Austrians who had
held domestic permits, and whose jobs had gone at the outbreak
of war. It was a piteous evening among lost people: a curious
island of unwanted, isolated women. We ended up with German
folk songs, all singing together. Mary (the pianist-travelling
friend) played all the things we sing after days skiing or walking
through marguerite fields, everyone sang and came alive again.
There were cooks by profession and psychoanalysts and scientists
and teachers.

Writer Noel Streatfeild felt enormous sympathy for the Italians caught up
in a similar way. In a letter to her brother and sister-in-law in Bangkok in
June 1940, she wrote:

I am surprised to find in these last days since Italy joined herself
with Germany how greatly the Italians are disliked in this
country. It's never been a matter of annoyance to us, has it, that
the majority of our best restaurateurs are Italian? But in the lower
walks of life it seems to have been a continual grievance that the
waiters of England were all Italian, while thousands of our young
men were unemployed. The answer to this was dozens of small
Italian shops all over the country had their windows smashed, on
the night that Italy declared war. It happened to one in Curzon
Street round the corner from me. Nobody could have been more
surprised than me.

By 1944 Lillibet Gruber, friend of campaigner Isabelle Granger in
Hampstead, had returned to the engineering profession. In a letter to a
friend, Isabelle wrote:

Lillibet is enjoying her job in Welwyn – sometimes rather
cynically, but she says the people in the office are friendly, and
in her job, assistant production engineer, she has a good deal to
do with the charge hands and foremen and operatives, which she
loves. She is good with people and they like her and it warms my
heart to confront with a German the sort of English people who
would not, in the normal way, have met one: it muddles them up

and makes them think, and then sometimes, I am certain, tidies up their views.

Dinner parties at the Granger/Gruber home continued to be multinational affairs with guests from China, Australia, Germany and America.

> We met a young German (now since '39 a US citizen) in a theatre through programme-sharing the other evening: he is coming to us for his leave soon – such a nice person, in the Army, and I imagine, training for special duties in Europe. Why don't we adopt our aliens and, if they serve us, make them at once, one of us – if indeed they feel any desire to be one.

Many aliens were 'adopted' by Britain. The chemist Dr Enoch returned from enforced exile in Canada in February 1941. His research led to the production of a tetanus anti-toxin and a vivicillin for swine fever which he tested on himself, his success hitting the headlines in April 1944. Klaus Ulrich was given a scholarship to Clifton College in Bristol, where he was educated with the help of an anonymous benefactor. He became an engineering apprentice and a British citizen and went into the British aircraft industry. He never saw his mother again: she died in a concentration camp.

Prisoners of war were also pressed into war service in Britain. In the Orkney Islands, Italian POWs built a tiny chapel, complete with Italianate frescos and a concrete statue of St George. All over the country prisoners of war were building sea defences and working on farms and in forestry.

Mariele Kuhn, whose husband was half Jewish, was asked to act as an interpreter at the Head Injury Hospital at St Hugh's College, Oxford. Many of the German conscripts she met had been wounded in the Allied advance after D-Day in 1944. On 28 September she met Johann Mosig from Silesia. He had been captured in France and flown to England after a few days in a field hospital. The 18-year-old had been wounded in the back and his spine was broken in two places.

> I was rung by the hospital to come over and do some interpreting while the neurologist examined Mosig more closely. I was to find out exactly how he was hurt – it seems he was running, when he

felt a big blow in the back, tumbled forward and could not get up again. He has no pains in his legs now, is just completely 'dead' from his chest downwards.

She recorded her visits to the damaged man in her diary.

October 3rd – Found Mosig, called Fritzly by the nurses, on his tummy, his face buried in his arms, his back had become so very sore from lying on it. The nurses are really sweet to him, anxious to see him happy and make him comfortable. Why wasn't he happy they asked me? Well, I thought being a physical wreck at the age of 18, a prisoner of war, in a foreign country, were quite good enough reasons for not being radiantly happy!

After a few days 'little Mosig', as Mariele called him, started to chat, though his dialect was hard to understand.

Showing me stacks of photos from home, father, step-mother, brothers, sisters, half-sisters, goats, kids, and chickens! He read the two books I took to him as well as the magazines. Told him that some of the books we'd collected for German Pows, were given by Jewish emigrants. When I tell him anything like that he just shuts his eyes and can't look at me. It does not fit in with all the things he has been told all his life.

Mariele Kuhn's humanity towards the German POWs is extraordinary, bearing in mind that she and her half-Jewish husband had been forced to flee Germany. She took sweets and souvenir postcards of English cities; she knitted scarves, and wrote letters home for those who were paralysed or blind. When patients died, she wrote letters of condolence to their families and even took photographs of their graves to send as a memento. While most of the young men she helped were not pro-Nazi, there were exceptions – including Walter Barr, who mistrusted the medical staff.

To him they are still 'enemies' I believe, and try to make him forget about it. He was also asked to make a toy rabbit (occupational therapy), but scorned the idea, probably thought they wanted him to make 'toys for British children'. I told him it was for his own good and if he wanted he could make it for my little Nicholas. Oh, how difficult it all is, and very depressing really, one can't even be angry with him.

Mariele had volunteered to interpret for the wounded POWs, but was soon employed by the British Red Cross as an official visitor. This official status, and the Red Cross armband, made her feel more at ease, particularly when she was abused by Allied prisoners who were in the same hospital. In April 1945, after Hitler's suicide, the Allies were liberating concentration camps, and horrifying pictures were released in the press.

> When leaving the ward, one of the lady helpers said bitterly to me – in front of all the others – 'Why don't you look after the people of Buchenwald?' It hurt me most terribly, I only answered, 'I wish I could'. Feeling is running high these days, since the horrors have been published with pictures etc. Actually one of the POWs, has himself been more than once in the camps, as a 'Marxist'.

Professor Dr Robert Munz, a veteran of World War I who had escaped from Berlin in 1938, was one of a group of German-Jewish academics who were in Oxford during the war. He was impressed by the tolerance of the British people.

> I think it is very remarkable that during the war it was possible to hold divine service in public, in German, in one of the finest churches in Oxford.

Extraordinary friendships were forged across the divide of war. Evidence of this is in a small collection of letters in broken English addressed to Percy Patten in Brighton.

> Dear Patten, I am very sorry that you was not able to come see us in this late time. Last week I received you letter and the strings for guitar. I was very please to read you kind letter that show me your complete interessamento for we. Money I hope to give you hand by hand when you come again. Sincerely your De Paolo Pietro.

Italian prisoners of war savour a taste of normal life as they make friends with London evacuees. These POWs worked on a farm, others did forestry work, all bolstering the Home Front workforce. Thousands of young Germans and Italians married local girls.

Percy and his wife, referred to as Lady Minnie, gave another POW toothpaste. But evidence of his greater kindness comes from a former POW writing from his home town of Hannover in December 1946.

> I am really glad to be a free man again. On this place I will have to thank you for all the kindness you have done to us. What this means for a prisoner of war I can't tell, and you have taught us that we are human beings. Through you I have got such a good impression from the English people I thought I will never get. You will never be forgotten by me and always remain an example for me.

12
KISSING COUSINS

Such a thrill! Our stars and stripes flying beside the Union Jack all up and down the High Street! English speaking people should stick together. People of common heritage should be united. We feel this very strongly Dick and I. And we found much in Falmouth to strengthen our belief.
(Peg Cotton, 4 July 1941)

Five months before the USA entered World War II, a prominent American couple attended Independence Day celebrations in a small Cornish town. America had fought alongside the Allies for the last few months of World War I. The transatlantic relationship was long and complex, tangled in the web of history. Britain's wartime Prime Minister, Winston Churchill, was born to an American mother; Lady Astor, the first woman to take her seat as an MP in the House of Commons, was an American; and many American heiresses had married into the British aristocracy in the late 19th and early 20th centuries. But to the bulk of the British population, America meant one thing: the movies. By the end of World War II, the GIs were the stars of their own movie, carrying off the hearts of 70,000 British 'GI brides'.

Long before GIs crossed the Atlantic to join the war, the 'Bundles for Britain' scheme brought clothes, blankets and hospital supplies from well-wishers in America. Britain's first year of the war was fought mainly at sea, and it was the plight of men serving in North Atlantic waters that stirred US sympathies, as Mrs Bingham, wife of the former American Ambassador to London, recorded.

Newspapers carried vivid and stirring descriptions of the hardships and constant peril endured by these men [on trawlers and minesweepers in the North Sea and Atlantic], and survivors of torpedoed vessels began to straggle into our ports after harrowing experiences and miraculous rescues at sea, in pitiful condition and in increasing numbers. So Bundles for Britain was started. By February 1 1940 the first shipment of 1,000 sweaters, 1,000 helmets, 300 pairs of mittens and 1,000 scarves was on its way to Britain. The first of 234 shipments.

Torpedo victims even found bundles waiting for them in such out-of-the-way places as Ponta Delgada in the Azores. An American-built British minesweeper was christened *Miss Bundles* in recognition of this American help. When the Blitz started, Bundles for Britain were sent to help victims of the raids. Constance Logan Wright reported back to the American well-wishers after a trip round recipients in Britain.

> The Lady Mayoress of Portsmouth said that she had been continually handing out 'Bundles' of garments, for after the raids it had been her job to tend to the people who had been bombed out and find clothing for them. She said it was remarkable the difference these gifts had made in the people. When they arrived to see her without any proper clothes, they were dirty and depressed, but when they left clean, and with new things to wear from Bundles their depression vanished. They were bright and cheerful once more and had gained courage to face their troubles. Bombed families had been without any clothes at all, except for what they stood up in, and very often those had been torn to pieces by the blast. With the clothes that Bundles had sent they had been able to clothe 4,000 women.

The naval base at Devonport made the city of Plymouth a constant target for German bombers. At the height of the Plymouth blitz, special trains were organized to take civilians from the city into the relative safety of the countryside. Passengers snatched what sleep they could in fields and under hedgerows. Mrs Bingham visited the city in 1942 to see what American aid had achieved and what more was needed.

> After 57 consecutive nights of bombing during the enemy's savage attack on their city, the people of Plymouth emerged to find Bundles for Britain on hand to help – the first civil relief agency to reach them.

This aid was not just for the civilian population. Anti-aircraft gunners, and many other servicemen and women, were supplied with refreshments at their posts by 105 mobile canteens provided by the Americans. A young British airman wrote to them:

> I am an authority on the tea car, for I am a pilot at this RAF station and what I am telling you comes straight from a grateful stomach. If only the unseen, unknown, kind hearts who gave us this welcome Bundle for Britain could pay one visit to our aerodrome to see for themselves how much this daily spot of comfort and cheer means to us.

City hospitals had to cope with routine medical care as well as those injured in air raids. Among them was Cardiff Royal Infirmary, one of the hospitals that was sent a mobile surgical unit from America. Constance Logan Wright reported back.

> Cardiff Royal Infirmary's working capacity was reduced by two thirds. When the buildings became practically useless through enemy action, this hospital built up an efficient mobile division. American ambulances rushed to the scene wherever bombs had fallen.

Ambulances, bedding and surgical instruments were sent to 57 London hospitals and 91 provincial ones. But it was the plight of British children, bombed out or orphaned, that prompted extraordinary kindness from their transatlantic cousins. According to a 'Bundles for Britain' leaflet, two very small children from Niagara Falls adopted the Sunshine Home for Blind Children.

> These youngsters heard something of the plight of their less fortunate British cousins and wanted to do something to help. They pledged themselves to save a cent a meal a day toward that end. The idea was quickly adopted in the city's schools and Sunday schools and funds sufficient to endow a Sunshine bed in perpetuity was the result.

The American town of Barnstaple funded a wartime nursery for orphans in its Devon namesake. Once America had entered the war, some US servicemen 'adopted' and sponsored war orphans, and at Christmas in 1943 Santa Claus arrived at orphanages and children's hospitals in a 'four-engined sub-stratosphere bomber' courtesy of the US Air Force.

Some Americans and Canadians had joined the British Forces long before America joined the war. Bob Raymond served in the RAF before joining his compatriots in the USAF. He was well placed to observe the tensions which existed between these allies.

> Every Canadian I've met, dislikes the officers of the RAF. I believe it is due to the fact that the officers cannot conceive of anyone not talking in the breezy staccato manner that is their natural mode of expression, and their being equal to them – the officers – in intelligence and efficiency. That rule applies to the English, for all but the well-educated classes, speak with an accent and act in every way as inferior beings. But the rule certainly does not apply to the Dominions personnel over here. I'm wondering what's going to happen on some of the long flights. The Canadian aircrew get along fine with English sergeants and other colonials, but they are as flint and steel to RAF officers.

British society and its class distinctions were incomprehensible to many American and Canadian personnel. Bob Raymond wrote in his diary:

> I sometimes feel that England does not deserve to win the war. Never have I seen such class distinctions drawn and maintained, in the face of a deep effort to preserve a democracy. With powers of regulation and control centred in the hands of a few, the abuse and preservation of the Old School Tie is stronger than it ever was on every side. In that, I am not affected and can remain aloof, and claim an unprejudiced onlooker's viewpoint. It has been well and truly said that General Rommel of the German Army Afrika Korps would never have risen above the rank of NCO in the British Army. This nation seems inexplicably proud of defects in its national character.

Efforts were made to promote a harmonious understanding between the natural allies. Dick Cotton, head of the Rola factory, which had relocated to North Devon, was drafted in to talk to the British while the USA was still neutral, as his wife Peg wrote in 1941,

> . . . and help the English people to understand the how and why of our actions nowadays; that our sympathies are with England, but that we are a very large nation peopled by a very large and varied public and governed by a system that is truly impelled by the people. And the American people, as a whole, are not yet ready to enter this war. They have no desire to. Who can blame them? But I believe that they will do so eventually – hating war as much as the English do, loving liberty too much to let it be strangled, believing in the rights of man, willing to die for all this, as the English do, but still not sure that this war is their war, America's. The Atlantic Ocean is a barrier in more ways than one.

Phyllis Warner, who had spent a year in the USA on a teacher exchange scheme, was also recruited as a lecturer to the British Forces, teaching troops about the Americans.

> I made my debut as an approved lecturer to his Majesty's Forces, by visiting an isolated AA Battery to deliver an oration on America. I felt very shy about it, but a powerful drink in the Officers' Mess as soon as I arrived gave me Dutch courage, which I needed when I entered the hall to the sound of a stentorian 'Eyes Front'. There are several hundred men on the site so I had a lively audience who asked good questions – for once they kept off Hollywood and gangsters. Afterward I was charmingly entertained to dinner by the officers, so it was quite a social function.

The silver screen was much to blame for the British view of Americans, as GI bride Avice Wilson recalled.

> Due to weekly visits to the local cinema I vaguely thought of Americans as being movie versions of New Yorkers and the soldiers would be the same, but in uniform, highly mechanised and rushing around.

Some Britons simply resented the Americans 'bossing them around'. Phyllis Warner, with many friends in the United States, was listening to the wireless when the news broke that Pearl Harbor had been bombed on 7 December 1941.

I devoured the headlines, then sat frozen with the effort to realise this appalling extension of suffering and misery that drags in fresh millions all over the globe. As the day wore on more details came in. The Americans seem to have been caught napping at Pearl Harbour and Guam. There's a good deal of irritation and some malicious pleasure at this which people are not doing much to conceal. Of course we want the Americans to win resounding victories – if they get defeated we'll have to take the consequences – but God knows that after all we have had to put up with in the way of American reproof and criticism and patronising surprise at our inefficiency, it wouldn't be human not to feel a wry satisfaction when they show a weak spot. Nobody could be more pro-American than I am, but even I think a defeat or two would do the Americans a power of good psychologically. The trouble is that we aren't allowed to say these things officially. The Press is politely muzzled on this point, and in public we're only allowed to kow-tow to the Americans, and keep saying how profoundly grateful we are to them, whilst they can shoot off their mouths at us as much as they please – officially and unofficially. This is why feeling towards America has cooled of late, particularly since the Russians are fighting tooth and nail whilst the Americans have been going on strike and scrapping amongst themselves and telling us off. It's silly to get more irritated with your good friends than your deadly enemies, but this incident I heard the other day is typical of a number lately. American visitor – 'I don't see why you English get sore with your people who have stayed over in the States through the war.' Englishman – 'Well for one thing, they're often people with brains and we need their brains over here.' American – 'I'll say you do need brains over here, and how you need them.' This is the sort of remark one doesn't forgive a visitor, and it accounts for the smirk that some people are trying to smother today.

In her California home, Londoner Florrie Elkus had been avidly following the war news from Britain, concerned for her large circle of friends and family all over England. Her parents living in Walthamstow and the rest of the family in south and east London were of particular concern. Her sister Ethel Mattison wrote to Florrie on 13 December 1941:

> Now we know how you felt when our part of the war started. I think of you when I am coming home from work in the blackout, and wondering if you hate it as much as we all do. One gets used to it but it is always unpleasant except on moonlight nights. I hate to think of you personally suffering any discomfort from the war (you've had enough to put up with worrying about us) but all the same, the general feeling is one of satisfaction that America is now in with us. At first I was very depressed about it and thinking it would mean fewer arms for us and the Soviet Union, but Roosevelt has assured us that this will not be so. What does amaze us is that America appeared to be caught napping. Surely they didn't really trust the Japanese? The Press stated here repeatedly, that they were only playing for time.

Ethel, like many diarists and letter writers in this period of the war, overflowed with admiration for the Russian struggle to expel the invading German army.

> *December 20th 1941* – The Russian successes are staggering – it's no wonder that everyone is bounding with enthusiasm for our Eastern allies. At the moment it's a big contrast with our lukewarm attitude to America. The press is largely to blame. For months it has uttered paens to America – whilst for years previous to 1941 practically every newspaper had proclaimed that Russia was a corrupted and weakened tyranny.

America's entry into the war in December 1941 brought with it an invasion of GIs. Even now the term 'GI' (an acronym for General, or Government, Issue – referring to their kit) conjures up images of dances, jazz, jitterbugging, and gifts of the unobtainable: nylon stockings, chocolate and chewing gum. The first Yanks arrived in the small Somerset

The Stars and Stripes and a model aeroplane decorate the walls at this dance at a Women's Land Army camp in Suffolk in 1943. Some of these American flyers appear to be teaching their partners how to jitterbug, the dance the GIs brought when they first landed in Britain.

town of Wellington in 1942, as Anne Lee Michell wrote in her diary,

> . . . followed by trails of children who can't leave them alone. Three hundred have now arrived and there's a forest of tents in the field behind the Griffins – lovely for them as they're woken at 5am by terrific chatteration, laughter and blowing of whistles!

The free and easy reputation of the GIs had already reached Somerset when Anne returned home one evening in October.

> Electrified to find a huge Negro in the kitchen – Gertie much flustered, explained it was her 'coloured friend, cycled over from Cross Keys' to see her. When she brought my supper she said he

had brought a bottle of beer and would I like a glass!! She then asked if she might go out for a bit with him, from which I sternly dissauded her, pointing out that Nasty Incidents happen in the Blackout. Gathered from Gertie's face that any such incidents happened weeks ago!

Bottled beer was at a premium in wartime Britain, so this was a handsome gift. This was the era of segregation, when black and white Americans served in separate companies. In Anne Lee Michell's quiet corner of the West Country, black faces were previously unknown – unknown and possibly therefore to be feared. The rumour mill got to work.

Lurid tale going round of a respectable Mrs Burton, who, followed by a negro last night, lost her nerve, and broke into a run under some dark trees. In a flash he was on her stabbing and slashing her neck with a knife. She screamed, luckily was heard by a cyclist (her brother in law) who came to her rescue, and took her dripping gore, into Mrs Ball's for First Aid. Man since arrested, but another one is missing from the camp. I trust I don't encounter him in the hay shed when I go in there of a dark evening. Wish the camp were further from our goats.

Anne's goats were on the small 'farm' where she and a friend, Babs, also kept hens and ducks and grew vegetables. Anne did war work at a munitions factory, and in the office in November 1942 there was more palpable evidence of the misbehaviour of another American GI.

Two policemen in the office this afternoon closeted with one of the girls, taking a statement from her – walking back to Rockwell Green last night she was followed by a US soldier (a white one) who knocked her into the hedge saying 'Scream and I'll knock your head off'. She managed to get away but lost her brooch and was badly shaken. Old Smith hearing this, said, 'You ought to be in Cardiff, where I've come from today, murder someone every night they do there – of course it's nearly always women, but they knifed a British soldier last night they did.'

Mrs E Innes-Ker had fled from Singapore as the Japanese advanced in 1941. She found temporary refuge in Bedford, another garrison town full of GIs.

> They would cluster around in groups in the town of an evening. Everyone had stories of being 'picked up' – mostly a good-natured attempt to find friendly and sympathetic company. I was followed one evening as I returned home from a concert, and wondered what on earth I should do. There did not seem to be anyone else around, though one could not see much in the blackout, and I could just hear my footsteps and those following me. In the end I decided I had better stop and tell him he was wasting his time, before he got too far out of town. He was very polite, and with a 'sorry Ma'am' and a salute he turned back and left me.

Troops of any nationality have always acquired a reputation when billeted amongst civilians. But whether these and other recorded incidents were apocryphal or not, they still reflect a certain unease about the proximity of GIs amongst the locals. Peg Cotton was aware of the faults of her countrymen.

> Almost always, alas, it is the small incidents brought about by small people that build up an adverse 'blanket' opinion. For instance, the reckless driving here of American jeeps and motorcycles along the narrow, twisting English roads. In Instow alone, we have four different smashed walls from accidents. The walls are private property. Their owners don't think much of Americans! Frank Heaver's car was run into by an American Jeep. Its driver – in a tearing hurry, and on the wrong side of the road at that – hops out and goes up to Frank, who was ruefully looking at his damaged hood. 'Can't you get out of the way? Don't you know there's a War?' I feel gratified and proud when I see and hear of all the nice things, the decent things, that most of our American boys do here in England. And they love children. They will go out of their way to speak to a youngster. I was standing in a bus queue at Barnstaple one day when an American Jeep drove into the adjacent parking place and stopped. The driver slid down behind the wheel, dug a piece of gum out of a pocket, and

commenced to chew. In a detached way he looked us over –
a line of women with laden shopping baskets, and the usual
lot of children, too young to be in school or left at home alone.
As though someone had pulled a few strings, the young man
suddenly straightened up, reached over into the back of the jeep,
and then climbed out. Both hands were full of candy and gum.
He went down the long queue, giving every child (even those in
their Mother's arms) a share of the sweets. 'Hi, Buddy!' or 'Here,
young lady!' he'd say – and grin shyly when the women thanked
him. 'Shucks! It's nothin', Ma'am.' He went back to the jeep.
And was asleep before our bus appeared. But the queue buzzed
with happy appreciation. And the corners of the little children's
mouths now turned up, rather than down, as they busily chewed
and chewed. I rather think that gum has come to stay here, in
England – in more ways than one. You should hear what the staff
of hotels, pubs, and snack bars have to say about the small, gray,
adhesive ornaments they now scrape from under chair seats and
table edges.

When 300 *more* Americans arrived in Wellington, Somerset, at the end
of October 1943, Anne Lee Michell (like many other war-weary Brits)
welcomed the diversion.

The camp behind the Griffins is a clamour once more, while
groups of greenish-grey figures lope about the streets. Curious
how a slight change in uniforms gives a foreign air. I hear the
officers are a nice lot. Let's hope they'll brighten our winter for
us, like Leslie and Briggs and the rest did last year.

On the whole, British families took the GIs into their hearts and homes.
Through a hospitality scheme, British families opened their doors in a
gesture of friendship to GIs on leave. The Americans had a reputation
for abundance. Kathleen Crawley, who entertained troops and war
workers with ENSA, wrote home from Colchester:

On Friday we went to the famed American camp and found
all that had been promised us – to begin with, at each of our

places at table were 40 Chesterfield cigarettes, 2 Mars, 2 packets of fruit sweets and a packet of chewing gum. After that we had hamburgers and chips and beans and I had two large plates of delicious coffee ice cream. After that we were given sherry and koka kola, and after that there was a sort of dance. It was great fun – most of the officers were extremely nice.

Peg Cotton opened her Devon home to fellow Americans, convalescents and servicemen on leave. They provided an exciting diversion for the whole household, including her granddaughter Penny.

They come over to Springfield – big, husky chaps with a real appreciation for a sing-song, a game of Bridge, a meal in a home, even though the meal is a distinctly wartime one. They come like the Greeks, bearing gifts – of tomato juice, candy, gum, cigarettes, and even a cake now and then. They remember Penny with special fruit drops and oranges. They talk of their homes – their parents – their wives – their children – their girl friends. They exhibit snapshots of all these human bits and pieces that make up the whole special 'Heart Experience' of each man – the thing he's eventually going to fight for, Home and Family and his Right to enjoy these things in Independence and Peace.

Peg Cotton's husband Dick was one of the team in charge of procurements for the Allied invasion of Normandy. In the run-up to that campaign, Bill Virgil Evans breezed into the lives of Anne Lee Michell and her husband Mike one evening in March 1944.

Our USA, one Bill Virgil Evans the 1st, arrived after lunch, a nice young lad with fair hair and blue eyes, feel I can deal with him fairly easily. Thrilled with home comforts and a big bed, his first for two years. We now await Bill, to whom Mike intends to give solemn warning of the perils of Wellington Women. Tonight he's told us all about the war, the colour question, sex ditto, and Americas 'attitood'. He doesn't talk as much as *hold forth,* but is very delightful and I s'pose we too had everything taped at 22.

The tall handsome Texan loved to dance, play cards and share the details of his life 'back home'.

> Quite overcome by Bill's showing me a photo of fine twin baby
> boys – his own – and the smiling blonde he told me was 'one of
> his best girls' is his wife! His first baby, a girl, died at 5 months
> and he has only seen his sons once, they are nearly two now. And
> he seems such an infant himself! Amazing! He slept out on field
> manoeuvres last night, and says it was not so bad, he covered
> himself over with leaves. Enlivening tales of his tough upbringing
> in Texas – his Ma used to go out drinking and leave him alone, he
> found her liquor once (aged 7) and was comatose under the table
> when she returned. He thinks the world of 'Mom' I may add – 'A
> fine little woman, plenty tough, yes Ma'am'!

It was their mores, money and easy manner that made the Yanks such a novelty. War-weary British civilians enjoyed their encounters with their ebullient allies.

> While doing the farming a USA van drew up, full of officers, and
> Babs in her best attire enthroned among 'em, clutching three
> carnations. She'd been whisked off to be Matron of Honour at a
> USA wedding in Taunton! Bride and groom complete strangers,
> but still. Great party at Sanford to celebrate this, we rushed
> back to cobble supper and take Bill into the Snells for a party,
> inebriated wedding guests and the band, they played and we
> danced in and out of chairs and drums. Bill consumed lots of
> neat whisky and whirled us round Texan-fashion, and when we
> got back at 12.30am, insisted on playing blackjack.

Peg Cotton recognized the cultural differences as her part of Devon swarmed with American troops.

> The swaggering, boisterous antics of thousands of GIs bewilder
> the Devonians. In the pubs the American soldier treats the
> English beer and 'whiskey & soda' like soda-fountain or
> milk-bar drinks. That is, he drinks all he wants – without

discrimination. He mixes drinks – and, in treating his English girl friend, he mixes her drinks! The result is not one to enhance the reputation of American young manhood. Windows are broken. Heads are broken. Hearts are broken. The English, because they do not understand, look askance at the Americans' free and easy ways.

Whatever British views of the Americans had been before the Yanks arrived, GIs were destined to have the romantic lead in this movie. Where once the Poles had held sway over the hearts of British women, the Yanks were about to take over. Avice Wilson was a teenager in Chippenham, Wiltshire.

In January 1944 the second lot arrived, the 4th Armored Division. By the time they left many of the boys had been adopted by families, every girl in the town had an American boyfriend, sometimes two, and some had worked fast enough to get married. As a family I think we were impressed with the 'action' of the GIs. Something needed doing or getting? Right we had it as soon as possible. Admittedly the Americans had greater resources than we had at that time, but it was the combination of drive and confidence that never failed to dazzle us.

Peg Cotton was watching on the sidelines, with some misgivings.

To the GI, no matter who the girl is, she becomes Millie, or Jane, or Babe, at once! There is no formality. The girl, to begin with, is uneasy when the American boy tightly links his arm in hers, as though they were very close friends. But in a very short time she accepts this as natural. She walks with nonchalance, hand-in-hand, with her American boyfriend. She chews gum. She boasts of the candy and sugar (both strictly rationed here) that he gives her. She is more leg-conscious than she ever was – wearing sheer American stockings – from the PX [American Forces supermarket]. She thinks all Americans are millionaires – and would like to marry one – and go to live in that country where everything is done by Modern Magic. I creep inwardly at the disillusion of some of these girls in the future.

Cliffs and beaches along the Devon coast were closed off as troops rehearsed for D-Day. Machine-gun fire, explosions and loud American voices disturbed the peaceful wartime countryside. Peg Cotton witnessed all this and sympathized with the locals who had to put up with it.

> In some ways there are compensations – the dances at
> Headquarters and the American boyfriends the English
> girls now have. There are decidedly mixed opinions on these
> Anglo-American Relations! But again, the matter rests with
> the individual. Martha has met a lot of nice young officers
> at Woolacombe. They take her and Alix to the dances – those
> fabulous dinner dances of an American Army HQ where the
> food is like ambrosia to a people so long on rations and sharply
> curtailed variety.

Aware of the needs of their troops far from home, the American Red Cross started clubs for GIs in major cities. Anne Chalmers volunteered as a hostess at the American Red Cross club in Bristol.

> There was no mistaking that we were on American territory, since
> it was their flag that was visible, their music that was being played
> on a radiogram, and the whole atmosphere was alien to any Brits,
> who, at least temporarily, left their native soil. Hand painted
> portraits of wolves heads with their bodies clad in American
> uniforms, graced the walls of the club. I talked to one of the Red
> Cross women and asked what hostesses were supposed to do.
> She replied that we had to dance with the men, talk to them and
> circulate. We were not supposed to stay with one particular one
> all the evening. There was a room with a piano, a lounge where
> soldiers could read quietly or write letters, a games room and a
> large ballroom with a stage, upon which well known bands would
> play for the Saturday night dances. There was also a canteen
> downstairs where food was provided, the kind that every resident
> in the United Kingdom currently dreamed about, since there was
> a plentiful supply of bacon and eggs and other 'goodies' which
> were severely rationed, and sometimes unobtainable as far as our
> own population was concerned. There were also bedrooms and

bathrooms upstairs, so that soldiers who visited Bristol, but were
not stationed there, could stay and enjoy the club's amenities.
In the club there was often a sense of unreality, away from what
was going on outside, with an exciting, stimulating feeling of not
knowing what was going to happen from one day to the next. The
American soldiers had brought with them a new dance called the
Jive, and taught it to us, which was just as well, as most of them
were not very good ballroom dancers.

This club was only for white GIs. Black GIs had their own club elsewhere
in Bristol, where they were allowed to bring their white girlfriends. Many
of them were very homesick, and though the new environment could mean
freedom and fun, some were miserable and lonely off duty. There were
reports that troops from the southern states took violent action on one
occasion when they heard of black troops going out with white girls: several
were stabbed. The next morning black and white officers held a combined
meeting to decide how best to separate the warring factions. Black soldiers
were to be allowed out on alternate evenings, and this applied to the whites
too. When dates were made, girls had to make sure whether it was a 'black'
night or a 'white' night.

Sally Peters was a 'donut girl', one of the hundreds of American girls who
arrived in the wake of the GIs to bring them some home comforts. She
wrote to her mother in Virginia:

All day I handed out cigs, life savers and chewing gum – The
'boys' are wonderful – they are so glad to talk to an American
girl. I have been running the Donut Dugout this week. That is
the small building taken over by the Red Cross to give the boys
some place to go other than pubs. It opens at 3pm and serves
only coffee and donuts but has writing rooms, lots of fireplaces
and big comfortable chairs. Tonight the Special Service Officer
was supposed to have one of the bands appear for a concert at
the Dugout, but they never showed up, so I gave some of the boys
dancing lessons while one of the GIs played the piano. We also
did a little singing of songs.

I was out dancing with a naval flyer last night, they are all such
grand guys. It sort of makes you feel strange to think that they

won't all come back . . . somehow I just can't blame them for getting drunk on their leave and staying that way for a couple of days – I think that the most good I've done so far is listening to the several I've been out to dinner with – one lad from California overstayed his leave a day and a night because he wanted to go out again with me – not that it was just me, but he had someone to listen to him and be interested in what he had to say – I got a letter from him yesterday thanking me. Saturday night was very gay – evening dress dancing etc. Could have been any Saturday night at home. I had a wonderful time and even pinned a decoration on the Colonel – Danger Hangover Under Construction.

She also visited the Grosvenor House Hotel in London, which had been requisitioned for US Army officers. It served 4,000 meals daily in the hotel's grand ballroom. The American Red Cross sent mobile canteens over with the troops. Although Sally wasn't able to tell her mother in her letter, she was serving GIs in special training for D-Day at Ilfracombe in Devon.

5.4.44 – Today I drove a 4 ton truck! Our clubmobile, for the 1st time. It wasn't so hard, just had to remember to drive on the left hand side of the road, know when to double clutch and how to use the 4 gears! Edna drove out to the camp where we picked up a jeep to lead us out to the boys who were to be served. The terrain changed from lovely rolling downs to rolling sand dunes and that's where we got stuck! We put a couple of urns of coffee and 5 or 600 doughnuts into a jeep and I went with the major and the jeep through the sand dunes to the place we were looking for. We placed the urns on top of the hood of the jeep, made the boys line up on both sides and served them coffee, letting them help themselves to the doughnuts. Incidentally, the major made me wear one of the GI steel helmets, but as I was wearing a bunch of narcissi in my hair I objected. Besides the helmet is most unbecoming – but he was firm. I got the best of him, sticking the flowers in the strap right in front. One of the GIs made some comment about my Easter bonnet, so I stuck it in the netting they wear on their helmets. I met the same boy three hours later and he was still wearing it! If only you could see me bouncing around in that jeep holding on to one sloshy coffee urn and that helmet bouncing around on my head.

In June 1944, Sally was on hand to serve those waiting to embark for France.

> There were so many girls that a few of us just sat around on the quay and talked. As we had the Victorola blaring away, a GI asked me to dance with him, so regardless of his pack we started out and in about two seconds had a huge audience gathered around us. Frank was a professional dancer and was he good? There was I struggling in my heavy boots and trousers to keep up with him. I tell you it was a sight.

As the war in Europe came to an end in May 1945, there were already many GI brides – and more to come. It was a trend frowned upon by many in Britain. Mrs Paroutaud's father was one of them.

> Our English relatives were appalled to see 100s of their young women being 'shipped to the US' to join husbands whom they scarcely knew and families they had never seen. I never saw my father again. He was old and broken by the grief of the war. My brother who would have been 21, was missing in action at Tobruk.

Despite her father's opinion, she was married in June 1945, and joined the other GI brides being shipped out Stateside the following year. They were allowed a baggage allowance of 200lb and were housed in a camp staffed by German prisoners of war.

> Everything at that camp was an acute embarrassment – there was a physical inspection with all clothing removed.

Avice Wilson's husband-to-be, Johnnie, was one of the team organizing the operation.

> Between the Army and the Red Cross everything the girls

Thousands of British women succumbed to the transatlantic charms of the American GIs, and some couples were married after only a few weeks. Sergeant Henri Paroutaud and his wife are pictured here after their wedding at Cheltenham in Gloucestershire in June 1945.

could possibly need was supplied, from baby bottle nipples to notepaper. Some girls neglected their children shamefully, others didn't know how to take care of them. Here the Red Cross girls did a valiant job, they took the children while their mothers were being processed, dried the tears of the homesick and bolstered the courage of girls who were having doubts about their journey. We embarked on the troopship *George W Goethals*. I stood at the rail watching a bombed Southampton receding. The girl next to me waved to her family on the dock until they were out of sight. Then she watched a church steeple near her home until that vanished. Some girls were sad, but there were more feelings of excitement and anticipation of a new life than of sadness.

To while away some of the time on board, Avice wrote letters home to her parents.

> There are 36 in a cabin, about 50ft by 13ft, so we are very crowded. Two tiered bunks, no proper place for hanging clothes so they are all around the sides. The bunks have a canvas bottom and mattress, and Hilda's is next to mine almost like a double bed. As this is a troopship there isn't much comfort, but it's worth any discomfort to join Johnnie. Three mothers and babies went off the ship, as the babies were ill. One girl received a cable 'Don't come, not wanted' and her passage was cancelled.

Avice and the other women were well fed; food was in such abundance that many of them gorged themselves.

> The ship's newspaper reported that the House of Commons sat until 4 am debating on porridge, which makes me feel guilty about the food wasted, due to such generous portions and the endless variety. I have tried not to waste or overeat, although it is wonderful to buy candy whenever I like. I am using American expressions I know, but I am bound to eventually, anyway I'm determined not to lose my English accent – some girls seem to be trying to do so on this ship. After dinner we had another talk by two Red Cross girls, on fashions and food. I suppose I shall have to wear hats and stockings more in future. One girl asked 'Do you have fish and chip shops' which made us laugh and blush at the same time.

Just as they were ignorant of the American way of life, some of these women knew very little about the husbands and fiancés they were going to join. In the postwar years, hundreds of illegitimate GI babies have tried to track down their fathers. Others, who were given up for adoption by ashamed or abandoned mothers, have also tried to discover the truth about their transatlantic origins.

13
STING IN THE TAIL

Sitting on a seat on Tooting Common one sunny morning this week, I looked across the road at the 80 gun rocket battery spread at regular intervals over a great square of grass commandeered some three years ago from the Common, wired off, cut up, hutted, utterly spoiled for years to come whatever happens. And I wondered if in the next few weeks, maybe before all the May blossom has been forgotten or the horse chestnuts quite gone, we shall know that the guns will never be used again – or not in this war.
(C Jory, 7 May 1944)

By 1944 an optimistic note was palpable in diaries and letters. The population was exhausted but felt victory was in sight. Hitler was on the run, and the country had survived the onslaught of thousands of bombs. But like any cornered and wounded animal, the Nazi beast would make a final vindictive and terrifying attack on the weary civilians on the Home Front. Unaware of this sting in the tail, the population talked of little else but the opening of the Second Front. It had been predicted and anticipated by some since 1942: soon the great day would arrive. With hindsight, it is known that the D-Day landings were the beginning of the final Allied victory over Hitler. But as he quietly mused in the beauty of a spring morning in May 1944, Mr C Jory could not predict certain victory.

Are we in this coming invasion going to get one more set back, is the purely bad luck or the criminally unforeseen and mismanaged going to put us back from peace for another year or more? A lot of people must be wondering the same thing, and many thousands, millions maybe, with men and boys in it looking with dread to what the next few weeks will bring to them, whether it is victory *or* defeat.

In the West Country, Americans were massing for this invasion, troops blocked the roads and soldiers slept under hedgerows. Jory went down to the West Country for a few days and was impressed by the American hardware as the US Army readied itself for D-Day.

> By day and night their lorries and trains and all sorts of queer
> vehicles with mysterious loads are on their way to the west. There
> is more purely American traffic on the main road all the 24 hours
> than used to be there on the busiest summer day in peacetime. One
> marvels where all the petrol comes from! The high spot for me of
> this road traffic was to see one of the huge amphibious vehicles
> overturned across the main road. It is a six wheeled open truck on
> land but underneath is a propellor shaft and quite a useful looking
> propellor. This particular craft overturned by hitting a wall in
> swerving to avoid a lorry that cut in front. The job of righting it (or
> her) was done most expeditiously.

In Somerset, Anne Lee Michell recorded the unbearable tension of this waiting game.

> Such a perfect day again, this loveliness almost frightens me, it
> seems as if it's the end of everything, nothing so perfect can last.
> Yet each day brings new wonder. Today it is the lilac opening. I
> think we are all jumpy over the 2nd Front, we expect to hear it's
> begun every day, yet it's always the same old news; raids, raids,
> raids. Such a lot of heavy gunfire yesterday rumbling, I really
> thought it had started.

Anne and her friends had been entertained and charmed by many of the Americans camped on the town, including her lodger Bill Virgil Evans I.

> Found Babs and Marion in the Sanford [a local pub] very gloomy
> because they think all the favourite US officers have gone. Long
> and tender goodbyes last night though no one said they were going.
> Bill came in late and had a sad little chat, asking us to look after his
> trunk 'in case anything happens' and giving me his folks' addresses.
> He seems to feel he may go off to battle any day now. How grim it is.

A woman steps from a London bus, unaware of the destruction caused by a V-1 flying bomb behind her, though others farther down the street appear to have noticed the disaster. This picture was taken on 30 June 1944 moments after the bomb fell on the Aldwych Theatre.

We both lay awake last night, tossing and turning and thinking of
all our friends waiting for the fateful zero hour.

That was at the end of April, and had she but known it, there was still more
than a month to go. The gorgeous weather and the suspense continued.

May 11th – More lovely weather, and sunbathing – these hot days,
smell of lilac, and general air of well-being certainly helps one to
bear the suspense. If it were not for the terrific air activity – fleets
of giant bombers, transport planes, and gliders – I'd think the
Second Front only an evil dream. Alas! I fear it's bound to come.

When at last D-Day arrived, streams of hyperbole, patriotism and the
possibility of peace poured into diaries and letters. The nation had held
its breath and released it in one prolonged cheer. Unkindly, just when the
future looked rosy, Hitler's new weapon (promised via Lord Haw Haw's
broadcasts) burst from the skies. After nearly five years of war, this was
devastating. Londoner Bill Regan, hardened to the sight and sound of
bombs by his job as a rescue worker, was not alone in his feelings.

Peculiarly, everyone is unanimous in their dislike of these things.
They make a bigger mess than the bombs ever did. Some have
a different note somewhat like an outsize bee, and they have a
proportionate sting. Bill Brackin told me he dreaded nightfall;
Wright and Pryor have said the same. There is not one man I
know who is getting used to it; if anything it is getting everyone
down. The sound of a motor far or near, brings everyone to their
feet with no exceptions. Not only is this so at the depot, but also
in the streets. Kids playing happily, grown ups going about their
affairs, next minute the streets clearing, as if by magic. You can
see by their expressions, and the way they seem to go – 'let me get
out of this'. You can feel the uneasiness. Unlike the old days when
everyone waited to help everyone else.

It was the RAF who nicknamed the jet-powered V-1 flying bombs
'doodlebugs', but they were also known as buzz bombs. Miss Andrews was
living in Tonbridge in Kent where the local population had their eyes glued

to the skies, watching the clouds of silver barrage balloons and listening for the buzz of the V-1s.

> People tend to be more jittery because of the inhuman aspect of the thing – once the engine stops, you know nothing can prevent disaster, and in London you don't see the fighters intercepting. We had guns all round us for a week or two, making it dangerous to move about outdoors, then they moved away and balloons have gradually crept closer. There are thousands of them (literally) stretching about 35 miles in width, and from here to London in depth, and at all heights. They are very successful in exploding doodles in the air; though sometimes a fast one will merely break the cable and sail on (one is going over as I write).

Mr Jory, who was a journalist, summed up the first week of living with the V-1s, which Hitler's propaganda chief Goebbels had proclaimed as the first of the new secret weapons designed to bring Britain to its knees.

> A week's intimate experience of this secret leaves us slightly bloody, but unbowed, and he will have to try something a lot better than that! First was on Sunday night or early Monday, just one that put a railway out of action, quite a lucky shot in the dark, as beyond setting the missile in a general direction and loading it with fuel for a certain (or more or less uncertain) distance, that is all the control there can be over it. Two nights later there were more and it was announced that they *were* flying bombs or pilotless or robot planes. By Friday they were coming regularly and quite frequently, day and night and we fired at every one enough stuff to sink a battleship without doing them any harm, and upsetting the populace by the increasing row all night. By night they were easily seen in flight, level and straight about 1,000 feet up, because of the red glow from the petrol driven engine placed on top of the plane, itself not quite half the size of a Spitfire. Fuel exhausted, noise would stop, light go out and ten or 15 seconds later there would be a loud explosion as 1 ton of bomb in the nose struck ground. Blast was tremendous and mostly lateral and buildings for good quarter

of a mile radius were wrecked. By Saturday night (when one fell 100 yards from flat and broke windows in it, killing 6 in houses in Downton Avenue opposite) they were coming over from 50 to 100 in night and alerts were more or less continuous. We seemed to have no answer, and it was obvious that if something effective were not done quickly there would be a considerable amount of panic; exodus on quite biggest scale since 1940 Blitz began. Goebbels and crew were telling the world London was in flames, that MPs had fled, that we all lived in shelters.

The following week, which he recorded as the '42nd week of the fifth year of the war', Jory declared that he could not write about the wider war, because he had to write about the war as 'it affected me in particular'. He was in bed with a bad cold in his top-floor London flat on the night of 24 June.

Listening to pilotless planes in large numbers passing over and bursting near and far when one did *not* pass over, but hit the roof of my flat over dining room with engine still running. The final noise before the burst was a fierce menacing roar like the snarl of a thousand tigers. Then came the explosion and everything seemed to be going down in a ruin about me. I was not more than 25 feet away from point of impact, with the concrete roof, the walls of the corridor between my bedroom and dining room all there was between us. I was at that moment half turning left towards bedroom window in opposite direction from where the plane came. I felt I had been hit in the face from direction of window, a sharp and hot blow. For a minute I could not see owing to cloud of black dust and I suppose smoke. Meanwhile the building rocked, debris rained down and I got to the centre of small room feeling blood already running from left side of face and head. Then for an appreciable but short time there was absolute silence, then shouting began in the street and lower down in building.

On hands and knees he looked for his torch, searching through the head-high rubble in his bedroom. By its light he surveyed the random damage. The wardrobe doors had been ripped off but the clothes inside were unscathed. The dressing-table mirrors were unbroken, although the grandfather clock had been blown from one end of the room to the other. He went to what remained of the window and shouted for help.

> A fireman in the yard below heard me and shouted that he would get on fire escape. I said: 'Don't do that come up the stairs instead.' So he and another did, though in places the landings had been blown away, stepping from one top rail of stairs over a three foot span with a 60–70 foot drop he got to my room window sill and came in. He agreed that the only way out was via the window, so I went first dropping in to the other fireman's arms at last.

His dog, Bill, had been lying under the bed when the flying bomb hit.

> The three of us passed out the Airedale, Bill, who was so amenable that he must have been dazed. Then I was helped to walk over piles of debris, every floor being wrecked but main stairs intact, to first floor, where in corridor my wife had been sheltering and was unhurt. In opposite corridor several people were buried under debris from ceiling and flats on either side.

One hundred pieces of debris were removed from his face and head when he arrived at the hospital. As he lay waiting to go down to theatre for an operation to remove a piece of glass from his left eye, the flying bombs still droned overhead.

> I had no idea then if my left eye had been saved. It was heavily bandaged and was a bit troublesome. So was my head, part of which had been stitched. A fractured skull had been feared I learned later.

The next afternoon he was transferred to hospital in Chertsey, Surrey, to recuperate. He travelled in a Green Line bus converted into an ambulance. The 30-mile journey took over five hours, as the ambulance had to pick up so many other casualties along the route. In September that year he returned to work – the surgeons had saved his eye.

Hospitals had to postpone their normal work to treat the casualties. Anne Lee Michell had an agonizing wait to have a breast lump removed in the summer of 1944, and could hear the rockets overhead as she lay in her hospital bed.

Homes all over the country were prepared to receive a new wave of evacuated mothers and children. Lucy Kemp's daughter Julie was in Canada, so she took two boys from London into her Cheshire home.

I have two boys here from Peckham, wherever that may be. Two quite good boys, from a very poor home, but clean and generally well-behaved. I get quite a lot of amusement from them and both have settled down well. Donald is only 6, rather younger than I bargained for, but is a nice child and fallen into habits of bath and bed at 7–7.30pm without a murmur. I'm told he never went to bed until 10.30 at home. They both eat well and are fascinated by puddings, (known as afters) cooked and eaten every day. Billy is quite canny too and has found a farm where he is allowed to help. They had only the clothes they stood up in, but we have got them fixed up better now, apparently there was little 'to follow' from home. They have lived in an old tenement, gas lighting no hot water etc etc so everything here is lovely and they happen to appreciate the change, and are not scared by it. We are full up with evacuees some settling well, but mothers with babies are the difficulty. I was thankful to be asked to take children, I went to volunteer and didn't know what might arrive. The accent is terrific, I can hardly understand young Donald at times, complicated by the fact that he can't say all his words properly anyway. However, the least I can do is to take some in, seeing that Julie has been so well cared for all this time – but it rather makes my heart ache to have children around and not her. I wish to goodness she would be coming home soon.

In Tonbridge, Miss Andrews watched the skies as Spitfire pilots tackled the new enemy, shooting the V-1s down over the Kent countryside.

At school we had to quarter the children close to indoor

shelter (for fear of shrapnel hitting them outside and also because there isn't time to get out). We kept a spotter who blew a whistle on hearing a bomb approach and then all dived for shelter. The worst worry was the approaching public exams. A very sympathetic notice from the university empowered us to postpone or alter times of exam, but where were we to hold it, were we to make them shelter? And in any case the strain on the children would be great. For no one could get much refreshing sleep as night was the great time for them now.

In the middle of the night a doodlebug fell perilously close. She was woken up by the screams of a child in the street below.

I raked out my uniform from a drawer splintered at the side, put on old thick shoes for fear of glass, had time to notice that our windows were alright and was out of the house in about three minutes. The street was in a haze of dust, people were already sweeping piles of broken glass from the roadway, and before we had gone far the back of my old shoe gave way, so that I had to 'dot and carry one', putting on belt and tie the while. The plane had fallen on the Woodward's tennis court in Bosdyke, and one could hardly see down there for dust cloud. Everyone was running or cycling to his ARP job. As we entered the First Aid Post we found almost all windows out and ceilings down in the kitchen and surgical pantry. My job was to sterilise instruments, and Mrs Besant had already put a pail on the gas ring in the kitchen, where dust and rubble inches thick was scarcely conducive to asepsis!

The next secret weapon Hitler had up his sleeve was the rocket-powered V-2. Miss Andrews wrote:

It is said to be an enormous rocket fired into sub-stratosphere from Germany. There were some twenty odd in the week and we could hear the explosion and feel the concussion from miles away. They make a much deeper crater than the flying bomb but blast damage is not so heavy.

As a Fleet Street journalist, Mr C Jory was privileged to have access to information about the rockets.

> No mention of them in the Press, by order, though every day
> evacuees were streaming back, flying bomb danger being
> apparently over. But even this restarted on Saturday morning
> when I heard the first alert since my return. No alert can be
> given for the rockets as they are not seen or heard till the last few
> seconds. They appear to have set us a pretty problem.

As Jory and many others anticipated the end of the war in January 1945, he recorded the impact that the V-2 rockets were still having on the population.

> They are much more numerous and nearer the centre of the
> London target than ever before. It is a strange way of living,
> when quite feasibly one may be dead next minute, next hour, or
> tomorrow, with no warning and no escape . . . a slaying which
> is purely a matter of luck. Day and night light and dark it is the
> same. These things fall and the matter is settled – and they may
> fall anywhere. Yet people show very little fear and except when
> there is one close enough to shake them or be heard rather louder
> than usual, take very little notice. Most of us may get, as I do,
> some consolation from the thought that if we do get a direct hit,
> we shall know nothing about it and our worries will be over – or
> we hope they will!

The combined death toll from V-1s and V-2s was 9,000 people. Among those killed by the V-2s were 20 women from the WVS in Lambeth; a further 100 volunteers were injured.

14
THE LIGHTS GO ON

The light is on at the corner, and I was playing under it last night,
and the night before.
(Donald Gulliver, spring 1945)

Donald Gulliver was too young to remember ever before playing under a street lamp aglow in the darkness. So when he wrote to his father in early 1945, the news that the lights had come on at last took up most of his letter. Vera Lynn had wished for the lights to come on all over the world, in a popular wartime song, but life is never so clean cut. First of all, the nation and the Allies celebrated Victory in Europe: VE day was on 8 May 1945. Practical difficulties abounded for those on the Home Front and those returning to it. Peg Cotton had spent a large part of the war in North Devon near her husband's munitions factory. When VE day arrived she found the idea of carrying on more of a challenge than before.

> Reality is catching up with us again. There are still the Japs to
> lick. The war goes on in the East. Casualty lists continue to pour
> in. Rationing is tight – tighter than ever, with only one ounce
> of lard instead of two per week. Distribution of food is uneven.
> Queues are longer. 'Points' [ration units] don't go so far. More
> articles hibernate beneath the counters. The feeling of anti-climax
> is so great that everywhere one hears these remarks. 'I think we
> miss having the War here – the air raids, the bombs, the rockets
> (V-1's and V-2's). There seems nothing to keep up for now!' I
> think we miss the war on the Continent. The European War
> furnished an excitement and an incentive that bolstered morale
> to high endurance. The war in the Pacific has not the same effect;
> it's too far away. If this aftermath of the European War is so hard

to bear, what will it be like when the Jap War is over – and VJ Day breaks upon us? Dick makes only the gloomiest of predictions. He says the two years following the end of World War II will be more difficult and harder to bear, in England, than the War years themselves. He's been right in his predictions most of the time. So I don't feel too happy.

Added to the hardships of postwar Britain was the challenge that faced couples who had made wartime marriages, sometimes after a brief romance. Mary Hooper (née Ross) had known her husband for a decade before she had married him in the spring of 1941, but as he was away in the army they had spent only brief euphoric 'leave' together. He was still in Germany as part of the army of occupation when the war finally ended. She wrote to him:

I've been doing a lot of thinking about life after you do get home pet. It's strange to reflect that although we've known each other ten years we don't really know what sort of people we're like to live with. I mean ordinary everyday sort of life. How you go out to school, how you spend your evenings – when you've years of evenings to spend as you like and things like that. It's going to be difficult at first and we must be intelligent about it.

Munitions worker Louie White had found some comfort through her job at Blackburn's Aircraft Factory in Leeds when her husband Jack and his brother Peter were both shot down within a few weeks of each other. But when victory came, she revealed the cost of 'her' war in her diary.

Jack Missing 97 weeks. The war is over in Europe. Everyone in suspense. I am not bothered. Worked over. At 9.0 the news was given that it was over in Germany and tomorrow will be VE day. At this moment someone is singing 'None but the weary heart'. How appropriate for me just now. I feel so miserable. There is only one whom I shall miss. Made a Red Flag, but as I won't be at work tomorrow I shan't be able to use it.

It rained in Leeds on VE Day, in empathy with her mood.

Victory celebrations in Plymouth had particular poignancy: in March and April 1941 the Devon port and naval dockyard had been hit by a more concentrated series of raids than any other southern port. The city's MP, Lady Astor, organized daytime dances to boost morale.

> **Had a holiday. In the afternoon went to see Hotel Berlin. Very Good, came home and stayed in.**

An essential part of the grieving process was taken from many war widows: they did not always know where their husbands' bodies lay. Jack White's brother Peter, who went missing in a bombing raid in 1943, was buried in the Steinhalden Cemetery at Bad Cannstatt. Louie did not record whether her husband Jack had a known grave.

Anne Lee Michell never discovered the fate of the Texan, Bill Virgil Evans I, who had brightened up her home in the months before D-Day. She was told by some of his fellow GIs that he had 'left the company'. The war in the Far East did not end until the Japanese surrender on 14 August. On 16 August Anne made her final diary entry.

All happy and joyful because of the war being over, and
looking forward to getting our POWs back from Japan. But
our larders are very bare and there are no houses for the
returning soldiers to live in. And many of them are coming
back to find small unwelcome black or American babies in
their families – not so good. Workhouses and nursery schools
crowded with little bastards, and a wave of crime is sweeping
Wellington. Boy of 16 has been forging cheques, a young
soldier's wife has murdered her baby (not his). Everyone's
house needs painting and plastering, our clothes are getting
very shabby, and you can not buy a sheet or a blanket unless
you have been newly wedded or bombed out. Life is going to
be every bit as strenuous.

More than 50,000 British service personnel were taken prisoner by the Japanese;
12,400 of them died in captivity. Those who survived the Japanese POW camps
were mentally, as well as physically, maimed by the experience. Miss ME
Littleboy had no idea whether the happy, handsome boyfriend who went to
fight the Japanese was even alive, until she received a telephone call in 1945.

The call was from the docks at Southampton. I could hardly
believe it, and was not a little perturbed, for I was rather involved
with my present boyfriend, and angry to be involved in something
I had not bargained for. I was also disturbed by this voice from
a long distant past; far too disturbed. It was as if a life had
suddenly come back from the dead.

She agreed to see him, with misgivings.

I felt vulnerable, not in command of the situation. He stood there
and I couldn't believe my eyes. This was not the young man I had
known. I was stunned. Misshapen. Pitted, scarred. Only the eyes
were the same. I could have wept. So while we had been fighting,
that is what the poor wretch had been turned into. I thought of
the handsome boyfriend I was to meet next weekend. Dark, tall, in
command of every situation. I looked at this hulk of humanity and
my heart bled. It was as if all that was left of my youth was gone in

the moment I saw him. He was part of the glamorous pages of my past and now it was there no longer and never would be again.

Her returning POW suffered from bouts of malaria, and she nursed him through. He insisted that the couple marry.

Here was the challenge given to me for peacetime. Could I meet it? London and the BBC were empty after my wartime activities. Could I keep this man alive and help him get back into life again? I loved the spirit of the man, but could love nothing else. I had to do it. There was no other way. He represented the challenge which was my future, the help I alone could give him.

The couple married, but it was only after his death that she felt able to commit this tragic story to paper.

ACKNOWLEDGMENTS

I would like to thank the ever-patient staff at the Imperial War Museum Department of Documents in particular Amanda Mason and Roderick Suddaby; special thanks to Simon Offord for his help over the months of research. This book would not have been possible without the foresight of those who kept and treasured the diaries and letters deposited in the archives and allowed extracts to be used in the manuscript. Thanks to Anne Orange for giving me a space to write, and to my parents for sharing their memories. Lastly to my family, Alan, Thomas and Stephen, who supported me throughout.

CHRONOLOGY

1939
1 September Germany invades Poland
3 September Britain declares war on Germany
November Soviet Union attacks Finland

1940
January Ration books come into use
April Germans invade Denmark and Norway
May Churchill becomes leader of the wartime coalition
May Germany invades the Low Countries
27 May 4 June Evacuation from Dunkirk
June Italy declares war on Great Britain and France
June France signs armistice with Germany
July Channel Islands occupied
July September Battle of Britain
24 August First air raid on London
September Blitzkrieg begins
October Italy invades Greece

1941
March United States Lease and Lend Bill
May Germany invades Greece and Yugoslavia
June Germany invades Soviet Union
October Attack on Moscow
December Japanese attack Pearl Harbor
13 December United States enters the war
December Japanese capture Hong Kong
December Conscription of women announced

1942
February Fall of Singapore
June Rommel captures Tobruk
September Battle of Stalingrad begins
October British victory at El Alamein
December Beveridge Report published

1943
January Casablanca Conference: Roosevelt and Churchill agree policy of unconditional surrender
May Allied victory in North Africa
July Sicily invaded by Allies
September Italians surrender
December Germans surrender at Stalingrad

1944
January Allied landings at Anzio
February Yalta Conference
March Battle of Monte Casino
6 June D-Day landings begin
June Allies capture Rome
13 June First V-1 lands
20 July Plot to assassinate Hitler fails
August Liberation of Paris
8 September First V-2 lands
September Battle of Arnhem
October Allied landings in Greece

1945
January Soviet Union invades Hungary, Poland and Austria
March Allied firebombing of Dresden
April Liberation of first concentration camps
30 April Hitler commits suicide
7 May Germany surrenders unconditionally
May Liberation of Channel Islands
July Labour Government elected
6 August Atomic bomb dropped on Hiroshima
9 August Atomic bomb dropped on Nagasaki
2 September Japan surrenders

INDEX OF CONTRIBUTORS

GENERAL INDEX

PICTURE CREDITS

Title Page Getty Images; 9 Imperial War Museum D17196; 13 Imperial War Museum CH1515; 19 Getty Images; 80
Imperial War Museum LN45590; 98 Imperial War Museum KY7763A; 132 Imperial War Museum LN7757C; 142
Bettmann/Corbis; 149 Imperial War Museum HU36177; 163 Imperial War Museum HU644; 187 Imperial War
Museum LDP325; 191 Imperial War Museum KY14185; 213 Imperial War Museum D18064; 223 Klaus Ulrich;
241 Imperial War Museum HU63802; 249 Imperial War Museum D14124; 264 Imperial War Museum HU638;
274 Plymouth Central Library; 39, 45, 65, 77, 103, 129, 155, 159, 179, 215, 260 courtesy of the Department of
Documents, Imperial War Museum

Mcleod